ood safety

Jeremy Stranks

THOROGOOD

Thorogood Publishing Ltd
10-12 Rivington Street
London EC2A 3DU
Telephone: 020 7749 4748
Fax: 020 7729 6110
Email: info@thorogoodpublishing.co.uk
Web: www.thorogoodpublishing.co.uk

A CIP catalogue record for this book is
available from the British Library.

PB: ISBN 978-185418379-8
RB: ISBN 978-185418384-2

Cover and book designed and typeset
by Driftdesign

Printed in Great Britain by Ashford Colour Press Ltd

Preface

Far too many people still suffer the ill-effects of poor levels of food safety and hygiene. These effects could be associated with a product purchased in a super-market, a meal in a restaurant or ready-prepared food purchased from a take-away premises. Despite the lessons learnt from the major food poisoning incidents of the last fifty years, far too many outbreaks of food poisoning still indicate a failure on the part of food business operators and their employees to follow basic principles of personal hygiene and the procedures for ensuring the preparation of food which is free from all forms of contamination.

There is no doubt that the safety of food is a matter which concerns everyone – food manufacturers, catering businesses, organisations in the supply and distri-bution chain, retailers and people preparing meals at home. Furthermore, recent legislation now requires food business operators to operate a food safety manage-ment system, such as Hazard Analysis: Critical Control Point (HACCP) with a view to reducing the toll of death and ill-health associated with unsound food.

This book has been produced as a ready-reference text for those engaged in the enforcement of food safety legislation, manufacturers of food products, caterers and others engaged in the operation of the wide range of food busi-nesses encountered today. It is further targeted at those studying for the range of food safety qualifications sponsored by professional bodies, such as the Char-tered Institute of Environmental Health, Royal Institute of Public Health, Royal Environmental Health Institute of Scotland and the Royal Society for the Promo-tion of Health, together with University and college students engaged in food technology and similar courses.

I hope that all who use this book will find it helpful.

Jeremy Stranks

Contents

A

B

C

D

F

G

H

I

J

L

M

N

Q

R

S

U

V

W

X

Y

Z

Appendices

A

Acaricide

A pesticide which kills mites.

Flour mite

Infestation prevention and control

Pest

Pesticides

Accelerated freeze drying

This is a process of food dehydration for certain foods such as peas, prawns and coffee. The process involves placing prepared pieces of quick-frozen food under vacuum and gently heating. As a result, 'sublimation' takes place where crystals of ice turn to water vapour without melting. On completion of the process, the food has a brittle and sponge-like texture. Foods treated in this way have a much longer shelf life providing the packaging is kept intact.

When water is added to the product, it enters much faster than with conventional dried products. Furthermore, when reconstituted (or re-hydrated), the food is similar in nature to that of the original food. Re-hydrated foods should be treated in the same way as fresh foods.

Blast chilling and freezing

Dehydration

Frozen food

Quick freezing

Acceptable daily intake

The quantity of a chemical substance which, according to current information, can be consumed day to day during a lifetime without adverse effects.

Acidity

The property of a chemical substance which, when combined with water, releases hydrogen ions. Solutions with a pH value of less than 7 are generally classed as acidic.

Alkalinity

pH value

'Act or default of another person'

If in any case the defence of *all reasonable precautions and all due diligence* involves the allegation that the commission of the offence was due to the act or default of another person, or to reliance on information supplied by another person, the accused shall not, without leave of the court, be entitled to rely on that defence unless:

a) at least seven clear days before the hearing; and

b) where he has previously appeared before a court in connection with the alleged offence, within one month of his first such appearance,

he has served on the prosecutor a notice in writing giving such information identifying or assisting in the identification of that other person as was then in his possession.

[Food Safety Act 1990]

[Food Hygiene (England) Regulations 2006]

All reasonable precautions and all due diligence

Food Hygiene (England) Regulations 2006

Food Safety Act 1990

Food safety requirements

Nature, substance or quality

Offences and penalties

Service of documents

Acute diseases

Those diseases in which the symptoms develop rapidly following infection.

Acute food poisoning

Acute food poisoning

Acute food poisoning produces an immediate response on the part of the individual, in many cases manifested by vomiting. This applies particularly in the case of certain hazardous substances.

Acute food poisoning implies a condition of very quick onset with severe symptoms such as sickness, vomiting and headache lasting for a short period of time, which may be hours or days. Fundamentally, the symptoms last as long as the pathogenic bacteria remain in the body.

Bacteria

Bacterial growth curve

Bacteriological standards

Diseases transmitted through food

Food-borne infection

Food poisoning (food-borne illnesses)

Food poisoning bacteria

Additives

Any substance intentionally added to food for a specific function, e.g. to preserve or colour food, that is not normally eaten as a food or used as a characteristic ingredient in food.

Additives include preservatives, stablilisers, sweeteners, colours, flavourings and other substances which may be added to food to increase shelf life, improve appearance and taste.

Antioxidant

Colours

Emulsifiers

Flavour enhancers

Flavourings

Gelling agents

Preservatives

Shelf life

Stabilisers

Sweeteners

Thickeners

Adulteration of food

The process of adding a substance to, or removing a constituent from, a food commodity which adversely affects the nature of that food.

Detention or seizure of food

Food safety requirements

Malicious tampering with food

Nature, substance or quality

Advertising food for sale

Any person who publishes, or is a party to the publication of, an advertisement (not being such a label given or displayed by him as mentioned in subsection (1) above) which

a) falsely describes any food; or

b) is likely to mislead as to the nature or substance or quality of any food, shall be guilty of an offence.

[Food Safety Act 1990]

False or misleading descriptions and information

Food Safety Act 1990

Aerobe

An organism requiring oxygen to survive.

Microbe

Aerobic Plate Count

This is a measure of organisms, described as 'colony-forming units' (CFUs), present during laboratory testing and expressed in CFU/gm. What is an acceptable level depends upon the food in question. However, levels above 10^4/gm are generally deemed unsatisfactory. This may be due to poor refrigeration or a significant degree of contamination.

Detection methods

Aflatoxin

Aflatoxins are endotoxins produced by certain fungi and, hence, referred to as mycotoxins. A number of varieties of mushroom and toadstool, together with some moulds, produce mycotoxins, particularly those of the *Aspergillus* genus.

In addition, certain species of *Penicillium*, which may be present in wet or moist stored foods, such as wheat, soya beans, oats and peanuts, can produce aflatoxin.

This toxin is highly resistant to heat.

Endotoxin

Fungi

Mycotoxin

Natural toxins

Air drying

This is a method of preservation used in many countries whereby vegetables, fruit and other foods are dehydrated simply through drying in the open air or in controlled drying plants.

Dehydration

Algae

These are simple plants capable of photosynthesis found in wet environments or damp soil, such as *Spirogyra*, commonly found in ponds as a bright green slimy mass, and seaweed.

Alkalinity

The property of a chemical compound whereby hydrogen ions are released when dissolved in water. Alkalis are generally classed as those chemical substances having a pH in excess of 7.0. They are comparatively rare in food but are corrosive and are used in disinfectants in small concentrations.

Acidity

pH value

Allergic reactions

Certain substances in food can cause an allergic response on the part of susceptible individuals. This is, fundamentally, an immunological response, triggered by a particular food, such as fish.

Food allergy implies an abnormal sensitivity to certain substances and foods and represents some response of the body's immune system. Typical allergic responses include hyperactivity, vomiting, gastro-enteritis, dermatitis and respiratory disfunction. The first consumption of the food generally produces no response but brings about sensitisation of the skin, lungs or some other part of the body. Once this sensitisation has taken place, subsequent consumption produces a body response.

Many foods can produce allergic responses, such as strawberries, fish, chocolate, food colouring agents common with many sweets, and milk.

All reasonable precautions and all due diligence

Where charged with an offence under the Food Safety Act and regulations made under the Act, the person charged may submit the defence that he took 'all reasonable precautions and exercised all due diligence' to avoid the commission of the offence. (Section 21)

Similarly, in any proceedings for an offence under the Food Hygiene (England) Regulations, it shall be a defence for the accused to prove that he took all reasonable precautions and exercised all due diligence to avoid the commission of the offence by himself or by a person under his control.

Proving 'due diligence'

In order to be able to prove 'all reasonable precautions and all due diligence', the following documents and procedures, together with evidence of their satisfactory implementation, are essential.

a) Policy Statement or Mission Statement on Food Safety, including specification of individual responsibilities of managers and employees

b) cleaning schedules

c) preventive maintenance schedules

d) documented temperature control arrangements

e) documented infestation control systems and records

f)   employee food hygiene training records

g)   food safety manuals, procedures, operating instructions, codes of practice

h)   records of ingredient and final product specifications in terms of quality, composition and safety

i)   evidence of pro-active inspections of food premises and reactive corrective action reporting procedures

j)   recorded analysis of consumer complaints

k)   documented product recall procedures

l)   formalised promotional activities, such as labelling, advertising, packaging, user instructions, information on storage, shelf life, 'eat by' dates and 'use by' dates

m)   written management procedures following enforcement action, e.g. service of improvement notices and emergency prohibition notices, or the making of a prohibition order

m)   procedures for liaison with food authority officers

n)   evidence of implementation of a food safety management system, such as HACCP (Hazard Analysis: Critical Control Point) or Assured Safe Catering covering biological, chemical and physical hazards to food

Assured Safe Catering (ASC)

'Clean person' strategies

'Clean place' strategies

Cleaning schedules

Complaints procedure

Enforcement procedure

Food hygiene inspections

Food Labelling Regulations 1996 (as amended)

Food Safety/Hygiene Policy

Food safety manuals

Hazard Analysis: Critical Control Points (HACCP)

Hygiene Emergency Prohibition Notice

Hygiene Emergency Prohibition Order

Hygiene Improvement Notice

Hygiene Prohibition Orders

Improvement Notices

Liaison with authorised officers

Offences and penalties

Preventive maintenance

Product recall systems

Prohibition Orders

Prohibition procedures

Regulation (EC) No 852/2004 on the hygiene of foodstuffs

Service of documents

Temperature control requirements

Training of food handlers

Alphachloralose

A chemical substance commonly used in pest control treatments for sparrows, pigeons and starlings infesting food premises.

Bird control

Infestation prevention and control

Integrated Pest Management

Pest

Pesticides

Ambient shelf stable

The feature of certain foods that enables them to be stored safely at ambient room temperature for a specified period.

Ambient temperature

The average or normal room temperature or that of the general surroundings.

Environmental control

Amenity areas

These are designated areas incorporating sanitary accommodation, washing facilities, clothing changing and storage arrangements, together with rest rooms and facilities for taking meals.

The minimum numbers of sanitation and washing facilities to be provided are incorporated in the Workplace (Health, Safety and Welfare) Regulations 1992, thus:

1	2	3
Number of people at work	*Number of water closets*	*Number of wash stations*
1 – 5	1	1
6 – 25	2	2
26 to 50	3	3
51 to 75	4	4
75 to 100	5	5

In the case of sanitary accommodation used only by men, the table below may be used as an alternative to column 2 of the Table above.

1	2	3
Number of men at work	Number of water closets	Number of urinals
1 to 15	1	1
16 to 30	2	1
31 to 45	2	2
46 to 60	3	2
61 to 75	3	3
76 to 90	4	3
91 to 100	4	4

An additional water closet and an additional washing station should be provided for every 25 people above 100 (or fraction of 25). In the case of water closets used only by men, an additional water closet for every 50 men (or fraction of 50) above 100 is sufficient provided at least an equal number of additional urinals are provided.

European food hygiene legislation

Food Hygiene (England) Regulations 2006

Regulation (EC) No 852/2004 on the hygiene of foodstuffs

Hand washing

Hand washing facilities

Personal protective clothing

Personal Protective Equipment at Work Regulations 1992

Toilets

Washing facilities

Welfare amenity provisions

Workplace (Health, Safety and Welfare) Regulations 1992

Anaerobe

An organism that does not require oxygen to survive.

Microbe

Animal by-products premises

Premises, other than a cold store, cutting plant, game-handling establishment or slaughterhouse, from which animal by-products are despatched to other premises.

[Animal By-Products (Identification) Regulations 1995 as amended by the Food Hygiene (England) Regulations 2006]

Ant control

Infestation by garden ants and Pharoah's ants, particularly in the summer months, can be a particular problem in food premises. Whilst garden ants tend to constitute a nuisance, Pharoah's ants are carriers of pathogens and tend to establish nests in inaccessible parts of a premises.

Typical control measures include:

a)   storage of food in closed containers off the floor

b)   concerted efforts to identify the location of nests and the use of ant-specific insecticides designed to destroy nests

c)   the use of syrup-soaked baits which trap the ants

d)   treatment of floor and wall surfaces with a residual insecticidal lacquer

e)   the use of juvenile hormone to control Pharoah's ants.

Attention must also be paid to structural defects, such as cracks in brickwork, defective pointing to brickwork, gaps around doors and windows, and spaces at the junctions of floor and wall surfaces which allow ants to penetrate a building.

As ants are particularly attracted to sweet food products, considerable attention must be paid to housekeeping activities, prompt removal of spillages and storage of such products in suitable sealed containers.

Infestation prevention and control

Structural requirements for food premises

Antibody

A blood protein which counteracts the growth and adverse actions of antigens, i.e. foreign substances, such as bacteria.

Antigen

Antiserum

Antigen

A substance, such as a bacterial toxin, that triggers the formation of an antibody.

Antibody

Antiserum

Antioxidant

Antioxidants are chemical substances which prevent oxidation reactions which result in, for example, rancidity in oils and fats and the browning of cut surfaces of certain fruits, such as apples.

The more common antioxidants are vitamin C (ascorbic acid or E300), vitamin E (tocopherol) and propyl gallate.

Additives

E-numbers

Antiseptic

Generally, a chemical substance which prevents bacterial and mould growth particularly in or on the human body.

Aseptic

Antiserum

Blood serum containing antibodies which act against specific antigens.

Antibody

Antigen

Antitoxin

Antitoxins are substances produced by the body or dosed to the body to reduce or control infection by bacterial toxins such as those produced by *Clostridium botulinum* or species of *Staphylococcus*.

Clostridium botulinum (Clostridium welchii)

Appeals against Notices, etc

Any person who is aggrieved by:

a) a decision of an authorised officer of an enforcement authority to serve a Hygiene Improvement Notice;

b) a decision of an enforcement officer, in the case of:

   i) a Hygiene Prohibition Order;

   ii) a Hygiene Emergency Prohibition Notice; and to refuse to issue a certificate to the effect that he is satisfied that the food business operator has taken sufficient measures to secure that the health risk condition is no longer fulfilled; or

c) a decision of an authorised officer of an enforcement authority to serve a remedial action notice, may appeal to a Magistrates Court.

[Food Safety Act 1990, Section 39]

On appeal against a hygiene improvement notice or a remedial action notice, the court may cancel or affirm the notice and, if it affirms it, may do so either in its original form or with such modifications as the court may in the circumstances think fit.

[Food Hygiene (England) Regulations 2006]

Emergency Prohibition Notices

Emergency Prohibition Orders

Food Hygiene (England) Regulations 2006

Food Safety Act 1990

Hygiene Emergency Prohibition Notice

Hygiene Improvement Notices

Improvement Notices

Appeals to Crown Court

A person who is aggrieved by:

a) the dismissal by a Magistrates Court of an appeal to it; or

b) any decision of such a court to make a Hygiene Prohibition Order or a Hygiene Emergency Prohibition Order, may appeal to a Crown Court.

[Food Safety Act 1990, Section 38]

[Food Hygiene (England) Regulations 2006]

Food Hygiene (England) Regulations 2006

Food Safety Act 1990

Hygiene Emergency Prohibition Order

Hygiene Prohibition Order

Ascaris lumbricoides

This is a large parasitic roundworm sometimes found in the intestines of pigs. Transmission to other pigs is through the eggs which are consumed by the pigs, setting up a further infestation in the intestines of those pigs. The larvae produced penetrate the intestinal walls and are taken by the bloodstream to the heart and lungs and, subsequently, to the trachea, where they are coughed up and swallowed. Classic manifestation of roundworm infestation is in the livers of pigs which show white areas (milk spots).

Humans can be similarly affected by this parasite whereby worms are excreted from the body in faeces or through the nose and throat which eventually mature to infective larvae in soil and water. The consumption of, for example, water or food contaminated by sewage can result in the process commencing in human beings.

Ascospores

An ascus is a sack-like structure which reproduces producing a sexual fungal spore or ascospore. An ascus may contain around 2 to 8 ascospores. Ascospores include unicellular yeasts and septate moulds, such as *Penicillium* and *Aspergillus*.

Aspergillus

Aseptic

This implies freedom from contaminations by micro-organisms.

Aseptic packaging

Aseptic packaging

This form of packaging is used in canning processes and in the filling of cartons of, for example, milk and fruit juices, whereby the actual closure of the pack or container is performed under aseptic conditions in order to control the bacterial load. Such a process implies complete control directed at preventing any form of bacterial contamination from entering the product.

Fundamentally, the process entails:

- filling a sterile product into sterile containers; and
- closing the container under sterile conditions.

Aseptic

Aspergillus

This group of moulds is commonly found in soil and decaying vegetation and is a common food spoilage organism, particularly in foods with a low water content. Aflatoxins may be produced by specific members of this group.

Aflatoxin

Natural toxins

Assured Safe Catering (ASC)

Assured Safe Catering can be seen as an extension to HACCP specifically directed at the catering industry. As a system, ASC analyses the various food hazards that can arise, and the controls necessary, at the various stages of catering activities, e.g. dealing with raw materials, storage, preparation, cooking, etc.

Broadly, ASC incorporates the following stages:

a) planning

b) getting organised, including training

c) development of a flow diagram showing the various catering steps

d) for each catering step:

   i)   list the food hazards;

   ii)   identify the control measures;

   iii) identify critical control points;

   iv)   develop a checking or recording system;

   v)   put the system into action;

   vi)   check the system

e) repeat stage 4 for each catering step

f) system check

g) system review

The Food Hygiene (England) Regulations place a duty on the proprietor of a food business to identify any step in the activities of the food business which is critical to ensuring food safety and ensure that adequate safety procedures are identified, implemented, maintained and reviewed.

The operation of ASC is designed to assist caterers to comply with hazard identification and control requirements. As with HACCP, there is no specific legal requirement to operate ASC.

BS EN ISO 22000: Food Safety Management Systems

Competent authority

Critical Control Points (CCPs)

European food hygiene legislation

Food Hygiene (England) Regulations 2006

Hazard Analysis: Critical Control Point (HACCP)

High risk foods

Regulation (EC) No 852/2004 on the hygiene of foodstuffs

'At risk' groups

Those groups of people who may suffer the greatest risk to health as a result of exposure to food-borne infections, including new and expectant mothers, mothers who are breast-feeding, breast-fed babies, the very young, the very old, those who are ill or convalescing from an illness and those with a weakened immunity to disease.

Audit

A systematic critical examination of an organisation's methods and procedures with the principal objective of minimising loss or adverse consequences.

Appendix D – Food Hygiene Audit

Authorised officer

A person authorised in writing by an enforcement authority, e.g. a local authority, to undertake certain functions and to act in specific matters.

In relation to an enforcement authority, means any person (whether or not an officer of the authority) who is authorised by them in writing, either generally or specially, to act in matters arising under the Hygiene Regulations.

[Food Hygiene (England) Regulations 2006]

Competent authority

Enforcement procedure

Environmental Health Officers

Food Hygiene (England) Regulations 2006

Liaison with authorised officers

Offences and penalties

Powers of entry

Autoclaves

An autoclave is a form of pressure vessel used to sterilise a range of materials by exposing them to moist heat under pressure. Generally, the greater the pressure inside the autoclave, the higher the temperature obtained and the shorter time required for total sterilisation. They are effective and quick in operation, and have their application in food manufacturing processes and microbiology laboratories.

Equipment requirements

Average illuminances and minimum measured illuminances (lighting)

Under the Workplace (Health, Safety and Welfare) Regulations 1992 there is a general requirement on employers for every workplace to be provided with 'suitable and sufficient lighting'.

Good standards of lighting are essential to ensure safe performance of tasks, the safe movement of people and vehicles, effective implementation of cleaning procedures and the maintenance of good housekeeping levels.

HSE Guidance Note *Lighting at work* [HS(G)38] makes recommendations for lighting in workplaces. The Guidance Note distinguishes between 'average illuminances' and 'minimum measured illuminances' according to the general activity undertaken and the type of location. Illuminance (the intensity of illumination) is measured in Lux (Lx), the metric unit of illuminance.

General activity	Typical locations Types of work Lux (Lx)	Average Illuminance	Minimum Measured Illuminance Lux (Lx)
Movement of people, machines and vehicles (1)	Lorry parks, corridors, circulation routes	20	5
Movement of people, machines and vehicles in hazardous areas; rough work not requiring any perception of detail (1)	Construction site clearance, excavation and soil work, docks, loading bays, bottling and canning plants	50	20
Work requiring limited perception of detail (2)	Kitchens, factories assembling large components, potteries	100	50
Work requiring perception of detail (2)	Offices, sheet metal work, bookbinding	200	100
Work requiring fine perception of detail (2)	Drawing offices, factories assembling electronic components, textile production	500	200

Notes

1. Only safety has been considered because no perception of detail is needed and visual fatigue is unlikely. However, where it is necessary to see detail, to recognise a hazard or where error in performing the

task could put someone else at risk, for safety purposes as well as to avoid visual fatigue, the figure should be increased to that for work requiring the perception of detail.

2. The purpose is to avoid visual fatigue; the illuminances will be adequate for safety purposes.

European food hygiene legislation

Food Hygiene (England) Regulations 2006

Lighting recommendations

Regulation (EC) No 852/2004 on the hygiene of foodstuffs

Workplace (Health, Safety and Welfare) Regulations 1992

A_W (water activity)

In order to support bacterial multiplication, water in a food product must be actively available. This availability of water is known as 'water activity' (A_W)

$$A_W = \frac{\text{Water vapour pressure of food}}{\text{Water vapour pressure of pure water}}$$

A_W x 100 = Equilibrium Relative Humidity

The A_W is an indication of the likelihood of a particular food to support bacterial growth.

The A_W of water is set at 1.0 and all foods other than water have a value below 1.0.

Most bacteria achieve optimum growth at values above 0.95, spoilage and pathogenic organisms growing the fastest at 0.98. Where the A_W is too low for growth, bacteria become dormant and, if particularly dry conditions persist, the cells will die.

Bacteria

Bacterial growth curve

Bacillus cereus

This is an organism commonly found in cereals, vegetables, dairy products and soil, and which causes two types of illness associated with different enterotoxins, namely vomiting illness and diarrhoeal illness. *Bacillus cereus* is a Gram-positive aerobic spore-forming bacterium which causes food poisoning through the release of an exotoxin.

Symptoms of vomiting illness arise very quickly and are similar to those of *Staphylococcus aureus* food poisoning with acute vomiting and, in some cases, diarrhoea. Foods associated with vomiting illness include cereals, such as boiled rice, but eaten cold as in the case of salads, fried rice and corn flour. Pasta, certain cheese products and potatoes have also been shown to be carriers of this micro-organism.

In the case of diarrhoeal illness, the mild symptoms resemble those of *Clostridium perfringens* food poisoning including diarrhoea and abdominal pain, sometimes with vomiting and nausea. Fish, milk, vegetables and meat are typical carriers of this micro-organism.

Bacteria

Fish and shellfish (food hazards)

Food-borne infection

Meat products (food hazards)

Milk and dairy products (food hazards)

Bacteria

Bacteria are single-celled micro-organisms with differing shapes, most of which are harmless. Bacteria play an important part in people's lives. Over 1700 species of bacteria are known to exist, but only a small number are pathogenic. They are used in food production, for example, in cheese and yoghurt manufacture.

Bacteria may be classified as:

a) pathogenic – responsible for a range of diseases;

b) spoilage – causing deterioration or degradation of the quality of food; and

c) commensal – harmless bacteria, some of which may be beneficial to mankind, existing in harmony with people and other hosts.

Aerobe

Anaerobe

Bacterial food poisoning

Bacterial growth curve

Bacterial toxin

Bacteriological control systems

Commensal

Food-borne infection

Microbe

Pathogenic agents (pathogens)

Spoilage of food

Bacterial food poisoning

The harmful bacteria that cause food poisoning are shown in the Table below.

Table: Food Poisoning Bacteria			
	Incubation period (Hours)	*Duration*	*Sources*
Salmonellae	12-36	1-8 days	Meat, poultry, eggs, rodents
Staphylococci	2-6	6-24hrs	Cuts, boils, in skin lesions
Clostridium perfringens	8-22	12-24hrs	Faeces, soil, dusts, insects, raw meat
Streptococci	4-36	1-3 days	Various

Bacteria

Bacterial growth curve

Bacterial toxin

Bacteriological control systems

Bacteriological standards

Bacteriology

Bacteriophage (phage) typing

Bacteriostatic

Botulism

Carriers of disease

Chronic food poisoning

Clostridium perfringens

Coliforms

Disinfection

Faecal coliform

Food-borne infection

Food poisoning bacteria

Food poisoning (food borne illnesses)

Gastro-enteritis

Incubation period

Infectious dose

Microbe

Reservoir of infection

Salmonellae

Staphylococcus aureus

Streptococci

Bacterial growth curve

This curve represents the changes in size in a colony of bacteria, i.e. the population development, recorded in graphic form. This growth curve identifies four specific phases:

a) *The Lag Phase*

  Here bacteria are adapting to a new environment, the stage lasting from a few hours to several days. The reproduction rate is minimal until bacteria have adapted to the new environment.

b) *The Log Phase*

  Reproduction takes place at the maximum rate to a point where there is a decrease in the growth rate due to scarcity of nutrients.

c) *The Stationary Phase*

  Reproduction and growth have reduced considerably to the point where the rate of reproduction equals the death rate. This may arise due to sudden changes in pH or loss of a growth factor, such as amino acid or vitamin.

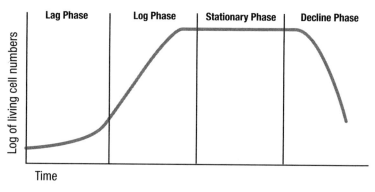

Bacterial growth curve

d) *The Death or Decline Phase*

  This is, fundamentally, the reverse of the Log Phase where the death of cells occurs at an exponential rate. The death rate far exceeds the rate of reproduction, mainly due to the accumulation of waste. Eventually the whole population will die.

Bacteria

Bacterial food poisoning

Bacteriological standards

Bacteriology

Bacteriophage (phage) typing

Bacterial toxin

A poisonous substance produced by pathogenic bacteria.

Bacteria
Bacteriological control systems
Natural toxins
Toxin

Bactericide

An agent which kills bacteria, such as disinfectant.

Bacteria
Bacterial toxin
Bacterial growth curve
Bacteriological control systems
Disinfectants
Disinfection

Bacteriological control systems

Bacteria which cause food poisoning multiply very quickly by simple cell division under the right conditions of temperature, moisture, time and the availability of food nutrients. Bacteriological control systems, therefore, are designed taking these factors into account.

Exposure to heat, perhaps through boiling for a specified period, is a common means of killing bacteria. Reducing the moisture content through various forms of drying process also has this effect. (Exposure to low temperatures, however, does not necessarily kill bacteria but merely reduces the rate of multiplication.) Certain bactericides, chemicals which will kill bacteria, are also used, together with exposure to ultra-violet light in certain cases.

Appropriate storage and temperature control of food is vital.

Bacteria
Bacterial food poisoning

Bacteriological standards

Bacteriological standards are concerned with ensuring the quality, shelf life and purity of food. Measurement is undertaken in a laboratory through assessing the number of micro-organisms present in a sample of a particular food. There are a number of laboratory methods available.

Total viable count (all living bacteria)

Where the number of micro-organisms/gram present is greater than 10^4, this indicates an unacceptable level of contamination.

Faecal organisms

The presence of faecal organisms indicates that contamination from the intestines of people or animals is present in the food.

Pathogens

Tests can be undertaken to detect the presence of, for example, *Salmonellae* species, *Staphylococcus* species, *Clostridium perfringens* and *Bacillus cereus*. The presence of these micro-organisms can indicate evidence of cross-contamination and, in some cases, poor personal hygiene.

Urgent action is required where there is evidence of *Salmonellae* species as, fundamentally, these micro-organisms should never be present. In the case of *Clostridium perfringens*, this should be below the safe level of 10^3/gram and for *Staphylococcus aureus,* 10^2/gram.

Clostridium perfringens

Coliforms

Detection methods

Escherichia coli (E. coli)

Personal hygiene

Salmonellae

Staphylococcus aureus

Bacteriology

Bacteriology is concerned with the study of bacteria.

Bacteria

Bacteriological control systems

Bacteriological standards

Bacteriophage (phage) typing

Bacteriophage

A form of virus that infects bacterial cells.

Bacteria

Bacteriological control systems

Bacteriophage (phage) typing

This is a process of identifying bacteria using particular strains of bacterio-phage, for example, *Salmonella enteritidis phage type 4*, which has been a causative factor in food poisoning outbreaks associated with the consumption of raw or inadequately cooked eggs. In this case, the organism is specialised in that it attacks only those members of a particular species or even the strains within a particular species.

Bacteria

Bacteriological control systems

Bacteriological standards

Detection methods

Bacteriostatic

The quality of a substance, such as an antiseptic, which stops the growth of bacteria but does not necessarily reduce the number of bacteria present.

Antiseptic

Bain marie

This is a form of equipment comprising a hot water bath into which assorted containers of, for example, sauces, can be immersed in order to keep them hot, but not to boil.

Equipment requirements

Batches, lots or consignments of food

Where any food which fails to comply with the food safety requirements is part of a batch, lot or consignment of food of the same class or description, it shall be presumed, until the contrary is proved, that all of the food in the batch, lot or consignment fails to comply with these requirements.

Authorised officers need reliable evidence before taking such action, but if there are serious doubts about the safety of the food the whole batch, lot or consignment should be detained. Part of the food may be seized later and then the notice may be withdrawn in respect of the remainder, if the officer is satisfied or has evidence from, for example, the public analyst or food examiner, that the problem affects only part of the batch, lot or consignment.

[Food Safety Act 1990]

Authorised officers must take the following matters into account when considering whether to seize or detain a batch, lot or consignment:

a) the nature of the contamination;

b) the nature and condition of any container holding the food;

c) the risk to health;

d) the evidence available; and

e) the quantity of food involved in relation to any sampling which has been undertaken.

Authorised officer

Enforcement authorities

Enforcement procedure

Food Safety Act 1990

Statutory Codes under the Food Safety Act

'Best before' date

This is a system of marking food products with a specific date before which the food will retain its original quality or 'shelf life'. The system is generally applied to low risk foods, some of which have long shelf-lives, such as canned goods, drinks, biscuits and other dry products.

Date marking

'Sell-by' date

'Use by' date

Binary fission

This is the process of cell division in unicellular organisms, which include bacteria. In this process one cell sub-divides into two cells (daughter cells) and the process continues with daughter cells further sub-dividing. Bacteria reproduce by this form of asexual reproduction about every 10 to 20 minutes under ideal conditions In this way literally millions of bacteria can be produced in a relatively short period of time.

Bacteria

Bacteriology

Microbe

Biochemistry

The study of the chemical substances and vital processes in living organisms.

Biocide

A chemical agent, such as a pesticide, that is capable of destroying living organisms.

Aerobe

Anaerobe

Bacteria

Microbe

Pesticides

Biodegradability

This is the ability of certain substances to be broken down into relatively safe non-toxic or non-polluting products.

Biotoxin

A toxic substance produced by a living organism.

Biochemistry

Natural toxins

Toxin

Bird control

Food manufacturing premises, such as bakeries and mills are commonly infested with large numbers of birds, such as feral pigeons, sparrows and starlings, who feed off food and the food spillages created both inside and outside these premises. The majority of birds carry food poisoning bacteria such as *Salmonellae* and their droppings may contaminate food in preparation and storage areas.

Control rests on:

- physical screening of all openings, such as doors and windows
- the use of nets on structural openings
- structural measures to discourage perching, such as the installation of spiked strips at perching points on roofs, sloping of external window ledges etc
- infilling of structural joints, such as that between a wall and roof
- narcotic treatments using alphachloralose.

Alphachloralose

Infestation prevention and control

Pest

Pesticides

Proofing of buildings

Blast chilling and freezing

Blast chilling is the process of using a fan-assisted refrigeration cabinet or room which lowers the temperature of cooked food very quickly to around 5°C prior to going into refrigerated storage. In order to prevent bacterial multiplication, the process should be completed within 90 minutes. Attention must be paid to the specific size of the food commodities being chilled, particularly in the case of meat joints. Ideally these joints should be no more than 2.5 kg in weight and regularly shaped.

Blast freezing takes place in similar manner to blast chilling. Here hot cooked food is quickly reduced to between -18°C and -22°C before being put into refrigerated storage.

Cold store

Cryogenic freezing

Fluidised bed freezing

Freezers

Frozen food

Plate freezing

Botulinum cook

This is a process used in food canning operations whereby the presence of *Clostridium botulinum*, which is particularly resistant to heat, is used as an indication of the effectiveness of the operations. The presence or otherwise of *Clostridium botulinum* is a process indicator for foods which have a pH in excess of 4.5. Clear evidence that the organism is destroyed is an indication that other bacteria will also have been destroyed, thereby achieving true sterility of the product.

Clostridium botulinum (Clostridium welchii)

Detection methods

pH value

Sterilisation

Botulism

This is the disease condition caused by the toxin of *Clostridium botulinum* which, in many cases, attacks the central nervous system. This micro-organism is associated with a range of foods including canned fish, certain pates and bottled vegetables.

The disease has an incubation period of 18 to 36 hours and initial symptoms are characterised by diarrhoea, headache and an overall tiredness. In serious cases, these symptoms may be followed by double vision, loss of balance, constipation and speech difficulties which, in some cases, can be fatal. Patients take a long time to recover and this recovery may be incomplete.

Bacterial food poisoning

Canned goods

Canning processes

Clostridium botulinum (Clostridium welchii)

Food poisoning bacteria

Incubation period

Toxin

Brining

The immersion in brine (a solution of approximately 25% salt, 3% sodium nitrate or potassium nitrate, and other substances, such as 1% sugar) of slices, joints or sides of pork during the preparation by curing of bacon.

Certain vegetables are also brined prior to pickling in order to reduce their water content.

Pickling
Preservation of food

BS EN ISO 22000: Food Safety Management Systems

BS EN ISO 2200: Food Safety Management systems: Requirements for any organisation in the food chain and *Guidance for organisations in the food chain* specifies the requirements for a food safety management system in the food chain. In many cases, an organisation needs to demonstrate that it can control food safety hazards and provide consistently safe end-products that meet both the customers' requirements and food safety legal requirements.

The standard incorporates key elements to ensure food safety along the food chain including:

a) interactive communication;

b) system management;

c) control of food safety hazards through pre-requisite programmes and HACCP plans; and

d) continual improvement and updating of the management system.

BS EN ISO 22000 applies to any organisation participating in the food chain, e.g. primary food producers, food processors, retail and food service outlets, transport and storage operators, manufacturers of equipment and packaging materials, manufacturers of cleaning agents and producers of food additives and ingredients.

Additives

Assured Safe Catering (ASC)

European food hygiene legislation

Food Safety/Hygiene Policy

Food safety management systems

Food safety risk assessment

General requirements for food premises

Hazard analysis

Hazard Analysis: Critical Control Point (HACCP)

High risk operations

Packaging

Processing

Regulation (EC) No 852/2004 on the hygiene of foodstuffs

Retailers

Structural requirements for food premises

Transport of foodstuffs

Wrapping

Wrapping and packaging of foodstuffs

Bulk transport in sea-going vessels of liquid oils, etc

In the bulk transport in sea-going vessels of liquid oils or fats and the bulk transport by sea of raw sugar, operators must comply with the specific requirements of Schedule 3 to the Hygiene Regulations.

[Food Hygiene (England) Regulations 2006]

Business

This includes the undertaking of a canteen, club, school, hospital or institution, whether carried on for profit or not, and any undertaking or activity carried on by a public or local authority.

[Food Safety Act 1990]

Food business (definition)

Food business operator

Responsibilities for food: food business operators

C

Campylobacter

There are several forms of the *Campylobacter* organism. The most common is *Campylobacter jejuni*, which accounts for approximately 99% of all infections. The epidemiology differs from *Salmonella* in that *Campylobacter* does not multiply on food and secondary infection is rare.

The most common food source of *Campylobacter* is poultry meat and around 50% of chickens are believed to carry *Campylobacter* organisms. It infects the human intestinal tracts and sometimes the bloodstream. Cases often occur during the summer months, the peak is in May.

Sickness occurs when undercooked chicken is eaten, or the organisms are transferred to the mouth inadvertently during cooking. Unpasteurised milk and untreated water can also pass on *Campylobacter*. Milk from bottles pecked by birds should never be consumed. 10% of infections reported in the UK are acquired whilst abroad, and Campylobacter can be passed on by contact with infected dogs and cats.

Campylobacter bacteria cause gastro-enteritis, characterised by blood diarrhoea, fever and abdominal cramps. The illness typically lasts 5 to 7 days and is usually resolved without antibiotics. Deaths are rare, with only one or two reported each year. However *Campylobacter* infections can provoke a paralysing neurological illness called Guillain Barre Syndrome in a small percentage of cases. Infected people continue to pass the organism in their faeces for up to a week.

To prevent sickness:

a) poultry should be thoroughly cooked, and anything that comes into contact with the poultry (hands and all utensils) should be washed with soap and water before they are used for other foods;

b) fresh meat should be wrapped in plastic bags to prevent blood dripping on to other foods;

c) foods should be refrigerated promptly, minimising any time they are kept at room temperature;

d) hands should be disinfected before and after food preparation;

e) cutting boards and counters should be washed and disinfected immediately after use and before further preparation of any food; and

f) raw milk or eggs or undercooked foods which contain these ingredients should be avoided.

[Source: Chartered Institute of Environmental Health]

Bacteria

Bacterial food poisoning

Bacteriological control systems

Bacteriological standards

Cross contamination

Disinfection

Food poisoning (food-borne illnesses)

Food-borne infection

Food handling (practice)

Gastro-enteritis

Hand contamination of food

Indirect contamination

Raw milk (restrictions on sale)

Temperature control requirements

Canned goods

Canning was one of the first processes directed at preserving food for long periods. These goods should be stored at ambient temperatures around 10 – 15°C in a dry area, such as a dry goods store. They can have extensive shelf lives from several months, in the case of canned tomatoes, to 20 or 30 years, as with corned beef.

Defects in cans, such as leaking seams, can be a source of contamination, particularly if dirty water is used to cool the can after processing, which results in water being sucked in through the defective seam. This can result in spoilage of the contents due to bacterial growth and the potential for food poisoning. Past outbreaks of typhoid fever in the UK were caused by canned meats contaminated by Typhoid bacilli from polluted cooling water.

Canned goods stored in moist atmospheres or for long periods may rust and develop minute pin holes through which organisms can pass.

Blown cans, which bulge at each end, due to the production of gas inside may also be encountered, particularly with products such as canned meats, tomatoes and fruits.

Where there is evidence of any the above faults in canned goods, the cans and contents should be discarded and not used.

Canning processes

Canning is an important means of preserving food and canning processes have been in operation for over 200 years since the days of Napoleon. It is a method in which food is hermetically sealed in metal containers and heat treated until it is commercially sterile.

The main objective of a canning process is to destroy pathogenic and spoilage micro-organisms through the application of heat in order to achieve commercial sterility. The quantity of heat applied to a food is directly related to its pH as micro-organisms do not survive or grow below a pH of 4.5. Heat treatment duration further takes into account can sizes and the nature of the contents, as solid contents require a longer period of treatment than liquids.

The construction of a can is critical. Generally cans are manufactured from tin-plated steel and incorporate a lacquer coating on the inside. Seams at the end of the can forming the lid must be correctly made and sealed as this is the principal point where leakage can occur. At the head of the can (the head space) a vacuum is created and this vacuum is critical. This vacuum can be measured and is an indicator of satisfactory processing and future shelf life.

Botulinum cook

Canned goods

Clostridium botulinum (Clostridium welchii)

Commercial sterility

Hydrogen swell

pH value

Carriers of disease

A carrier is, broadly, an individual who is infected by a pathogenic organism and who is capable of passing the organism on to other people. A carrier, in many cases, will not experience the symptoms of the disease. Many people who suffer a disease may make a full recovery but, in many cases, remain carriers of same without manifesting the symptoms.

These carriers can be classified as:

Healthy carriers

These persons are the most dangerous form of carrier particularly if employed in the handling of food in that, whilst they may not show signs of illness, may excrete the pathogenic micro-organisms and, through not paying such attention to personal hygiene, may contaminate food

Convalescent carriers

When people are recovering from a food-borne illness they may excrete micro-organisms although the symptoms have ceased.

Incubation carriers

People who are at the incubation stage of food poisoning may excrete micro-organisms without necessarily showing the symptoms.

In some cases, people may excrete pathogenic organisms throughout their lives (chronic carriers) whilst other casual carriers may excrete organisms for a limited period only.

Acute food poisoning

Bacteria

Bacteriological standards

Chronic food poisoning

'Clean person' strategies

Cross contamination

Diseases transmitted through food

Droplet infection

Epidemiology

Exclusion of food handlers

Excreter

Food-borne infection

Food contamination

Food handling (practice)

Food poisoning bacteria

Gastro-enteritis

Incubation period

Hand washing

Health surveillance

Healthy carrier

Persons suffering from certain medical conditions

Pre-employment health screening

Prohibition from handling food

Reporting of diseases (food handlers)

Reservoir of infection

Training of food handlers

Water-borne infections

Carry-over effect

The consequences of toxic substances present in one food being carried to another food until they accumulate in body fat tissue or organs of animals bred for human consumption or, in the case of humans, carried in breast milk.

Ceilings in food premises

Ceilings in food rooms and food preparation areas should be so constructed and surfaced so that they can be easily cleaned and maintained in a clean condition.

Food rooms
Structural requirements for food premises

Certificate that there is no longer a risk to health

A certificate issued by an enforcement authority under section 12 of the Food Safety Act following the service of an *Emergency Prohibition Notice* or the making of an *Emergency Prohibition Order,* to the effect that they are satisfied that the proprietor has taken sufficient measures to secure that the health risk condition is no longer fulfilled with respect to the business.

[Food Safety Act]

Emergency Prohibition Notices
Emergency Prohibition Orders

Food Safety Act 1990

Health risk condition

Cestoda

These are various forms of tapeworm found in animals and fish which seriously affect fitness for human consumption. They include *Taenia saginata* (cattle), *Taenia solium* (pigs) and *Diphyllobothrium latum* (freshwater fish).

Tapeworms commonly incorporate a head with four suckers and, in some cases, a ring of hooklets. Behind the head are a number of segments, each containing male and female reproductive organs. The more posterior segments contain ripe eggs which are excreted with faeces. When the eggs are consumed by another animal the embryo developing from the egg enters the system and forms a small water bladder or cyst in the flesh or organs. If the flesh is eaten by a suitable host, the cysts develop in the gut to adult tapeworms. Evidence of such cysts is found during the meat inspection process.

The most important tapeworms, from a food safety viewpoint, are those of man, i.e. *Taenia saginata* (measly beef), *Taenia solium* (measly pork) and the dog, i.e. *Taenia hydatigena, Taenia multiceps* and *Echinococcus granulosus*.

Fish and shellfish (food hazards)

Taenia saginata

Taenia solium

Tapeworms (Cestodes)

Changing facilities

Suitable and sufficient facilities must be provided for changing clothes where people have to wear special clothing for the purposes of work.

Changing facilities should be readily accessible from workrooms and eating facilities, if provided. They should be provided with adequate seating and should contain, or communicate with, clothing accommodation and showers or baths if provided. They should be constructed and arranged to ensure the privacy of the user.

The facilities should be large enough to enable the maximum number of persons at work expected to use them at any one time, to do so without overcrowding or unreasonable delay. Account should be taken of starting and finishing times of work and the time available to use the facilities.

[Workplace (Health, Safety and Welfare) Regulations 1992 and ACOP]

Amenity areas

Food Hygiene (England) Regulations 2006

Regulation (EC) No 852/2004 on the hygiene of foodstuffs

Welfare amenity provisions

Workplace (Health, Safety and Welfare) Regulations 1992

Chartered Institute of Environmental Health Risk Categorisation of Food Premises

1. Preparation premises	Risk level
Hotels, restaurants, cafes	High
Take away outlets (excluding fish and chip shops)	High
Fish and chip shops	Medium
Public houses – where food is prepared	High
– no food prepared	Medium
All other kitchens (including educational establishments, prisons, canteens, hospitals, etc.)	High
Butchers – raw meat only with no preparation	Medium
– raw and coked meat and/or further preparation	High
Fishmongers	High
Delicatessens	Medium
Bakers and confectioners	High
Agricultural enterprises, e.g. farm vegetables	Low
Slaughterhouses	High
2. Retail premises	Risk level
Market stalls – e.g. vegetables	Low
fish	Medium
meat	High
Food hawkers – fish and chip vans	Medium
– beefburgers, hot dogs, sandwiches	High
Multiple stores (including supermarkets)	–
Retail stores	–
Greengrocers	Low

3. Manufacturing premises	Risk level
Alcoholic drinks	Low
Bread and flour products	Medium
Chocolate and confectionery	Medium
Processed vegetables – canning, vacuum packing	High
– other packaging	Low
Fish products	Medium
Oils and fats	Medium
Meat and meat products	High
Milk and dairy products	High
Infant and baby foods	High
Other dietetic products	Medium
Raw materials	–
Soft drinks and mineral water	Low
Beverages	Low
4. Storage premises	Risk level
Deep freezing and cold storage	Low/Medium
Importers, wholesalers, warehouses	–
5. Packers	Risk level
Egg packers	Medium
Canning, bottling and drying	Low
Fruit packers	Medium

Enforcement authorities

Enforcement procedure

Environmental Health Officers

Inspection of food premises

Chemical contamination of food

Chemicals, such as pesticides and cleaning substances, can cause contamination of food resulting in chemical food poisoning.

Careful control over all chemicals is required. This includes the provision of information, instruction and training, in particular, to cleaners and pest control staff, and ensuring any process involving chemicals follows the procedures outlined by the manufacturers in their safety data, including the correct dilution of cleaning agents and their application to surfaces in food rooms, together with the effective rinsing of such surfaces.

Specific storage areas should be designated for the storage of cleaning agents and cleaning equipment. A system of stock control and rotation should be operated, together with ensuring the regular cleaning of these areas.

Food safety management systems should take into account the potential for contamination of food by chemical substances used and stored on the premises. Control must be exercised over the location of rodent baiting trays and in the use of insecticidal sprays in food production and catering areas.

Cleaning, disinfection and housekeeping

Cleaning schedules

Contaminant

Contamination

Detergents

Detergent-sanitisers

Disinfectants

Food contact materials

Fumigation

Fungicides

Hazard Analysis: Critical Control Point (HACCP)

Insecticides

Pesticides

Chemical residues

These are chemical substances intentionally or accidentally brought into contact with, or added to, a food during its growth period. These include pesticides, herbicides and additives in feed and veterinary products.

Chemical contamination of food

Insecticides

Pesticides

Chill control

Chill control is an essential element for ensuring the safety of high risk foods.

Schedule 4 of the Food Hygiene (England) Regulations deals with temperature control requirements for food with particular reference to:

a)   chill holding requirements;

b)   upwards variation of the 8°C temperature by manufacturers, etc; and

c)   chill holding tolerance periods.

Chilled storage

Chill holding requirements

Chill holding tolerance periods

Food Hygiene (England) Regulations 2006

High risk foods

Temperature control requirements

Upward variation of the 8°C temperature by manufacturers, etc

Chilled storage

The process of storing high risk foods under refrigeration (1 – 4°C) in order to extend the shelf life for several days.

High risk foods

Temperature control requirements

Chill holding requirements

Any person who keeps any food:

a)   which is likely to support the growth of pathogenic micro-organisms or the formation of toxins; and

b)   with respect to which any commercial operation is being carried out,

at or in food premises at a temperature above 8°C shall be guilty of an offence.

[Food Hygiene (England) Regulations 2006]

Subject to sub-paragraph 2 and paragraph 3 (general exemptions from chill holding requirements) any person who keeps any food:

a) which is likely to support the growth of pathogenic micro-organisms or the formation of toxins; and

b) with respect to which any commercial operation is being carried out,

at or in food premises at a temperature above 8°C shall be guilty of an offence.

Sub-paragraph 1 shall not apply in relation to any food which, as part of a mail order transaction, is being conveyed to the final consumer.

Subject to paragraph 3, no person shall supply by mail order any food which:

a) is likely to support the growth of pathogenic micro-organisms or the formation of toxins; and

b) is being or has been conveyed by post or by a private or common carrier to the final consumer,

at a temperature which has given rise to or is likely to give rise to a risk to health.

[Food Hygiene (England) Regulations 2006]

General exemptions from chill holding requirements

Sub-paragraphs 1 and 3 of paragraph 2 (chill holding requirements) shall not apply in relation to:

a) food which
   i) has been cooked or reheated;
   ii) is for service or is on display for sale; and
   iii) needs to kept at or above 63oC in order to control the growth of pathogenic micro-organisms or the formation of toxins;

b) food which, for the duration of its shelf life may be kept at ambient temperatures with no risk to health;

c) food which is being or has been subjected to a process such as dehydration or canning intended to prevent the growth of pathogenic micro-organisms at ambient temperatures, but not where:
   i) after or by virtue of that process the food was contained in a hermetically sealed container; and
   ii) that container has been opened;

d) food which must be ripened or matured at ambient temperatures, but not when the process of ripening or maturation is completed;

e) raw food intended for further processing (including cooking) before human consumption, but only if that processing, if undertaken correctly, will render that food fit for human consumption;

f) food to which Council Regulation 1906/90 applies; and

g) food to which Council Regulation 1907/90 applies.

[Food Hygiene (England) Regulations 2006]

Chill control

Chilled storage

Chill holding tolerance periods

Food Hygiene (England) Regulations 2006

Upward variation of the 8°C temperature by manufacturers etc

Chill holding tolerance periods

In any proceedings for an offence consisting of a contravention of sub-paragraph 1 of paragraph 2, it shall be a defence for the accused to prove that the food:

a) was for service or on display for sale;

b) had not previously been kept for service or on display for sale at a temperature above 8°C or, where a recommendation has been made pursuant to sub-paragraph 1 of paragraph 4, the recommended temperature; and

c) had been kept for service or on display for sale for a period of less than four hours.

In any proceedings for an offence consisting of a contravention of sub-paragraph 1 of paragraph 2, it shall be a defence for the accused to prove that the food:

a) was being transferred:

i) from premises at which the food was going to be kept at or below 8°C or in appropriate circumstances the recommended temperature to a vehicle used for the purposes of a food business; or

ii) to such premises from such a vehicle; or

b) was kept at a temperature above 8°C or, in appropriate circumstances, the recommended temperature for an unavoidable reason, such as:

 i) to accommodate the practicalities of handling during and after processing or preparation;

 ii) the defrosting of equipment; or

 iii) temporary breakdown of equipment,

and was kept at a temperature above 8°C or, in appropriate circumstances, the recommended temperature for a limited period only and that period was consistent with food safety.

[Food Hygiene (England) Regulations 2006]

Chill control

Chilled storage

Chill holding requirements

Upward variation of the 8°C temperature by manufacturers, etc

Chronic diseases

A disease whose symptoms may last for many years and which develop slowly after infection.

Acute food poisoning
Chronic food poisoning

Chronic food poisoning

Food poisoning that develops slowly over a long period of time and which, in some cases, may be irreversible.

Acute food poisoning

Ciguatera poisoning

This is a form of neurotoxin food poisoning, which is similar to paralytic shellfish poisoning, and caused by consumption of various tropical species of fish, such as barracudas and snappers, which have been contaminated by a species of toxic algae.

Natural toxins

Neurotoxin

Scombrotoxin

Clean-as-you-go

'Clean-as-you-go' is one of the basic principles of food hygiene requiring food handlers to clean surfaces, such as floors and work surfaces, and to clear up waste items and spillages as they occur, sooner than doing so at the end of the production run or when there is time available.

Cleaning, disinfection and housekeeping

Cleaning, disinfection and housekeeping

Cleaning implies the removal of dirt, soil, food residues, grease and other unwanted matter from surfaces. There is a duty on both employers and occupiers of premises under both the Workplace (Health, Safety and Welfare) Regulations 1992 and Food Hygiene (England) Regulations 2006 to keep a food premises, equipment and other items clean. Evidence of poor or inadequate levels of housekeeping are, in the majority of cases, a direct indication of poor management control of the food premises. Poor housekeeping is commonly a contributory cause of foreign body contamination and accidents.

Disinfection implies the reduction of the number of micro-organisms to an acceptable and safe level. This may not entail total destruction or a significant reduction in the numbers of spores, however. Disinfection entails the use of a range of disinfectants. Heat through water at 82° C applied for one minute is a common means of disinfection. A range of chemical disinfectants, such as hydrogen peroxide and hypochlorites, are also used for disinfection purposes, together with ultra violet light. In the case of chemical disinfectants, it is essential that that be prepared and used according to the manufacturer's instructions in terms of contact time on equipment.

It is essential that there be an effective system for maintaining high standards of cleaning and housekeeping, particularly in the case of food premises. This is best achieved through the operation of a cleaning schedule, supported by regular inspections to:

a)   assess the efficiency of implementation of the cleaning schedule; and

b)   assess standards of housekeeping.

Cleaning-in-Place (CIP) systems

CIP systems are commonly installed in those premises manufacturing and/or bottling liquid products, such as beer, milk and mineral waters. The system involves extensive pipework connected to all items of equipment which come into contact with the product at various stages of the process.

At the completion of the food manufacturing process, or following the completion of a particular batch, the whole of the plant is flushed with a series of detergents and/or detergent/sanitisers followed by hot and cold water rinses. Detergents may be held within the system at a particular temperature for a specified length of time with a view to clearing soiling, food residues and other deposits.

Most CIP systems tend to be fully automatic and controlled from a central location.

Cleaning schedules

The main problem with cleaning operations is that, in many cases, responsibilities for the various cleaning activities are not clearly defined. A cleaning schedule, which identifies each area and item of plant, machinery, structure, the method, materials and equipment to be used, the frequency of cleaning, precautions necessary, and responsibility for implementing each cleaning operation, should be established. A manager should have specific responsibility for monitoring compliance with the cleaning schedule on a regular basis.

The following are the principal components of a formal cleaning schedule or programme:

- *The item or area to be cleaned* – the item of plant and equipment, wall surface, floor surface, etc. should be specified.

- *The frequency of cleaning* – this could be, for example, once per hour, once per week, or at the end of each production run.

- *Individual responsibility* – specific responsibility, either by name or job title, for ensuring the cleaning operation takes place to the appropriate hygiene specification should be clearly identified in the cleaning schedule.

- *Equipment* – there should be principal emphasis on the use of mechanical cleaning equipment, such as floor scrubbers, industrial vacuum cleaners, as opposed to the use of brushes, brooms and string mops.

- *Materials* – the choice of the correct cleaning preparation for the type and degree of soiling is important; manufacturers' instructions should be followed closely.

- *Method* – the method of cleaning should be clearly identified and the need to train people in the method of cleaning appropriate to the item of plant or surface concerned should be appreciated.

- *Special precautions* – in certain cases, it may necessary to clearly identify the hazards from the use of certain cleaning compounds or preparations and the precautions needed on the part of staff.

Inspection by a responsible person, such as an appropriately trained hygiene officer, should be directed to ensuring that the cleaning schedule for a particular room, area, item of plant or equipment has been implemented satisfactorily.

In order to achieve uniformity of approach, check lists should be used. Such lists should incorporate all specific items requiring visual or other forms of examination, the date of the inspection of same, details of the person undertaking the inspection and an indication of action necessary wherever deficiencies in cleaning and housekeeping procedures are noted.

Cleaning, disinfection and housekeeping

'Clean place' strategies

Contact time

Detergents

Detergent-sanitisers

Food Hygiene (England) Regulations 2006

Hygiene inspections

Hygiene managers/officers

Regulation (EC) No 852/2004 on the hygiene of foodstuffs

Appendix E – Cleaning schedule

'Clean person' strategies

These strategies are concerned with people, in particular food handlers, and include the following aspects:

- Personal hygiene
- Provision, use and no misuse of personal protective equipment
- Careful actions in ensuring personal hygiene
- Health surveillance
- Selection and placement of staff
- Adequate supervision and control
- Competent and trained operators

Aim – An increase in the subjective perception of hygiene risks by food handlers and staff generally.

'Clean place' strategies

Food handling (practice)

Health surveillance

Information, instruction and training

Personal hygiene

Personal protective clothing

'Clean place' strategies

These strategies are concerned with the structural, environmental and organisational aspects of hygiene control, and include the provision and maintenance of:

- Clean premises
- Clean plant and equipment
- Clean processes
- Clean environment
- Clean systems of work
- Adequate supervision and control
- Competent and trained operators

Aim – A reduction in the physical, chemical and biological conditions likely to lead to a food hygiene incident.

Cleaning, disinfection and housekeeping

Cleaning schedules

'Clean person' strategies

Food hygiene inspections

Information, instruction and training

Clean seawater

Natural, artificial or purified seawater or brackish water that does not contain micro-organisms, harmful substances or toxic marine plankton in quantities capable of directly or indirectly affecting the health quality of food.

[Regulation (EC) No 852/2004 on the hygiene of foodstuffs]

Clean water

Clean seawater and fresh water of a similar quality.

[Regulation (EC) No 852/2004 on the hygiene of foodstuffs]

Regulation (EC) No. 852/2004 on the hygiene of foodstuffs

Water supply

Clostridium botulinum (Clostridium welchii)

This micro-organism is one of the most deadly food poisoning bacteria. It is a Gram-positive anaerobic bacillus which forms spores and can survive high temperatures.

Consumption of food contaminated by *Clostridium botulinum* may result in botulism due to the release of a neurotoxin. There are seven types of botulism (A to G), each of which is recognised by the toxin produced in each strain, types A, B, E and F causing botulism in humans. Death may result due to disturbances of various brain centres, particularly that regulating the control of breathing.

Many foods are associated with the micro-organism, principally those with a pH above 4.5. Those which are common are poorly processed or contaminated bottled or canned products, which provide the anaerobic conditions necessary. Contamination of meat and fish may also arise since spores of the organism are widely spread.

Bacteria

Bacterial food poisoning

Bacteriological control systems

Bacteriological standards

Botulinum cook

Botulism

Clostridium perfringens

Food poisoning (food-borne illnesses)

Hot holding requirements

Clostridium perfringens

This anaerobic bacterium is commonly associated with meat and meat dishes, such as rolled joints of beef, stews and other meat dishes which have gone through a long slow cooking and storage process. Where they have not been cooled rapidly or refrigerated after cooking, or where they have not been re-heated thoroughly, the risk of infection can be significant. Contamination may be from excreta, raw meat and poultry and from soil. This disease has been associated in the past with institutional cooking arrangements, such as in hospitals, schools, factory canteens and prisons, where large quantities of food are prepared many hours before service and kept below a recognised hot holding temperature.

Clostridium perfringens is a spore-forming bacterium which often survives normal cooking and food poisoning symptoms arise as a result of an entero-toxin released during spore formation in the digestive system. Growth takes place between 15°C and 50°C and it usually requires an extremely large number of the organism to be present in the food for food poisoning, which is rela-tively mild, to occur. The onset period for the disease is 8 to 22 hours with duration of illness between 12 to 48 hours. Symptoms include abdominal pain, diarrhoea, occasional vomiting and nausea.

Bacteria

Bacterial food poisoning

Bacteriological control systems

Bacteriological standards

Clostridium botulinum (Clostridium welchii)

Enterotoxin

Food poisoning (food-borne illnesses)

Hot holding requirements

Cockroach control

The two forms of cockroach encountered in the UK are the German cockroach (*Blatella germanica*) and the oriental or common cockroach (*Blatella orientalis*) also known as the 'black beetle' or 'black clock'.

The oriental cockroach can measure up to 25mm in length and has a shiny dark red appearance whereas the German cockroach tends to be smaller in length (10 to 15mm) and has a yellowish-brown external colouring.

Both species of cockroach are capable of climbing rough vertical surfaces, such as brickwork, and often congregate around sources of water. They are commonly found anywhere where it is warm, damp and dark, such as basements, cellars, drains and certain items of equipment. In particular, cockroaches tend to be nocturnal in habit so that infestations can increase in size if the premises are not used at night. Bakeries are particularly prone to cockroach infestations in that they provide all the elements necessary for breeding.

Cockroaches are capable of carrying a range of micro-organisms, particularly certain food poisoning bacteria, such as *Staphylococcus aureus* and *Salmonella typhimurium*, which can contaminate food and equipment.

Reproduction takes place through the laying of eggs in an oothecae or purse-like structure, taking approximately two months to hatch. After hatching the immature cockroaches take between 6 to 12 months to reach maturity where there is a plentiful food supply and heat.

Preventing cockroaches getting into a building is of prime importance. They may be unwittingly brought into a building with laundry, raw materials and in food containers. The need, therefore, for vigilance is essential and, where necessary, inspection of suppliers' premises to ensure freedom from such infestation prior to taking on a supplier.

Control of cockroaches, in most cases, entails a formal programme of structural improvement and maintenance supported by sound cleaning and housekeeping procedures, backed up by the use of cockroach traps and insecticidal sprays. Structural proofing should include the sealing of cracks and crevices and around pipe holes, ducting and conduits passing through walls, ill-fitting panels and other items which allow access to a building. High levels of cleaning and housekeeping should also be maintained, including the regular removal of spillages.

Insecticidal control entails the use of residual insecticides containing fenitrothion. Before commencing any treatment, however, a full survey of the premises must be undertaken at night using a torch to ascertain the scale of the infestation. In daytime, the use of an insecticide incorporating a flushing action, such as pyrethrum, may be used. Ideally an insecticide should kill both mature adults and the nymphs, the immature insects. Deep-seated infestations can take many months to eliminate and very rarely is elimination achieved through one treatment session.

Cleaning, disinfection and housekeeping

Infestation prevention and control

Insecticides

Pest

Proofing of buildings

Structural requirements for food premises

Codes of Recommended Practice – Food Hygiene (England) Regulations

For the guidance of food authorities, the Secretary of State may issue codes of recommended practice as regards the execution and enforcement of the Hygiene Regulations and any such code shall be laid before Parliament after being issued.

The Food Standards Agency may, after consulting the Secretary of State, give a food authority a direction requiring them to take any specified steps in order to comply with a code so issued.

Every food authority:

a) shall have regard to any relevant provision of any such code; and

b) shall comply with any direction which is given and requires them to take any specified steps in order to comply with such a code.

[Food Hygiene (England) Regulations 2006]

Food Hygiene (England) Regulations 2006

Food Standards Agency

Cold chain

A term used to describe the continuing and uninterrupted storage requirements of certain high risk chilled foods from the final production stage to actual consumption. The cold chain incorporates a number of stages of storage, including that after production, during transport and at the premises of wholesalers, retailers and ultimate consumers.

Chill control

Chilled storage

Chill holding requirements

Cold holding/service

Temperature control requirements

Cold holding/service

Where cold food is being held for service it should be contained in suitable shallow cold holding containers that can keep cold foods at 5°C or lower.

Internal food temperatures should be measured at least every two hours using a calibrated thermometer. Cold food should be protected from contamination with covers or food shields.

Ice used on display should be self-draining and drip pans should be sanitised after use.

Hot holding/service

Ice

Temperature control requirements

Temperature measurement equipment

Cold store

Any premises, not forming part of a cutting plant, game-handling establishment or slaughterhouse, used for the storage, under temperature controlled conditions, of fresh meat intended for sale for human consumption.

[Animal by-Products (Identification) Regulations 1995 as amended by the Food Hygiene (England) Regulations 2006]

Temperature control requirements

Coliforms

Coliforms or, more correctly, faecal coliforms are a group of bacteria commonly found in the colon (large intestine) and include *Eischerichia coli* (*E. coli*), *Vibrio cholerae* and *Shigella dysenteriae*. Evidence of their presence in food may be an indication of sewage contamination. Coliforms are also responsible for much food spoilage, causing the production of 'off' flavours.

Bacteriological standards

Escherichia coli (E. coli)

Faecal coliform

Faecal organisms (bacteriological standards)

Shigella

Colony count

A microbiological technique which, fundamentally, involves counting the number of colonies of micro-organisms present in or on a particular food sample after a specified period of time.

Bacteriological standards

Detection methods

Colour coding of equipment

This is a simple system of controlling cross-contamination by using different coloured items of equipment, such as knives and cutting boards, in specific areas or for dealing with particular foods.

A typical colour coding scheme operates on the basis of:

- Raw meats   Red
- Poultry meat   White
- Cooked meats   Yellow
- Raw fish   Blue
- Vegetables   Brown
- Fruit   Green

Cross contamination

Equipment requirements

Colours

Artificial or natural colours are used to replace the natural colour lost during food processing or storage, or to make products a consistent colour. Commonly used colours are caramel (E150a), in products such as gravy and soft drinks, and curcumin (E100), a yellow colour extracted from turmeric roots.

Additives

E-numbers

Commensal

A biological relationship whereby one organism gains benefits without necessarily harming another organism. It is a form of symbiosis.

Symbiosis

Commercial freezing

The quick freezing and storage of food products at a temperature below -18°C. In some cases, products may be stored at -22°C or below that temperature.

Cold chain

Cook-freeze

Freezers

Plate freezing

Quick freezing

Thawing of frozen food

Commercial operation

In relation to food or any contact material, means any of the following, namely:

a)   selling, possessing for sale and offering, exposing or advertising for sale;

b)   consigning, delivering or serving by way of sale;

c)   preparing for sale or presenting, labelling or wrapping for the purpose of sale;

d)   storing and transporting for the purpose of sale;

e)   importing and exporting,

and, in relation to any food source, means deriving food from it for the purpose of sale or for purposes connected with sale.

[Food Safety Act 1990]

Contact material

Delivery of food

Labelling requirements

Transport of foodstuffs

Wrapping and packaging of foodstuffs

Commercial sterility

A term used in canning of goods, in particular, to describe the virtual total destruction of all micro-organisms and spores. Whilst some non-pathogens may survive the sterilisation process, the product is generally considered safe.

Botulism

Canned goods

Canning processes

Clostridium botulinum (Clostridium welchii)

Heat treatment

Sterile

Sterilisation

Community Instruments and Regulations

For the purposes of the Food Hygiene (England) Regulations, 'the Community Regulations' means:

- Regulation 852/2004 on the hygiene of foodstuffs
- Regulation 853/2004 laying down specific hygiene rules for food of animal origin
- Regulation 854/2004 laying down specific rules for the organisation of official controls on products of animal origin intended for human consumption
- Regulation 2073/2005 on microbiological criteria for foodstuffs
- Regulation 2075/2005 laying down specific rules on official controls for *Trichenella* in meat.

European food hygiene legislation

Food Hygiene (England) Regulations 2006

Meat

Meat products (food hazards)

Microbiological criteria

Regulation (EC) No 852/2004 on the hygiene of foodstuffs

Trichinella spiralis

Compensation

Compensation may be payable to the owner of food under section 9(7) of the Food Safety Act when:

a) a Detention of Food Notice is withdrawn; or

b) a magistrate refuses to condemn food which has been seized.

Compensation is payable to the owner of the food for any depreciation in its value resulting from action taken by the authorised officer. Where there is disagreement between the owner of the food and the food authority as to the amount of compensation payable, arbitration should be applied for.

Compensation for losses suffered

Where an Emergency Prohibition Notice is served on the proprietor of a food business, the enforcement authority shall compensate him in respect of any loss suffered by reason of his complying with the notice unless -

a) an application for an Emergency Prohibition Order is made within the period of three days beginning with the service of the notice; and

b) the court declares itself satisfied, on the hearing of the application, that the health risk condition was fulfilled with respect to the business at the time when the notice was served;

and any disputed question as to the right to or the amount of any compensation payable under this subsection shall be determined by arbitration or, in Scotland, by a single arbiter appointed, failing agreement by the parties, by the sheriff. [Section 12(10) FSA]

[Food Safety Act 1990]

Detention Notices

Emergency Prohibition Notices

Emergency Prohibition Orders

Health risk condition

Competent authority

The central authority of a Member State competent to ensure compliance with this Regulation or any other authority to which that central authority has delegated that competence; it shall also include, where appropriate, the corresponding authority of a third country.

[Regulation (EC) No 852/2004 on the hygiene of foodstuffs]

Food authority

Complaints procedure

One of the principal criticisms, from both enforcement agencies and consumers, is that food manufacturing, distribution and catering organisations do not handle complaints in a professional manner.

People who complain about food products, whether they are off the shelf of a supermarket or served in a hotel restaurant, are frequently perceived as 'trouble makers', idiots, cranks or as those who 'want something for nothing'. In most cases, people who have taken the trouble to complain, which may entail some degree of inconvenience or the risk of an embarrassing 'scene', are the very ones who seek the support of the enforcement agencies if they do not get satisfaction.

Whilst fines in a court for offences under the Food Safety Act may not be excessive, it is the adverse publicity following such cases that can be damaging to an organisation's image in the market place on a long term basis, particularly if reported in the press or on television. It is essential, therefore, that food manufacturers and others operating in the food chain, have a formal procedure for dealing with complaints from consumers, the principal objective of which is to ensure appropriate, fair and consistent handling of all product-related complaints and incidents.

Initial stage of the complaints procedure

All complaints/incidents, from whatever source should be reported immediately through a senior manager direct to a manager responsible for quality assurance. Judgement of priority and appropriate action should be made only by this manager and not by line managers. The importance of immediate reporting should be emphasised at all levels of the organisation. It is vital that no time is wasted!

The following information should be collected initially for all complaints:

1. Who received the complaint?
2. Where was the complaint received from?
3   The date and time the complaint was received.
4. The product type and brand.
5. Nature of complaint/incident.
6. Sample obtained or arrangements in progress to obtain same.
7. Date of purchase.
8. Product code number.
9. 'Best before' date.
10. Product purchase location.
11. Product purchase date.
12. Other parties knowing of the complaint/incident.
13. Action taken so far, if any, by the complainant.
14. Name of complainant, address and telephone number.

Follow-up procedure

Following receipt of the complaint, the responsible manager must assess whether the complaint is of a serious, major or minor nature. Depending upon this judgement, different levels of the organisation will be involved and appropriate action taken.

In certain situations it may be necessary to operate a product recall procedure but, in the majority of cases, a quick response at local level, aimed at reassuring the complainant may be sufficient. Any meeting with a complainant should take place in the presence of a third party. The principal objective of such a meeting must be the examination of the food product complained about with a view to identifying the reasons for the complaint and establishing the cause of the defect in the product, e.g. foreign body, mould.

Much will depend upon the nature of the complaint and the attitude of the complainant, e.g. hostile, friendly, as to the action to be taken at this stage. Under no circumstances should an admission of liability be made, however. The complainant should be informed that a report will be made to senior management, a copy of which will be sent to the complainant in due course. At this stage the examining manager should depart, reassuring the complainant that action will be taken to remedy the situation.

At the final stage, the complainant should be informed of the action taken by the organisation, the decision reached with respect to the complaint and any measures the company wishes to take to regain the confidence of the consumer. Such measures could include free replacement of the offending product or the provision of vouchers to a certain value to use in their food premises.

'Best before' date

Food safety management systems

Foreign bodies

Moulds in food

Nature, substance or quality

Product recall systems

Compositional requirements

The compositional requirements for a range of foodstuffs, including those containing additives, colourings, antioxidants, preservatives and flavourings are commonly incorporated in specific regulations, in some cases applying to particular industries.

For example, compositional requirements are laid down in:

- Cocoa and Chocolate Products Regulations 2003
- Condensed Milk and Dried Milk (England) Regulations 2003
- Fruit Juices and Fruit Nectars (England) Regulations 2003
- Honey Regulations 2003
- Jam and Similar Products (England) Regulations 2003
- Specified Sugar Products Regulations 2003

Additives

Antioxidants

Flavourings

Nature, substance or quality

Regulations

Confused flour beetle *(Tribolium confusum)*

A small dark-coloured beetle, approximately 6mm in length, found in stored cereal products, particularly flour. Evidence of infestation is seen by the meandering pathways taken by the beetle in flour dust on floors in particular.

Insecticides

Infestation prevention and control

Pest

Pesticides

Consumer protection provisions (Food Safety Act)

Any person who sells to the purchaser's prejudice any food which is not of the *nature* or *substance* or *quality* demanded by the purchaser shall be guilty of an offence. This section is not new and has been the principal means of protecting consumers against foreign bodies, moulds and other extraneous items found in food.

Any person who gives with any food sold by him, or displays with any food offered or exposed by him for sale, or has in his possession for the purpose of sale, a label, whether or not attached to or printed on the wrapper or container, which:

    a)   falsely describes the food; or

    b)   is likely to mislead as to the nature or substance or quality of the food,

shall be guilty of an offence.

[Food Safety Act 1990]

Without prejudice to the more specific provisions of food law, the labelling, advertising and presentation of food, including their shape, appearance or packaging, the packaging material used, the manner in which they are arranged and the setting in which they are displayed, and the information which is made available about them through whatever medium, shall not mislead consumers.

[Food Safety Act 1990 as amended]

Food Labelling Regulations 1996 (as amended)

Food Safety Act 1990

Foreign bodies

Moulds in food

Nature, substance or quality

Offences and penalties

Contact material

Any article or substance which is intended to come into contact with food.

[Food Safety Act 1990]

Equipment requirements

Food contact materials

Food contact surfaces

Food contamination

Food Hygiene (England) Regulations 2006

Regulation (EC) No 852/2004 on the hygiene of foodstuffs

Structural requirements for food premises

Wrapping and packaging of foodstuffs

Contact technique

A technique used in rodent control whereby a rodenticide dust, such as broma-dialone, is spread along runs and in harbourage areas. The dust is picked upon the feet of the rats and may be taken into the mouth, as part of the grooming process common to rats, or pass through the skin. Both routes of entry result in rapid extermination.

This technique is limited in its application to those part of a premises which are not classified as food rooms.

Food rooms

Infestation prevention and control

Pest

Pesticides

Rodent control

Contact time

The length of time for a disinfectant chemical compound, such as a hypochlorite, to be in contact with a particular surface to achieve the desired effect. This period can vary from 3 minutes in the case of a hypochlorite to 30 minutes in the case of other chemical compounds.

Cleaning, disinfection and housekeeping

Disinfectants

Disinfection

Hypochlorites

Contaminant

Any extraneous or unwanted physical, chemical or biological substance, or object, encountered in food.

Contamination

Food contamination

Contamination

The presence in food of contaminants or the process of contaminating food.

The presence or introduction of a hazard.

[Regulation (EC) No 852/2004 on the hygiene of foodstuffs]

Contamination of food is associated with:

a) plants, vegetables and fruit – yeasts, moulds and bacteria;

b) water – viruses and bacteria;

c) food equipment and structural surfaces – bacteria, moulds and yeasts;

d) air – fungal spores, bacteria and viruses;

e) animals, poultry, birds – bacteria;

f) food handlers – bacteria and viruses;

g) soil – bacteria, yeasts and moulds; and

h) sewage – bacteria and viruses.

Bacteria

Bacterial food poisoning

Contaminant

Equipment requirements

European food hygiene legislation

Fish and shellfish (food hazards)

Food handling (practice)

Food Hygiene (England) Regulations 2006

Food poisoning (food-borne illnesses)

Food safety management systems

Food safety requirements

Freshness and fitness of food

Meat

Meat products (food hazards)

Milk and dairy products (food hazards)

Moulds in food

Poultry (food hazards)

Regulation (EC) No 852/2004 on the hygiene of foodstuffs

Spoilage of food

Sporulation

Viruses

Water-borne infections

Yeast

Contractors on site

Organisations should have a formal procedure to regulate the activities of contractors on site, whether they be main contractors involved in project work or small-scale contractors involved in activities such as window cleaning and electrical work. Whilst company contractors' regulations are largely concerned with ensuring appropriate levels of health and safety performance, many instances of food contamination can be associated with contractors' employees failing to recognise the significance of working in food premises.

The briefing of contractors in the food safety requirements, physical segregation of specific areas in certain cases and control over all potential contamination-producing activities in the work need constant attention.

Contamination

Food contamination

Food safety requirements

Food safety management systems

Structural requirements for food premises

Controlled atmosphere

This process is used in the storage of fruit, vegetables and meat whereby carbon dioxide is introduced to delay ripening and slow down the process of the growth of microbes.

Meat

Meat products (food hazards)

Microbe

Controlled atmosphere packing

The precise adjustment of the composition of the air surrounding packaged food in order to extend its shelf life.

Controlled atmosphere

Shelf life

Wrapping and packaging of food

Conveyances and containers

Regulation (EC) No. 852/2004 on the hygiene of foodstuffs lays down requirements with respect to the hygienic transport of foodstuffs.

1. Conveyances and containers used for transporting foodstuffs are to be kept clean and maintained in good repair and condition to protect foodstuffs from contamination and are, where necessary, to be designed and constructed to permit adequate cleaning and/or disinfection.

2. Receptacles in vehicles and/or containers are not to be used for transporting anything other than foodstuffs where this may result in contamination.

3. Where conveyances and/or containers are used for transporting anything in addition to foodstuffs or for transporting different foodstuffs at the same time, there is, where necessary, to be effective separation of products.

4. Bulk foodstuffs in liquid, granular or powder form are to be transported in receptacles and/or containers/tankers reserved for the transport of foodstuffs. Such containers are to be marked in a clearly visible and indelible fashion, in one or more Community languages, to show that they are used for the transport of foodstuffs, or are to be marked 'for foodstuffs only'.

5. Where conveyances and/or containers have been used for transporting anything other than foodstuffs or for transporting different foodstuffs, there is to be effective cleaning between loads to avoid the risk of contamination.

6. Foodstuffs in conveyances and/or containers are to be so placed and protected as to minimise the risk of contamination.

7. Where necessary, conveyances and/or containers used for transporting foodstuffs are to be capable of maintaining foodstuffs at appropriate temperatures and allow those temperatures to be monitored.

[Regulation (EC) No 852/2004 on the hygiene of foodstuffs]

Cleaning, disinfection and housekeeping

Cleaning schedules

Food contamination

Food purchase and delivery

Food safety management systems

Hazard Analysis: Critical Control Point (HACCP)

Regulation (EC) No 852/2004 on the hygiene of foodstuffs

Temperature control requirements

Temperature measurement equipment

Transport of foodstuffs

Cook-chill

This is a method of mass food preparation used by hospitals, airlines and super-markets, in particular, where there is a high demand for ready-prepared meals on a continuing basis. In this process food is prepared, cooked to a core temperature of 70°C and then chilled rapidly to 3°C. It is then stored at that temperature and, on demand, regenerated (reheated) to 70°C.

The success of this process is dependent on effective temperature control at all stages. This entails regular temperature checks using probe thermometers and should the food, during its storage period, reach 5°C, it must then be consumed within 12 hours. Where the food commodity temperature reaches 10°C, it must be rejected.

This is, fundamentally, a five day process although some operators of the system may reduce this time. The storage period lasts three days with a further day for regeneration and eventual consumption on the fifth day.

Cook-freeze

Cooking of food

Food Hygiene (England) Regulations 2006

High risk foods

Temperature control requirements

Cook-freeze

This process is similar in theory to that for cook-chill products. In this case, the food commodity is stored at -18°C giving it an extended shelf life.

Cook-chill

Cooking of food

Food Hygiene (England) Regulations 2006

High risk foods

Temperature control requirements

Cooking of food

One of the principal objectives of cooking fresh food is the prevention of bacterial growth which could cause food poisoning.

Food cooked at a high temperature for a short period of time is generally safer than food which has been prepared over a long period of time at lower temperatures. This is due to the fact that the temperature at which bacterial growth can take place is quickly passed and the food reaches a temperature where bacteria actually die. Thus the time/temperature relationship is crucial to ensure safe cooking. Similarly, in the subsequent cooling of food, bacterial growth may take place if the food is allowed to cool too slowly.

Cooling of food

Core (centre) temperature

Temperature control requirements

Cooling of food

The risk of bacterial growth can be significant where cooked food is to be prepared for eventual cold service. To reduce this risk, cooked food should be cooled to between 10°C and 15°C within 90 minutes before being refrigerated. This prevents bacterial multiplication.

In the case of meat joints and other large items, such as turkeys, they should be cooked in pieces weighing no more than 2.5 kg. Similarly, in the case of liquids, such as soups and gravies, these should be split into smaller quantities of no more than 25 litres and cooled in wide shallow containers which assist rapid cooling.

Bacterial growth curve

Cooking of food

Temperature control requirements

Core (centre) temperature

This is the temperature at the centre or thickest part of food during cooking.

Cooking of food

Temperature control requirements

Corporate offences

Offences by bodies corporate

Corrective action

Corrective action implies any form of action directed at preventing contamination of food and is an important feature of the HACCP process. Other food safety monitoring techniques, such as food safety risk assessments, food hygiene inspections and audits, may identify deficiencies in cleaning procedures, inadequate storage temperatures and other breaches of food hygiene legislation. Inspection reports should specify corrective action required and the time scale for such action.

Certain notices served under the Food Safety Act and Regulations, such as an Improvement Notice and a Hygiene Improvement Notice, specify the corrective action necessary within a stated period, e.g. 28 days.

Audit

Food hygiene inspections

Foods safety risk assessment

Food Standards Inspection

Hazard Analysis: Critical Control Point (HACCP)

Hygiene Improvement Notice

Improvement Notices

'Minded to' Notice

Appendix D – Food Hygiene Audit

Creuzfeldt-Jakob disease

This disease takes the form of a transmissible spongiform encephalopathy in humans and can be fatal within 6 months of contracting same. It has been described as the human equivalent to bovine spongiform encephalopathy ('Mad cow' disease). Symptoms of the disease include brain disfunction resulting in dementia, loss of memory and disorientation.

Criminal offences

Breaches of the Food Safety Act and Regulations made under the Act give rise to criminal liability.

Principal offences under the Food Safety Act are:

Food safety

- rendering food injurious to health (Section 7)

- selling food not complying with food safety requirements (Section 8)

Consumer protection

- selling food not of the nature or substance or quality demanded (Section 14)

- falsely describing or presenting food (Section 15)

All reasonable precautions and all due diligence

Consumer protection provisions (Food Safety Act)

Food safety provisions

Nature, substance and quality

Offences and penalties

Critical Control Points (CCPs)

These are stages in HACCP at which operators of food preparation processes should exercise controls directed at preventing or minimising the risk of food hazards.

Corrective action

Hazard Analysis: Critical Control Point (HACCP)

Critical limit

In HACCP, a dividing line between what is safe and unsafe with respect to food preparation.

Hazard Analysis: Critical Control Point (HACCP)

Cross contamination

Cross contamination implies the transfer of, particularly, bacterial contamination from one contaminated food product, such as uncooked poultry, to another uncontaminated food product, such as cooked meats.

Contamination

Food contamination

Cryogenic freezing

This is a form of quick freezing whereby food is immersed in liquid nitrogen. It is mainly used for the preservation of commodities such as prawns and strawberries.

Frozen food

Quick freezing

Cryptosporidia

These are various unicellular protozoa, such as *Cryptosporidium parvum*, which can be ingested by a host, normally animals. This protozoon has a two-stage life cycle commencing with the development of oocysts, a form of cyst which, when ingested, causes the preliminary stage of infection.

The secondary stage takes place when sporozites, increasingly mobile cysts, enter the body cells of the host producing new oocysts. These oocysts are subsequently excreted in the faeces of the host and can contaminate natural waters, such as rivers and ponds. Normally, the cysts can survive water treatment, such as chlorination.

Infection, (cryptosporidiosis) occurs through drinking contaminated or unpurified water, consumption of contaminated food or through personal contact. Symptoms appear after an incubation period of approximately 10 days and include diarrhoea, abdominal pain, loss of weight and vomiting. Much depends on the state of health of the individual infected but those suffering form debilitating illnesses or damaged immune systems, such as those suffering from AIDS, are at greatest risk.

Definitive (primary) host

Faecal coliform

Host

Incubation period

Parasites

Personal hygiene

Protozoa

Sporulation

Water-borne infections

Curing of food

This is a method of preserving food, in particular, meat and fish. In this case, the food is immersed in a solution of salt and sodium or potassium nitrate or alternatively, the brine solution is injected into the carcase, as with the preparation of bacon. The subsequent increase in osmotic pressure reduces the available water and produces conditions which are difficult for bacterial growth to take place.

Brining

Preservation of food

Cutting plant

An establishment which is used for boning and/or cutting up fresh meat for placing on the market which:

a) is approved or conditionally approved under Article 31(2) of Regulation 882/2004; or

b) (although lacking the approval or conditional approval that it requires under Article 4(3) of Regulation 853/2004) was, on 31st December 2005, operating as licensed cutting premises under the Fresh Meat (Hygiene and Inspection) Regulations 1995 or the Poultry Meat, Farmed Game Bird Meat and Rabbit Meat (Hygiene and Inspection) Regulations 1995.

[Food Hygiene (England) Regulations 2006]

Cysticerci

These are the cystic stages of a number of tapeworms, namely:

- *Cysticercus bovis – Taenia saginata* (Cattle)
- *Cysticercus cellulosae – Taenia solium* (Pigs)
- *Cysticercus tenuicollis – Taenia hydaginata* (Dogs)

Taenia saginata

Taenia solium

Tapeworms (Cestodes)

D

Danger zone

This is the ideal temperature range, 5°C to 63°C, at which bacterial multiplication can take place.

Chilled storage

Chill holding requirements

Cold chain

High risk foods

Hot holding requirements

Temperature control requirements

Date marking

A date mark is a date or coded date indicating the period in which food should be consumed. Foods must be marked with either a 'use by' date or a 'best before' date.

Labelling requirements

'Sell by' date

'Use by' date

Deep freeze

This is the process of storing a range of foods at -18°C and below at which the growth of many micro-organisms is virtually reduced and the shelf life greatly increased. However, storage at these temperatures does not necessarily kill pathogenic bacteria and, on thawing, bacteria will commence to multiply.

Spoilage enzymes are also inhibited at these temperatures, but long term storage may result in loss of quality.

Bacteria

Enzymes

Frozen food

Shelf life (definition)

Spoilage of food

Thawing of frozen food

Defences

Food safety law provides a number of defences in the case of persons charged with offences.

Food Safety Act 1990

Where charged with an offence under the Act, the accused may be able to plead that:

a) the offence was due to the fault of another person;

b) the accused had taken all precautions and exercised all due diligence; and

c) the accused received the advertisement in the ordinary course of business and did not know and had no reason to suspect that its publication would amount to an offence.

'Act or default of another person'

Advertising food for sale

All reasonable precautions and all due diligence

Publication in the course of a business

Food Hygiene (England) Regulations 2006

In any proceedings for an offence under these Regulations, it shall, subject to paragraph 2 below, be a defence for the accused to prove that he took all reasonable precautions and exercised all due diligence to avoid the commission of the offence by himself or a person under his control.

If in any case the above defence involves the allegation that the offence was due to the act or default of another person, or to reliance on information supplied by another person, the accused shall not, without leave of the court, be entitled to rely on that defence unless:

a) at least seven clear days before the hearing; and

b) where he has previously appeared before a court in connection with the alleged offence, within one month of his first appearance,

he has served on the prosecutor a notice in writing giving such information identifying or assisting in the identification of that other person as was then in his possession.

'Act or default of another person'

All reasonable precautions and all due diligence

Food Hygiene (England) Regulations 2006

Food Safety Act 1990

Offences and penalties

Definitive (primary) host

This is the host in or on which a parasite undertakes its sexual stage and the terminal host of a parasite.

Host

Parasites

Dehydration

This is a technique of food preservation whereby water is removed from food products thereby reducing the potential for bacterial growth.

The technique is used in:

a) *spray drying* of milk, soups and other liquids whereby a concentrated liquid is sprayed into a hot air stream, usually in a spray drier chamber;

b) *roller drying* using a heated roller or series of rollers, the food being spread onto the rollers and the subsequent residue being scraped off;

c) *tunnel drying* whereby food is placed in trays and passed through a tunnel incorporating hot air blowers;

d) *air or sun drying,* a technique in which the food is simply spread out in the open air and used, particularly, in the drying of fruits, such as grapes (sultanas, raisins), currants, apricots, etc.; and

e) *freeze drying* where the liquid product, such as coffee or soup, is subjected to rapid freezing, removing the extraneous water and creating small ice crystals which are subsequently reheated in a vacuum; the steam is removed leaving a powdered residue which can be reconstituted by the addition of hot or boiling water.

On reconstitution by the addition of water, such foods should be treated as fresh foods, particularly in the case of milk, soups and gravies.

Preservation of food

Delivery of food

Food may be subjected to risk of contamination and loss of temperature control during the delivery process. On this basis, there is a need for the recipients of delivered food to undertake a number of checks to ensure the safety of that food. Such checks should include:

- date codes
- the integrity and state of any packaging
- correct temperatures of chilled and frozen foods
- the segregation of certain foods to prevent risk of contamination
- the level of hygiene of the delivery vehicle with particular reference to:
    - internal surfaces, which should be capable of being readily cleaned
    - temperature control of chilled (5 – 8°C) or frozen foods (-18°C or below)
    - refrigeration and insulation of vehicle
    - the construction of food containers
    - segregation of high risk from low risk foods
- and the personal hygiene of people delivering the food

Cross contamination

Date marking

Food purchase and delivery

Food receptacles

Packaging

Personal hygiene

Temperature control requirements

Transport of foodstuffs

Appendix G – Temperature Control Record – Deliveries

Depuration

The process of purification/cleansing of shellfish.

Fish and shellfish (food hazards)

Shellfish

Shellfish toxin

Detection methods

The physical contamination of food during preparation and processing can take place in many ways. Detection methods are directed at identifying physical contamination and include a number of scanning systems:

a) *Metal detectors* are magnetic devices located at the end of a production process which scan the product for evidence of metallic items, such as nuts, bolts, nails and staples.

b) *Bottle scanners* are used in dairies and drinks manufacturing operations and operate on the basis of sending beams of light through bottles passing along a filling line. Any contamination, such as dirty bottles or foreign bodies, breaks the beam resulting in the bottle filling system rejecting the bottle from the line.

c) *X-ray systems* are used in the large-scale production of convenience foods, in particular, such as ready-prepared meals. These systems readily detect extraneous materials which do not respond to metal detectors, such as glass fragments, plastic, bone and cardboard.

The visual inspection of products passing along a production line is still practised in many food manufacturing operations. Such a method relies heavily on the visual acuity, concentration and alertness of people undertaking this task, however, and is unreliable as the sole means of detecting contamination in continuous operations.

Extrinsic contamination

Food contamination

Foreign bodies

Detention of food

Under the Food Safety Act, authorised officers have the power to detain food which they suspect may be unfit or otherwise unsatisfactory.

In this case, the authorised officer must serve a *Notice of Detention of Food* by hand immediately on the person in charge of the food, and the owner of the food notified. The prescribed form for this purpose is covered by the Detention of Food (Prescribed Forms) Regulations 1990. Failure to use the prescribed form is a material irregularity.

Where an authorised officer exercises these powers, he must, as soon as is reasonably practicable and in any event within 21 days, determine whether or not he is satisfied that the food complies with the food safety requirements and, if he is so satisfied, must forthwith withdraw the notice (using the appropriate *Withdrawal of Detention of Food Notice*). The notice withdrawing the detention must be served as soon as possible to prevent further deterioration of the food. The notice need not be served by the officer but a person considered competent by the authorised officer. Where he is not satisfied he must seize the food and serve a *Food Condemnation Warning Notice* and take the food before a JP.

Detention Notices

Detention or seizure of food

Food Condemnation Warning Notice

Food Safety Act 1990

Appendix B – Food Safety Act forms

Detention or seizure of food

In circumstances where an authorised officer is of the opinion that any food is likely to cause food poisoning or any disease communicable to human beings, an authorised officer may either:

a)   give notice to the person in charge of the food that, until the notice is withdrawn, the food or any specified portion of it is not to be used for human consumption and either must not be removed or, alternatively, removed to a place specified in the notice; (Section 9(3)(a)) or

b)   seize the food and remove it in order to have it dealt with by a justice of the peace; (Section 9(3)(b))

and any person who knowingly contravenes the requirements of a notice under paragraph (a) above is guilty of an offence. ('Knowingly' requires proof of *mens rea* or intention.)

He must, at the same time, serve on the person in charge of the food a *Notice Warning of the Intention to Apply for Condemnation*.

Authorised officers should have regard to the chain of evidence where this might be crucial in any subsequent prosecutions and should make every attempt not to leave the food which has been seized unattended.

[Food Safety Act 1990]

Food Condemnation Warning Notice

Food Safety Act 1990

Appendix B – Food Safety Act forms

Detention Notices

An authorised officer of an enforcement authority may, at an establishment subject to approval under Article 4(2) of Regulation 853/2004, by a notice in writing (in this regulation referred to as a *Detention Notice*) served on the relevant food business operator or his duly authorised representative require the detention of any animal or food for the purposes of examination (including the taking of samples).

[Food Hygiene (England) Regulations 2006]

Detention of food

Detention or seizure of food

Food Hygiene (England) Regulations 2006

Detergents

Detergents are, fundamentally, cleaning agents which remove soiling from equipment, utensils and structural surfaces. They are described as surface active agents or surfactants in that the action of a detergent reduces surface tension.

The process of emulsification also takes place whereby grease is dispersed in water, suspended in water and prevented from re-settling on surfaces.

Detergents should be non-toxic and easily rinsed off.

Detergent-sanitisers

Detergent-sanitisers

This is a chemical substance which has the twin action of, firstly, removing soil from surfaces and, secondly, providing a degree of sanitisation of surfaces. It is vital that detergent-sanitisers are used at the correct concentration and water temperature. The use of automatic tap-dosing of detergent-sanitisers to utensil washing equipment, such as sinks, is designed to ensure correct concentrations.

Detergents

Disinfection

Equipment requirements

Diarrhoeal syndrome

A condition associated with frequent and excessive bowel loosening and movement.

Bacterial food poisoning

Direct contamination

A route of contamination passing direct from the contaminating agent to the food. Hand contamination of food, the dripping of contaminated fluid from food on to another food or where a contaminated food touches an uncontaminated food are typical examples of direct contamination.

Contamination

Food contamination

Hand contamination of food

Direct supply by the producer of small quantities of meat from poultry or lagomorphs slaughtered on the farm

This type of operation is covered by Schedule 5 of the Food Hygiene (England) Regulations.

Where a producer supplies meat to the final consumer or to a local retail establishment directly supplying meat to the final consumer, he shall ensure that it bears a label or other marking clearly indicating the name and address of the farm where the animal from which it is derived was slaughtered.

The producer shall:

a)   keep a record in adequate form to show the number of birds and the number of lagomorphs received into, and the amounts of fresh meat despatched from, his premises during each week;

b)   retain the record for a period of one year; and

c)   make the record available to an authorised officer on request.

A producer who fails to comply with the above requirements shall be guilty of an offence.

Food Hygiene (England) Regulations 2006

Offences and penalties

'Dirty'

A term implying varying degrees of soiling or contamination of a food, which may be of a physical, chemical or biological nature.

Bacteriological standards

'Clean person' strategies

'Clean place' strategies

Coliforms

Commercial sterility

Contaminant

Contamination

Cross contamination

Enforcement procedure

Examination of food

Faecal coliform

Faecal organisms (bacteriological standards)

Food injurious to health

Pathogenic agents (pathogens)

Personal hygiene

Diseases transmitted through food

A range of diseases and ill-health conditions can be transmitted by food as a result of contamination. These causes can be classified on the basis of physical, chemical and biological contamination thus:

Physical contamination

Contamination by a range of foreign bodies, such as fibres, hairs, false finger nails, pencil stubs, hair grips and earrings, some of which may cause interference with body functions, such as choking, or cause damage to teeth in particular.

Chemical contamination

Chemical contaminants include pesticides, cleaning and disinfecting chemicals, acids, alkalis, veterinary products, additives, heavy metals and dioxins, all of which, depending upon the concentration in the food, can cause a wide range of acute and chronic ill-health symptoms including diarrhoea, vomiting, stomach pains, dizziness, headaches, liver and kidney damage.

Biological contamination

This takes the form of microbiological contamination of food by pathogenic bacteria from a wide range of sources, such as food handlers, animals, birds, insects, food contact surfaces, water, waste materials, raw food, vegetables and fruit, meat and meat products, rice, cereals, dust and soil. This contamination produces the classic food poisoning symptoms, such as diarrhoea, vomiting, stomach pain and dizziness. In some cases, biological contamination can result in death of the consumer.

Acute food poisoning

Bacterial food poisoning

Canned goods

Carriers of disease

Chemical contamination of food

Chronic food poisoning

Coliforms

Contamination

Cross contamination

Direct contamination

Eggs and egg products (food hazards)

Extrinsic contamination

Faecal coliform

Fish and shellfish (food hazards)

Food-borne infection

Food injurious to health

Food poisoning (food-borne illnesses)

Foreign bodies

Gastro-enteritis

Hand contamination of food

High risk foods

Ice cream (food hazards)

Indirect contamination

Intrinsic contamination

Meat

Meat products (food hazards)

Milk and dairy products (food hazards)

Moulds in food

Pathogenic agents (pathogens)

Physical contamination

Poultry (food hazards)

Spoilage of food

Dish and utensil washing

This is an essential feature of maintaining good hygiene levels with a view to ensuring that food residues on which micro-organisms can grow are completely removed. Automatic dish washing equipment is used for the majority of dish and utensil washing.

Where such equipment is not available, or utensils are unsuitable for washing in same, a two-sink system should be used.

Equipment requirements

Two sink system

Washing of food and food equipment

Disinfectants

These are mainly liquids used to prevent or reduce bacterial contamination on the hands of food handlers, food contact surfaces, machinery and utensils. Application of water at around 80°C with a contact time of at least one minute is the more common disinfectant. A range of commercial chemical substances, such as those containing hypochlorites and hydrogen peroxide, are also used. In certain cases, ultra violet light has a disinfectant effect.

Contact time

Contamination

Disinfection

Hypochlorites

Disinfection

This is the destruction of micro-organisms, but not usually bacterial spores. Disinfection may not kill all micro-organisms but reduces them to a level which is neither harmful to health nor the quality of perishable goods.

Disinfection is the process of reducing the numbers of micro-organisms to a safe level only. Disinfection does not imply total destruction of micro-organisms nor a significant reduction in the number of micro-organisms, however.

Cleaning, disinfection and housekeeping

Disinfectants

Hypochlorites

Disposal and destruction of food

Food authorities are responsible for organising the destruction or disposal of food. This may be by total destruction, e.g. incineration, or disfigurement of the food commodity, such as the flattening of canned goods prior to disposal in a landfill site. Security provisions should ensure that such food cannot be returned to the food supply chain.

Enforcement procedure

Food Safety Act 1990

Distribution chain

This is the route of distribution of a food product from the manufacturer (or importer) to wholesaler, retailer and consumer. Contamination can arise at any of these stages of the distribution chain.

Delivery of food

Distributor

Fault of another person (defence)

Food business operator

Hazard Analysis: Critical Control Point (HACCP)

Distributor

A person who sells raw cows' milk that has been produced on a production holding of which he is not the occupier.

[Food Hygiene (England) Regulations 2006]

Distribution chain

Farm premises

Food business (definition)

Food business operator

Occupier

Production holding

Raw milk (restrictions on sale)

Shop premises

DNA (Deoxyribonucleic acid)

Inside a typical cell is the cytoplasm, (a liquid containing enzymes), metabolites (fats, products of digestion and proteins) and waste. The cytoplasm encloses vital structures, such as storage granules (proteins stored for subsequent use) and ribosomes, where genes, the units of inheritance, are replicated.

Genes are located on a linear chromosome comprising a strand of deoxyribonucleic acid (DNA). DNA fundamentally determines the species and individual nature of the bacterium, its reproduction rate, resistance to adverse environments and preferences for particular types of food.

Bacteria

Bacterial growth curve

Bacterial toxin

Enzymes

Doner kebab

This food product takes the form of minced lamb or beef which is spit roasted and then moulded on to a vertical rotating spit. The meat is further cooked as the spit rotates in contact with a vertical grill. The meat product is carved off the spit in slices and served with salad in a bread roll or similar product.

This is a particularly high risk food in many respects. Temperature control is vital during preparation and cooking due to the fact that contamination may have been introduced during the final shaping or moulding of the meat on to the spit. Raw kebabs should be refrigerated before use. Kebab meat should be thoroughly cooked at a high temperature, ensuring that the grill remains in operation at all times.

Cooking of food

Core (centre) temperature

Food handling (practice)

Food preparation

High risk foods

Temperature control (premises)

Temperature control requirements

Doors

Doors to food premises should have an impervious and smooth finish and be capable of being readily cleaned. Kick plates are beneficial in that they reduce the potential for damage and entry by rodents when the door is closed.

Proofing of buildings

Regulation (EC) No 852/2004 on the hygiene of foodstuffs

Structural requirements for food premises

Drainage of food premises

Food premises should be connected via a drainage system to a public sewer. The following points should be considered in ensuring effective drainage:

- design should ensure the system complies with current Building Regulations

- the floors of food rooms where a wet process is carried out or which are regularly cleaned by wet methods, such as hosing with hot water, should be laid to a fall of 1 in 60 to half-round floor channels covered by metal gratings

- outlets to sinks, wash basins, water closets and urinals should be connected to the drainage system via a trap

- filter traps should be fitted to outlets from certain items of equipment, such as potato peelers
- grease traps should be installed at outlets to sinks used for washing heavily soiled and greasy utensils, pans and containers, and should be emptied on a regular basis.

Equipment requirements

Food Hygiene (England) Regulations 2006

Food rooms

Regulation (EC) No 852/2004 on the hygiene of foodstuffs

Structural requirements for food premises

Washing of food and food equipment

Droplet infection

The transmission of infection by small liquid aerosols which carry bacteria. Mucus containing bacteria from the nose, mouth and throat can be expelled, particularly during sneezing, resulting in contamination of food. Many food poisoning cases are associated with droplet infection from food handlers and customers in food premises.

Bacteria

Cross contamination

Food contamination

Food handling (practice)

Food preparation

Personal hygiene

Training of food handlers

Dry goods

This term is generally taken to mean products such as canned and packaged goods, dehydrated products and other goods which are non-perishable. These items should be stored off the floor in a well-ventilated store at a temperature of 10-15°C.

Food storage

Structural requirements for food premises

Due diligence

The principal defence under the Food Safety Act.

All reasonable precautions and all due diligence

Consumer protection provisions (Food Safety Act)

Defences

Food Safety Act 1990

Food safety requirements

Dysentery

Dysentery is an acute infection of the intestines. There are two classifications of the disease.

Bacillary dysentery is associated with infection by *Shigella sonnei*. This micro-organism is spread through faecal-oral transmission from an infected person or may be contracted by the consumption of contaminated foods, including milk and water. Symptoms include diarrhoea, vomiting, stomach cramps and fever. In addition, faeces may contain blood, pus and mucus.

Amoebic dysentery, on the other hand, is caused by infection with a particular protozoon, *Entamoeba histolytica* and is relatively rare. Typical symptoms include abdominal pain, diarrhoea and, in some cases, constipation.

Bacteria

Bacteriological control systems

Shigella

Water-borne infections

Echinococcus granulosus

This is a parasitic tapeworm of dogs, the cystic stage of which may infect humans and food animals. Food contaminated with dog faeces is a common source of the infection.

Parasites

Tapeworms (Cestodes)

Ectoparasite

A parasite which survives on the body surface of its host

Endoparasite

Parasites

Eggs and egg products (food hazards)

Eggs and egg products have, in the past, been responsible for many outbreaks of *Salmonellae* food poisoning, particularly involving products containing raw egg, such as home-produced mayonnaise. However, in recent years, increased vaccination of poultry, together with improved flock hygiene measures, has reduced the incidence of food poisoning considerably.

Salmonella enteritidis phage type 4 is particularly invasive in poultry, causing clinical disease resulting in death of chicks together with pericarditis and peri-hepatitis in carcases on slaughter. Production of infected eggs by hens carrying the organism is sporadic.

Fresh eggs have glazed shells with a bloom on the surface. There should not be more than a quarter inch space between the contents and the shell and, when opened, an egg should have a pleasant smell with a clear white, yellow yolk and no spots. Cracked and broken eggs should be discarded.

Bacterial spoilage of eggs can result in changes in colour of the white, off-flavours and the putrid smell of rotten eggs. Fungal spoilage, such as 'pin spot' moulds of differing colours (green, pink, yellow, blue) on the surface of the shell and inside same.

Eggs should be stored and transported at an even temperature below 20°C, in dry conditions and should be consumed within three weeks of laying. Eggs should be sold under a 'use-by' date and stored in a refrigerator at below 8°C, with storage information being incorporated on the packages of eggs.

Pasteurised liquid egg is used in the catering and baking industries in particular. As a desirable substitute for raw eggs, liquid egg should be stored under refrigeration and used in the manufacture of products, such as mayonnaise, sauces, mousses and bakery confectionery products, such as meringues.

In the past, duck eggs have been associated with many cases of *Salmonellae* poisoning. On laying, the shells of duck eggs tend to be porous compared with hens' eggs which incorporate a wax-like coating. The environment of the duck pond also exposes the duck to a range of bacterial infections which can be transmitted to eggs. Generally, duck eggs should be treated with caution, held in refrigerated storage and cooked thoroughly.

Bacterial food poisoning

Cooking of food

Food poisoning bacteria

Pasteurisation

Salmonellae

Spoilage of food

'Use by' date

Emergency Control Orders and Ministerial Directions

Emergency Control Orders

If it appears to the Minister that the carrying out of commercial operations with respect to food, food sources or contact materials of any class or description involves or may involve imminent risk of injury to health, he may, by an order (in this Act referred to as an *Emergency Control Order*), prohibit the carrying out of such operations with respect to food, food sources or contact materials of that class or description. (Section 13(1)) Any person who knowingly contravenes an Emergency Control Order is guilty of an offence.

Under section 35, the offence is triable either way, with a £5,000 maximum penalty in a magistrates' court and an unlimited fine and/or 2 years imprisonment in the Crown Court.

The Minister may consent, either unconditionally or subject to any condition that he considers appropriate, to the doing in a particular case of anything prohibited by an Emergency Control Order. (Section 13(2))

It shall be a defence for a person charged with an offence under subsection (2) above to show:

a) that consent had been given under subsection (3) above to the contravention of the Emergency Control Order; and

b) that any condition subject to which that consent was given was complied with.

Ministerial Directions

Section 13(5) empowers the Minister:

a) to give such *directions* as appear to him to be necessary or expedient for the purpose of preventing the carrying out of commercial operations with respect to any food, food sources or contact materials to which an Emergency Control Order applies; and

b) to do anything which appears to him to be necessary under this section or expedient for that purpose.

Any person who fails to comply with a direction under this section shall be guilty of an offence. (Section 13(6))

If the Minister does anything by virtue of this section in consequence of any person failing to comply with an Emergency Control Order or a direction under this section, the Minister may recover from that person any expenses reasonably incurred by him under this section.

[Food Safety Act 1990]

Commercial operation

Contact material

Food Safety Act 1990

Food source

'Imminent risk of injury to health'

Offences and penalties

Emergency prohibition action

The power of an authorised officer to serve an Emergency Prohibition Notice and to apply to a court for an Emergency Prohibition Order in situations and circumstances where there is imminent risk of injury to health is an important feature of the Food Safety Act. This power was brought in to cover high potential risk situations, for instance, where there may be gross contamination of a premises due to flooding with sewage, serious infestation by rodents or where the risk of food contamination is excessive. The service of an Emergency Prohibition Notice ensures the immediate closure of premises or immediate prevention of use of an item of equipment or the operation of a particular process. Once the notice has been served, the authorised officer must then apply to the court for an Emergency Prohibition Order within 3 days.

An Emergency Prohibition Order cannot be made against a person.

Both an Emergency Prohibition Notice and an Emergency Prohibition Order shall cease to have effect on the issue by the enforcement authority of a certificate to the effect that they are satisfied that the proprietor has taken sufficient measures to secure that the health risk condition is no longer fulfilled with respect to the business (Section 12(9)). The enforcement authority must issue a certificate under subsection (8) above (*Certificate That There Is No Longer A Risk To Health*) within three days of their being satisfied as mentioned in that subsection. On the application by the proprietor for such a certificate, the authority must:

a) determine, as soon as is reasonably practicable and in any event within 14 days, whether or not they are so satisfied; and

b) if they determine they are not so satisfied, give notice to the proprietor of the reasons for that determination.

In the case of (b) above, the *Notification of the Continuing Risk to Health* must state the reasons for their dissatisfaction.

Emergency Prohibition Notices

Emergency Prohibition Orders

Enforcement procedure

Food Safety Act 1990

'Imminent risk of injury to health'

Offences and penalties

Appendix B – Food Safety Act forms

Emergency Prohibition Notices

If an authorised officer of an enforcement authority is satisfied the health risk condition is fulfilled with respect to any food business, he may by notice served on the proprietor of the business (in the Act referred to as an Emergency Prohibition Notice), impose the appropriate prohibition. [Section 12(1)]

Satisfaction as to the fulfilment of the health risk condition is, of course, based on a subjective judgement by the authorised officer at a particular point in time.

As soon as practicable after the service of an Emergency Prohibition Notice, the enforcement authority shall affix a notice in a conspicuous position on such premises used for the purposes of the business as they consider appropriate and any person who knowingly contravenes such a notice shall be guilty of an offence. [Section 12(5)]

Statutory Code of Practice No. 6 *Prohibition Procedures* recommends that the authorised officer, in the case of both an Emergency Prohibition Notice and an Emergency Prohibition Order, should if possible firmly affix the document inside the premises but in a position where it can clearly be seen and read by members of the public from the outside. A preferable position would be on the inside of the glass of a front display window. Where the authorised officer discovers that a notice has been removed or defaced, he should replace the notice as soon as possible, and consider starting proceedings for criminal damage. Where an order has been removed or defaced the officer should start proceedings under section 63(3) of the Magistrates Court Act 1980 to the court's requirement that it should not be removed or defaced.

An Emergency Prohibition Notice shall cease to have effect:

a)   if no application for an Emergency Prohibition Order is made within the period of three days beginning with the service of the notice, at the end of that period;

b)   if such an application is so made, on the determination or abandonment of the application. [Section 12(7)]

[Food Safety Act 1990]

Authorised officer

Emergency prohibition action

Emergency Prohibition Orders

Health risk condition

Offences and penalties

Statutory Codes under the Food Safety Act

Appendix D – Food Safety Act forms

Emergency Prohibition Orders

Where a Magistrates' Court or, in Scotland, the sheriff is satisfied, on the application of an authorised officer, namely by way of a complaint to the Magistrates' Court pursuant to section 53-57 of the Magistrates Court Act 1980, that the health risk condition is fulfilled with respect to any food business, the court or sheriff shall (mandatory, not permissive), by an order (in this Act referred to as an Emergency Prohibition Order) impose the appropriate prohibition. [Section 12(2)]

The authorised officer shall not apply for an Emergency Prohibition Order unless, at least one day before the date of the application, he has served notice (Notice of Application for an Emergency Prohibition Order) on the proprietor of the business of his intention to apply for the order. [Section 12(3)] The notice of application must be in the prescribed form as indicated in the Food Safety (Improvement and Prohibition) (Prescribed Forms) Regulations 1991.

Subsections (2) and (3) of section 11 shall apply for the purposes of this section as they apply for the purposes of that section, but as if the reference in subsection (2) to risk of injury to health were a reference to imminent risk of such injury. [Section 12(4)]

Similar provisions apply as in the case of an Emergency Prohibition Notice to an Emergency Prohibition Order with regard to service on the proprietor of the business and fixing in a prominent and secure position.

[Food Safety Act 1990]

Authorised officer

Emergency prohibition action

Emergency Prohibition Notices

Health risk condition

'Imminent risk of injury to health'

Offences and penalties

Emetic syndrome

A condition associated with acute (projectile, in some cases) vomiting accompanied by diarrhoea and abdominal pain, commonly associated with *Bacillus cereus* infection.

Bacillus cereus

Bacterial food poisoning

Emulsifiers

Additives, such as Lecithins (E322), which assist in the mixing of food ingredients that would normally separate, such as oil and water.

Additives

E-numbers

Endoparasite

A parasite living within its host, for example, in the organs, body tissues or a body system.

Ectoparasite

Endospore

An endospore is a heat resisting structure formed by some bacteria inside the growing or multiplying cell which is formed in inadequate environmental conditions, such as those with low nutrient and moisture levels and high temperatures. Endospores involve two groups of bacteria, the *Clostridium* group and the *Bacillus* group, both of which are significant as potential food poisoning agents. Endospore-forming bacteria are widely distributed but primarily inhabit soil. As such, they can survive for long periods in the soil as the outer coats make them resistant to adverse effects, such as dehydration.

From a food safety viewpoint, endospores are able to withstand the majority of food cooking and preparation processes. As such they are resistant to boiling water for up to 5 hours compared with other cells which are quickly destroyed in this situation. Spore-forming bacteria, such as *Bacillus cereus* and *Clostridium perfringens*, will form endospores as soon as there is a significant rise in temperature of a food product. When the temperature falls to below $63^{O}C$, they revert to the vegetative state within minutes. Temperature control of foods following cooking is, therefore, essential.

Bacillus cereus

Clostridium perfringens

Endotoxin

These are hazardous toxic substances which are released from the cells of bacteria and other micro-organisms, including various fungi. They remain within the cell during its normal life and it is only after the death of the cell, damage to the cell wall or during the formation of spores, that they may be released.

Endotoxins are associated with *Escherichia coli*, *Salmonellae* and *Clostridium perfringens* and the symptoms of infection include diarrhoea, fever and local tissue shock.

Bacteria

Clostridium perfringens

Enterotoxin

Escherichia coli (E. coli)

Salmonellae

End product testing

The physical, chemical and microbiological testing of finished products as a means of validating quality and determining their safety for consumption is a common feature of food manufacturing and catering processes. It has been successfully applied to drinking water, milk, milk products and egg products. However, such an approach has serious limitations and should complement, but not replace, an approach based on HACCP.

The limitations of end product testing to control, in particular, microbiological hazards, include:

a)   the problem of sampling and examining a sufficient number of sample units to obtain meaningful information on the microbiological status of a batch of food;

b)   the difficulty in defining a batch;

c)   constraints on time and cost to obtain results; and

d)   reliable and comparable laboratory methods.

Fundamentally, the microbiological safety of food can never be achieved solely by end product testing. Whilst this process will detect that some form of failure has occurred, it can only contribute indirectly to the identification and cause of the failure. Furthermore, no sampling programme can totally ensure the absence of pathogenic bacteria in a food and testing food products at the point of production, port of entry or when in the retail distribution chain is of limited value.

Detection methods

Food safety requirements

Hazard Analysis: Critical Control Point (HACCP)

Microbiological criteria

Sampling and analysis

Testing methods

Enforcement authority

The authority which, by virtue of regulation 5, is responsible for executing and enforcing the Hygiene Regulations.

[Food Hygiene (England) Regulations 2006]

Enforcement authorities

The food authorities in England and Wales, namely:

a) as respects each London borough, district or non-metropolitan county, the council of that borough, district or county;

b) as respects the City of London (including the Temples), the Common Council;

c) as respects the Inner Temple or Middle Temple, the appropriate Treasurer.

[Food Safety Act 1990]

1. In respect of any food business operator to whose operations Regulation 852/2004 applies but Regulation 853/2004 does not apply, the (Food Standards) Agency or the food authority in whose area the food business operator carries out his operations

2. In respect of any food business operator to whose operations Regulations 852/2004 and Regulation 853/2004 apply, the Food Standards Agency in the case of:

   a) a slaughterhouse;

b) a game handling establishment; or

c) a cutting plant.

[Food Hygiene (England) Regulations 2006]

Enforcement authority

Enforcement procedure

Food authority

Food Hygiene (England) Regulations 2006

Food Safety Act 1990

Food Standards Agency

Enforcement procedure

General and specific enforcement procedures for food authorities are laid down in the Food Safety Act 1990 and the Food Hygiene (England) Regulations 2006.

Food Safety Act 1990

A number of enforcement methods are available to the food authorities, the courts and the Minister. These include the powers of authorised officers to serve and enforce Improvement Notices and Emergency Prohibition Notices, together with powers of inspection and seizure of suspected food. Courts can make Prohibition Orders and Emergency Prohibition Orders and the Minister, Emergency Control Orders.

The main methods of enforcement by food authorities are dealt with in section 9 (inspection and seizure of food), section 10 (Improvement Notices), section 11 (Prohibition Orders), section 12 (Emergency Prohibition Notices and Orders) and section 13 (Emergency Control Orders) of the FSA.

Food Hygiene (England) Regulations 2006

An authorised officer of a food authority is empowered to serve and enforce Hygiene Improvement Notices, Remedial Action Notices and Detention Notices in addition to instigating prosecution of the offender. A court is empowered to make a Hygiene Emergency Prohibition Order.

Authorised officer

Detention Notices

Emergency Control Orders and Ministerial Directions

Emergency Prohibition Notices

Emergency Prohibition Orders

Food Condemnation Warning Notice

Hygiene Emergency Prohibition Order

Hygiene Improvement Notice

Improvement Notices

Inspection of food

'Minded to' Notice

Prohibition Orders

Prosecution

Remedial Action Notices

Enteric fever

A term used to describe both typhoid fever and paratyphoid fever.

Enteritis

Inflammation of the intestines, a common symptom of food poisoning.

Food-borne infection

Food poisoning (food-borne illnesses)

Gastro-enteritis

Enterotoxin

These are poisonous waste products which attack the stomach and intestine linings causing diarrhoea and vomiting. Both endotoxins and exotoxins fall within this group.

Enterotoxins are particularly poisonous and resistant to heat, being capable of surviving at a temperature of 100°C for 30 minutes. However, the bacteria which produce enterotoxins, such as *Staphylococcus aureus*, are less heat-resistant and the presence of bacteria in a food product is not vital for illness to arise.

Bacterial food poisoning

Endotoxin

Exotoxins

Food poisoning bacteria

Neurotoxin

Staphylococcus aureus

Enterovirus

This is a virus which can be transmitted by faeces. Transmission may be through direct contact, water and food which carry faecal contamination.

Coliforms

Faecal coliform

E-numbers

The term 'E-number' applies to the incorporation in food of a range of additives, such as antioxidants, colours, emulsifiers, stabilisers, flavour enhancers, flavourings, preservatives and sweeteners. Where a food additive is identified by an E-number, this implies it has been tested for food safety and is approved for use throughout the European Union. This approval is monitored, reviewed and amended in the light of new scientific data.

Antioxidants

Colours

Emulsifiers

Flavour enhancers

Gelling agents

Preservatives

Stabilisers

Sweeteners

Thickeners

Entertainment

This includes any social gathering, amusement, exhibition, performance, game, sport or trial of skill.

[Food Safety Act 1990]

Exposing food for sale

'Sale' (of food)

Environmental control

A term used to describe the control of certain environmental features in food premises, such as temperature, lighting, ventilation and humidity.

Average illuminances and minimum measured illuminances (lighting)

Food Hygiene (General) Regulations 2006

General requirements for food premises

Lighting recommendations

Regulation (EC) No 852/2004 on the hygiene of foodstuffs

Ventilation requirements

Environmental Health Officers

Duly qualified and appointed officers of a local authority who have a number of functions with respect to the enforcement of legislation including that relating to food safety, occupational health and safety, environmental pollution, housing and infectious diseases.

Authorised officer

Enforcement authorities

Enforcement procedure

Inspection of food

Inspection of food premises

Obstruction etc of an authorised officer

Powers of entry

Enzymes

An enzyme is a form of protein that can trigger chemical reactions in an organism without itself undergoing any change. They can cause food spoilage or decay under ideal conditions.

They operate best at body temperature and a neutral pH, their action reducing as temperature falls or rises. Enzymes continue to work in both freezers and refrigerators. They are destroyed by heat.

pH

Spoilage of food

Epidemiology

The study of the causes and transmission of disease.

Bacterial food poisoning

Equipment requirements

Generally, any equipment coming into contact with food must be in good condition and capable of being effectively cleaned.

Chapter V of Regulation (EC) No 852/2004 on the hygiene of foodstuffs lays down particular requirements with respect to equipment thus:

1. All articles, fittings and equipment with which food comes into contact are to be kept clean and:

    a) be effectively cleaned and, where necessary, disinfected. Cleaning and disinfection are to take place at a frequency sufficient to avoid any risk of contamination;

    b) be so constructed, be of such materials and be kept in such good order, repair and condition, as to minimise any risk of contamination;

    c) with the exception of non-returnable containers and packaging, be so constructed, be of such materials, and be kept in such good order, repair and condition, as to enable them to be kept clean and, where necessary, to be disinfected, sufficient for the purposes intended; and

    d) be installed in such a manner as to allow adequate cleaning of the equipment and the surrounding area.

2. Where necessary, equipment is to be fitted with any appropriate control device to guarantee fulfilment of this Regulation's objectives.

3. Where chemical additives have to be used to prevent corrosion of equipment and containers, they are to be used in accordance with good practice.

Chemical contamination of food

Cleaning, disinfection and housekeeping

Cleaning schedules

Food receptacles

Regulation (EC) No. 852/2004 on the hygiene of foodstuffs

Transport of foodstuffs

Eradication (infestation)

The process of treatment and removal of rodent, crawling and flying insect infestation in premises, particularly food premises.

Ant control

Bird control

Contact technique

Flying insect control

Food safety management systems

Hazard Analysis: Critical Control Point (HACCP)

Infestation

Infestation prevention and control

Pest

Pest control contracts

Pesticide

Rodent control

Structural requirements for food premises

Ergot

Ergot is a mycotoxin derived from a mould, *Claviceps purpurea*, and associated with grains, such as rye. The mould forms a hard black spur on the ears of grain and consumption of contaminated products, such as bread, may cause ergotism, a condition which can cause severe intoxication and even death following consumption of large amounts of the affected food. Moreover, continuing high levels of consumption of affected foods can cause gangrene.

Control is exercised by high levels of inspection and laboratory examination of grain supplied to a food producer.

Detection methods

Mycotoxin

Natural toxins

Escherichia coli (E.coli)

This micro-organism takes a number of strains and is found in the intestines of man, farm animals, dogs and cats. It is commonly found in raw foods, such as meat, poultry and fish and their by-products. It is easily destroyed by heat, through pasteurisation and effective cooking. The presence of *E. coli* is generally an indicator of poor standards of hygiene and/or inadequate processing of food.

Whilst the majority of strains are harmless, some strains cause a range of ill-health conditions due to the release of an enterotoxin, (which causes an illness similar to cholera in symptoms) and the invasion of the lining of the intestine (which causes an illness with symptoms similar to dysentery).

Infection from E. coli food poisoning has an incubation period of 8 to 72 hours and the illness may last for 1 to 7 days. Maximum growth of the organism takes place between 10°C and 40°C. Symptoms include watery or blood-stained diarrhoea, abdominal pain, vomiting and fever.

Enterotoxins

Food poisoning (food-borne illnesses)

Heat treatment

Incubation period

Pasteurisation

Raw foods

VTEC (Verocytotoxin)

Establishment

Any unit of a food business.

[Regulation (EC) No 852/2004 on the hygiene of foodstuffs]

European food hygiene legislation

This legislation:

- modernises, consolidates and simplifies previous EU food hygiene legislation;
- applies effective and proportionate controls throughout the food chain, from primary production to sale or supply to the final consumer;
- focuses controls on what is necessary for public health protection; and
- clarifies that it is the primary responsibility of food business operators to produce food safely.

As EU regulations, the legislation is directly applicable law. The regulations are:

- Regulation (EC) 852/2004 on the hygiene of foodstuffs
- Regulation (EC) 853/2004 laying down specific hygiene rules for food of animal origin
- Regulation (EC) 854/2004 laying down specific rules for the organisation of official controls on products of animal origin intended for human consumption.

The general hygiene requirements for all food businesses are laid down in Regulation 852/2004. Regulation 853/2004 supplements Regulation 852/2004 in that it lays down specific requirements for food businesses dealing with foods of animal origin. Regulation 854/2004 relates to the organisation of official controls on products of animal origin intended for human consumption.

The legislation introduces a 'farm to fork' approach to food safety, by including primary production in food hygiene legislation for the first time in the majority of cases.

All food businesses should be registered with the competent authority, such as the Meat Hygiene Service or the local authority environmental health department, depending upon the type of business.

The legislation requires food business operators (except farmers and growers) to put into place, implement and maintain a permanent procedure, or procedures, based on HACCP principles, although the legislation is structured so that it can be applied flexibly and proportionately according to the size and nature of the food business.

Assured Safe Catering (ASC)

BS EN ISO 22000: Food Safety Management Systems

Business

Commercial operation

Community Instruments and Regulations

Competent authority

Enforcement authority

Environmental Health Officers

Food business (definition)

Food business operator

Food Hygiene (England) Regulations 2006

Food premises

Food receptacles

Food rooms

Food safety risk assessment

Food Standards Agency

General requirements for food premises

Hazard analysis

Hazard Analysis: Critical Control Point (HACCP)

Layout of food premises

Liaison with authorised officers

Primary products

Registration and approval of food premises

Regulation (EC) No 852/2004 on the hygiene of foodstuffs

Rooms where foodstuffs are prepared

Structural requirements for food premises

Training of food handlers

Transport of foodstuffs

Welfare amenity provisions

Examination of food

Food authorities in England and Wales have a discretionary power to provide facilities for the examination of food. *Examination* means a microbiological examination.

[Food Safety Act 1990]

Authorised officer

Food authority

Microbiological criteria

Powers of entry

Samples, analysis of

Samples, procurement of

Sampling and analysis

Statutory Codes under the Food Safety Act

Exclusion of food handlers

No person suffering from, or being a carrier of a disease likely to be transmitted through food or afflicted, for example, with infected wounds, skin infection, sores or diarrhoea is to be permitted to handle food or enter any food-handling area in any capacity if there is any likelihood of direct or indirect contamination. Any person so affected and employed in a food business and who is likely to come into contact with food is to report immediately the illness or symptoms, and if possible their causes, to the food business operator.

[Regulation (EC) No. 852/2004 on the hygiene of foodstuffs]

Where food handlers are known to be suffering from food poisoning, they should not be allowed to handle food or to enter food rooms until they have been declared medically free from such infection. This implies that they must not have demonstrated symptoms of food poisoning for at least two days.

In the case of typhoid infection, food handlers should be able to demonstrate evidence of negative faecal samples for a period of, generally, at least 14 days before being permitted to handle food or work in a food room.

Other conditions which may warrant exclusion from food handling or work in a food room include septic cuts, whitlows, styes, boils and similar lesions, heavy colds and skin conditions.

Organisations should have a clearly written procedure covering the reporting of such conditions and the exclusion of food handlers where necessary.

Acute food poisoning

Bacterial food poisoning

Exclusion of food handlers

Excreter

Food business (definition)

Food business operator

Food handler

Food handling (practice)

Food Hygiene (England) Regulations 2006

Food poisoning (food-borne illnesses)

Food room

Gastro-enteritis

Health surveillance

Infection

Personal hygiene

Regulation (EC) No. 852/2004 on the hygiene of foodstuffs

Water-borne infections

Excreter

A person who persistently passes disease-carrying organisms in faeces and/or urine, whether or not displaying the actual symptoms of the disease.

Carriers of disease

Exclusion of food handlers

Personal hygiene

Exotoxins

A toxin released from the cell of a living bacterium, such as *Staphylococcus aureus, Bacillus cereus* and *Clostridium botulinum,* into its surroundings.

Bacillus cereus

Clostridium botulinum (Clostridium welchii)

Endotoxin

Staphylococcus aureus

Exposing food for sale

This term comes within the extended definition of 'sale' under the Food Safety Act. It means that if food is 'exposed for sale' there is a presumption that it is actually for sale. This applies particularly in the case of:

a) food exposed for sale by the organisers of any entertainment to which the public is admitted (whether or not they are admitted for money) where it is offered as a prize or reward or given away in connection with any entertainment;

b) where, for the purpose of advertisement or to further trade or business, it is offered as a prize or reward or given away; and

c) where it is exposed or deposited in any premises for the purpose of being so offered or given away.

[Food Safety Act 1990]

Entertainment

Food Safety Act 1990

'Sale' (of food)

Extrinsic contamination

This is the contamination arising from sources other than the raw food itself, namely external sources of contamination, such as foreign bodies. During manufacturing and catering processes, food can be exposed to extrinsic contamination from items such as glass particles, wood splinters, hairs, small personal items, such as pens, rings and hair grips, rodent droppings, dead insects, cigarette ends, plastic items and metal objects falling from badly-maintained plant and equipment.

Contamination may also be associated with poor standards of building maintenance resulting in flaking paintwork, rust from overhead pipes and contaminated water leaking from pipes, all of which could enter the product at some stage of preparation.

Food safety management systems should explore the potential for extrinsic contamination at the various stages of processing.

Contamination

Food contamination

Food safety management systems

Foreign bodies

Hazard Analysis: Critical Control Point (HACCP)

Intrinsic contamination

Structural requirements for food premises

Extrinsic factor

Any external factor, such as time, temperature and moisture, which affects or influences the survival and growth of a micro-organism.

Bacterial growth curve

F

Faecal coliform

A micro-organism, such as *E.coli*, the presence of which indicates faecal contamination of food.

Bacteriological standards

Coliforms

Escherichia coli (E. coli)

Exclusion of food handlers

Excreter

Faecal matter

Commonly excreta (stools) passed out from the alimentary canal of humans and animals containing indigestible residues and bacteria.

Bacteriological standards

Coliforms

Faecal coliform

Streptococci

Faecal organisms (bacteriological standards)

Bacteriological standards

Faecal coliform

Streptococci

False or misleading descriptions and information

Any person who gives with any food sold by him, or displays with any food offered or exposed by him for sale or in his possession for the purpose of sale, a label, whether or not attached to or printed on the wrapper or container, which:

a)   falsely describes any food; or

b)   is likely to mislead as to the nature or substance or quality of the food, shall be guilty of an offence.

[Food Safety Act 1990]

Farm premises

A farm occupied by the occupier of a production holding as a single farm and includes the production holding and any other building situated on that farm and occupied by the same occupier.

[Food Hygiene (England) Regulations 2006]

Fasciola hepatica

This is a liver fluke found in animals, particularly cattle and sheep, and in humans. The livers of animals may be unfit for human consumption where the bile ducts have become thickened, the condition known as 'pipey liver'.

Fault of another person (defence)

Where the commission by any person of an offence under the Hygiene Regulations is due to the act or default of some other person, that other person shall be guilty of the offence; and a person may be convicted of the offence by virtue of this regulation whether or not proceedings are taken against the first-mentioned person.

[Food Hygiene (England) Regulations 2006]

First aid arrangements

First aid is defined as 'the skilled application of accepted principles of treatment on the occurrence of an accident or in the case of sudden illness, using facilities and materials available at the time'.

First aid is rendered:

a) to sustain life;

b) to prevent deterioration in an existing condition; and

c) to promote recovery.

The significant areas of first aid treatment are:

a) restoration of breathing (resuscitation);

b) control of bleeding; and

c) prevention of collapse.

Health and Safety (First Aid) Regulations 1981

These Regulations apply to nearly all workplaces in the UK. Under the Regulations *first aid* means:

a) in cases where a person will need help from a medical practitioner or nurse, treatment for the purpose of preserving life and minimising the consequences of injury or illness until such help is obtained; and

b) treatment of minor injuries which would otherwise receive no treatment or which do not need treatment by a medical practitioner or nurse.

Duties of employers

An employer must provide, or ensure that there is provided, such equipment and facilities as are adequate and appropriate in the circumstances for enabling first aid to be rendered to his employees if they are injured or become ill at work.

Two main duties are imposed on employers by the Regulations:

a) to provide first aid; and

b) to inform employees of the first aid arrangements.

Self-employed persons must provide first aid equipment for their own use.

First aid rooms

Any first aid room provided pursuant to this regulation shall be easily accessible to stretchers and to any other equipment needed to convey patients to and from the room and be sign-posted, and such sign to comply with regulation 4 of the Health and Safety (Safety Signs and Signals) Regulations 1996 as if it were provided in accordance with that regulation.

Approved Code of Practice

The Approved Code of Practice to the Regulations emphasises the duty of employers to consider a number of factors and determine for themselves what is adequate and appropriate in all the circumstances. Furthermore, where there are particular risks associated with the operation of an enterprise, the employer must ensure that first aiders receive training to deal with these specific risks.

Factors to be considered in assessing first aid provision include:

a) the number of employees;

b) the nature of the undertaking;

c) the size of the establishment and the distribution of employees;

d) the location of the establishment and the locations to which employees go in the course of their employment;

e) use of shift working; (each shift should have the same level of first aid cover/protection); and

f) the distance from external medical services, e.g. local casualty department.

The general guidance suggests that even in a simple office there ought to be a first aider for every 50 persons.

First aid boxes

There should be at least one first aid box, the contents being listed in the HSE Guidance.

HSE Guidance

Contents of first aid boxes

A first aid box should contain the following items:

- 1 Guidance Card

- 20 assorted individually wrapped sterile adhesive dressings

- 2 sterile eye pads with attachment

- 6 individually wrapped triangular bandages

- 6 safety pins

- 6 medium sized individually wrapped sterile unmedicated wound dressings

- 2 large individually wrapped sterile unmedicated wound dressings

- 3 extra large individually wrapped sterile unmedicated wound dressings

and NOTHING ELSE.

A minimum 300 ml sterile water container should be provided where mains water is not available.

Equipment etc. for first aid rooms

The following equipment and other items are recommended for first aid rooms:

a)   a sink with running hot and cold water always available;

b)   drinking water when not available on tap, together with disposable cups;

c)   soap;

d)   paper towels;

e)   smooth topped work surfaces;

f)   a suitable store for first aid materials;

g)   suitable refuse containers lined with a disposable plastic bag;

h)   a couch with waterproof surface, together with frequently cleaned pillows and blankets;

i)   clean protective garments;

j)   a chair;

k)   an appropriate record (Form BI 510); and

l)   a bowl.

Travelling first aid kits

Where employees travel away from base, they must be provided with a travelling first aid kit. The minimum contents for a travelling first aid kit are:

- 1 Guidance card

- 6 individually wrapped sterile adhesive dressings

- 1 large sterile unmedicated dressing

- 2 triangular bandages
- 2 safety pins; and
- individually wrapped moist cleansing wipes.

[Health and Safety (First Aid) Regulations 1981]

First aid materials

The potential for food being contaminated by bandages and plasters worn by food handlers following cuts and other minor injuries must be considered.

Plasters should be of the specific type that are waterproof, coloured blue and which incorporate a fine metallic strip. In the event of a plaster being lost, such a plaster may be readily detectable by eye. In other cases, the plaster may be detected by a metal detector during the final stages of production.

In the case of injuries dressed with a bandage, much depends on the scale of injury. In certain cases, it may be possible to protect a cut finger with a rubber finger stall or a disposable rubber glove. In more serious cases, it may be necessary to withdraw the person concerned from food handling operations until the wound has healed completely.

Extrinsic contamination

First aid arrangements

Personal hygiene

Regulation (EC) No 852/2004 on the hygiene of foodstuffs

Testing methods

Fish and shellfish (food hazards)

All forms of fresh fish and shellfish deteriorate rapidly and should be treated as high risk foods, including strict temperature control and careful handling. They quickly contaminate other foods and should be separated from same. Evidence of unfitness in fish is shown by a dull, slimey surface, dark coloured blood in the gill pouches, limp bodies and sunken eyes. Spoilage largely takes place through bacterial growth and the actions of enzymes.

Fresh fish should be stored at 0°C using ice. Cooked fish and shellfish should be refrigerated or kept hot above the hot holding temperature (63°C). Fish which is to be eaten raw should be frozen at -18°C for at least a day.

Enzymes

Freshness and fitness of food

Hot holding requirements

Spoilage of food

Flatworms

These are worms lacking blood vessels and with a flat body. Many parasites take the form of flatworms.

Parasites

Flavour enhancers

Additives used to bring out the flavour in a wide range of savoury and sweet foods without adding a flavour of their own. A common flavour enhancer is monosodium glutamate (E621) added to processed foods, particularly soups, sausages and sauces. They are also used in a wide range of other foods including savoury snacks, ready-to-eat meals and condiments.

Additives

E-numbers

Flavourings

Flavourings

Additives in a wide range of foods, usually in small amounts, to give a partic-ular taste or smell. Flavourings are not allocated E-numbers.

Additives

E-numbers

Flavour enhancers

Floor surfaces

Floors are, perhaps, the most important feature of the structure of a food prem-ises. Floor surfaces must be impervious and capable of being cleaned effectively. They must incorporate a non-slip finish and, ideally, be coved to the adjacent wall surface to eliminate the dirt trap created at the junction between floor and wall.

Cleaning, disinfection and housekeeping

Cleaning schedules

Regulation (EC) No. 852/2004 on the hygiene of foodstuffs

Food Hygiene (England) Regulations 2006

Structural requirements for food premises

Flour mite

These mites have a colourless body and reddish/yellow legs, measuring around 0.5mm in length. Flour mite is a common pest of cereal products and is commonly found in food storage areas. Ideal breeding conditions arise in bakeries, in particular, where there are high ambient temperatures and humidity levels.

To prevent infestation, a high standard of cleanliness must be maintained together with regular insecticidal spraying of potentially affected areas. A good standard of ventilation of these areas is also essential along with regular stock rotation.

Cleaning, disinfection and housekeeping

Infestation

Infestation prevention and control

Pest

Pesticides

Stock control and rotation

Ventilation requirements

Fluidised bed freezing

This is a method of quick freezing, particularly in the case of garden peas and beans. The peas are frozen while suspended in a current of cold air blasted through a perforated plate. As a result of this process, the peas are not clustered together but individually frozen and the quality is excellent.

Quick freezing

Flying insect control

Flying insects, such as house flies, bluebottles, blow flies and fruit flies can infest food premises, particularly during hot weather. They represent a significant risk as they may carry bacteria on their bodies and feet. Moreover, flies feed through regurgitating partly digested food and may contaminate food in this way.

In many cases, flying insects, such as flies and bluebottles, lay eggs in food, particularly meat, resulting in the development of maggots in the food.

Control may be exercised through:

- flyscreening of doors, windows and other openings in the fabric of a building
- the use of plastic strips over external doors
- the use of ultra violet-emitting flying insect killers
- the use of fly-specific insecticides where there is no risk of contaminating food with same
- careful control over refuse and refuse storage areas.

Infestation prevention and control

Insecticides

Pest

Pesticides

Proofing of buildings

Waste food storage and disposal

Food Alerts

Previously known as *Food Hazard Warnings*, Food Alerts are the Food Safety Authority's method of alerting local authorities and consumers about problems associated with food and, in some cases, providing details of specific action to be taken.

Food Alerts are based on two categories:

a) Food Alerts for Action; and

b) Food Alerts for Information.

Food Alerts are often used in conjunction with product withdrawal or recall by a manufacturer, retailer or distributor.

Product recall systems

Food Assurance Schemes

Food Assurance Schemes are voluntary systems for food manufacturers and processors which set out production standards. These cover food safety, environmental protection, animal welfare issues and other characteristics that may be considered important by anyone buying their food products.

Additives

Consumer protection provisions (Food Safety Act)

End product testing

Food safety

Labelling requirements

Food Authentication by Spectrographic Techniques (FAST)

A laboratory technique using spectroscopy and nuclear magnetic resonance (NMR) to analyse the content of foods.

Consumer protection provisions (Food Safety Act 1990)

Food hazard

Food safety requirements

Nature, substance or quality

Food authority

This has the meaning that it bears by virtue of section 5(1) of the Act, except that it does not include the appropriate Treasurer referred to in section 5(1)(c) of the Act (which deals with the Inner Temple and Middle Temple).

[Food Hygiene (England) Regulations 2006]

Enforcement authorities

Enforcement procedure

Food Safety Act 1990

Food-borne infection

These illnesses are defined by the World Health Organisation as diseases, usually either infections or toxic in nature, caused by agents that enter the body through the ingestion of food. Every person is at risk of food-borne illness.

Bacteria

Bacterial food poisoning

Contamination

Diseases transmitted through food

Food contamination

Food poisoning bacteria

Food poisoning (food-borne illnesses)

Gastro-enteritis

Food business (definition)

Any undertaking, whether for profit or not, of whether public or private, carrying out any activities related to any stage of production, processing and distribution of food.

[Food Safety Act 1990 as amended]

Business

Commercial operations

Food business operator

Food business operator

The natural or legal person responsible for ensuring that the requirements of food law are met within the food business under their control.

[Food Safety Act 1990 as amended]

Food business (definition)

Food Condemnation Warning Notice

Where any authorised officer of a food authority has seized food with the intention of having it dealt with by a Justice of the Peace, a Food Condemnation Warning Notice must be given to the person in charge of the food and also the owner of the food.

According to Statutory Code of Practice No 4: *Inspection, Detention and Seizure of Suspect Food,* the notice should indicate the description, quantity and identification marks of the food and the intention of the authorised officer to apply to a justice at a particular date and time for the specified food to be condemned.

Authorised officer

Compensation

Detention or seizure of food

Disposal and destruction of food

Enforcement procedure

Inspection of food

Statutory Codes under the Food Safety Act

Appendix B – Food Safety Act forms

Food contact materials

These are any wrapping or packaging material with which food may come into contact. Such materials must be clean and, dependent on the food material with which they come into contact, capable of preventing contamination of food.

Packaging

Regulation (EC) No. 852/2004 on the hygiene of foodstuffs

Wrapping

Wrapping and packaging of foodstuffs

Food contact surfaces

These are work surfaces which may come into contact with food. Such surfaces must be kept clean and must be capable of being effectively cleaned, i.e. impervious and smooth surfaced. Food grade stainless steel and certain plastic finishes provide this degree of protection. Wood is unsuitable for all but the preparation of raw meat and fish.

Equipment requirements

Food Hygiene (England) Regulations 2006

Regulation (EC) No. 852/2004 on the hygiene of foodstuffs
Structural requirements for food premises

Food contamination

Contamination of food can arise at any point in the food manufacturing or processing chain, e.g. from contaminated raw materials, contaminated processing or cooking equipment, inadequate levels of personal hygiene and at the delivery or service stage. The sources of food contamination can be broadly classified into:

a) physical sources, such as soil and foreign bodies, e.g. metal and glassfragments;

b) chemical sources, such as cleaning agents and food additives; and

c) biological sources, namely those causing contamination by a range of micro-organisms, resulting in food spoilage, food poisoning and, in some cases, death.

Whilst physical and chemical sources can be controlled by appropriate management systems, the control of biological contamination is more difficult but, on the other hand, vital. Microbiological contamination is associated with a range of bacteria, viruses and moulds which, under the right conditions, will proliferate.

Principal causes of food contamination

These can be listed thus:

- Faecal contamination

- Hand to mouth/nose contamination

- Handling of food refuse

- Handling of cleaning materials

- Cross contamination from raw foods to cooked or partially-cooked foods

- Bad habits, such as nose picking

Bacterial contamination

Contamination by a range of bacteria is, perhaps, the most common form of microbiological contamination. Such contamination results in varying degrees of food poisoning. Sources of entry of bacteria into food premises include people, who may be carriers of a particular form of food poisoning, various forms of infestation, such as rodents, insects and birds, certain raw foods, the water supply, and various environmental contaminants, for instance, dust.

Viruses may be introduced through human carriers or raw foods, such as contaminated meat, and shellfish. Mould spores are commonly found on damp surfaces of structures and equipment, on mouldy food and in the air.

Some bacteria form poisons or toxins, and these are of great importance when considering food poisoning. Organisms of the *Clostridium* group will develop only in the absence of oxygen and are spore-bearing. Illness occurs after eating food, particularly meat, grossly contaminated with *Clostridia* which have multiplied during long slow cooling and storage of cooked meats, stews, pies or gravy. Many of the spores produced, which occur frequently in raw meat, may survive boiling, stewing, steaming or braising for as long as five hours. After cooking, these spores readily germinate into bacteria which multiply rapidly under favourable conditions, including temperatures up to 50C.

The toxin of *Clostridium botulinum* is a highly poisonous substance which affects the nervous system causing often fatal illness. This toxin is sensitive to heat, though in its pure form is destroyed by boiling. However, it is dangerous to rely on boiling for rendering toxic foods safe, because the toxin may be protected from the heat by protein and other substances present.

This toxin is produced in food by actively multiplying micro-organisms. It is lethal in very small doses and gives rise to symptoms quite different from other types of bacterial food poisoning, namely fatigue, headache and dizziness in the initial stages. Subsequent stages include effects on the central nervous system, such as disturbed vision and speech, and death often occurs within 8 days.

Aerobe

Anaerobe

Bacterial food poisoning

Botulism

Clostridium botulinum (Clostridium welchii)

Coliforms

Contamination

Cooking of food

Cross contamination

Endotoxins

Exotoxin

Faecal coliform

Hand contamination of food

Hand washing

Meat

Meat products (food hazards)

Moulds in food

Personal hygiene

Toxin

Viruses

Food (definition)

Any substance or product, whether processed, partially processed or unprocessed, intended to be, or reasonably expected to be ingested by humans. It includes drink, chewing gum and any substance, including water, intentionally incorporated into the food during its manufacture, preparation or treatment.

'Food' does not include feed, live animals unless they are prepared for placing on the market for human consumption, plants prior to harvesting, medicinal products, cosmetics, tobacco and tobacco products, narcotics or psychotropic substances, residues and contaminants.

[Food Safety Act 1990 as amended]

Food hygiene

Food Hygiene (General) Regulations 2006

Food injurious to health

Food Safety Act 1990

Foodstuffs – provisions applicable to

Regulation (EC) No. 852/2204 on the hygiene of foodstuffs

Food given away in connection with any entertainment

The extended meaning of the term 'sale' applies in circumstances where food is offered as a prize or reward or given away in connection with any entertainment to which the public are admitted, whether on payment of money or not.

[Food Safety Act 1990, section 2]

Entertainment (definition)

Food Safety Act 1990

'Sale' (of food)

Food handler

A person who engages in the handling of food in a food business.

Food business (definition)

Food (definition)

Food handling (practice)

Food handling (practice)

Any operation which involves the production, preparation, processing, packaging, storage, transport, distribution and sale of food.

Food handler

Food hygiene

Hand contamination of food

Hand washing

Personal hygiene

Food hazard

A food hazard is any physical, chemical or biological contamination of food that could harm the consumer.

Food products are presented to consumers in a variety of ways, as canned goods, dried food products, chilled or frozen products and in the fresh state, as with fruit and vegetables, bread and confectionery. The majority of products also incorporate an 'Eat by' or 'Best before' date on the container which advises the consumer on the relative 'shelf life' of that product. Food may be stored on shelves at ambient temperatures, in refrigerators and chill display units. Refrigeration generally implies storage at a temperature below 0°C, whereas chill temperature can be between 5°C and 8°C.

Common hazards associated with food and food products include:

Meat and meat products

Mould is frequently encountered on imported meat as black spot or white spot. These moulds are caused by variations in temperature during refrigeration. Black spot mould penetrates below the surface of the meat and must be removed by trimming, whereas white spot mould can be wiped off. Where mould is accompanied by sliminess, indicating bacterial spoilage, the meat would generally be unfit for human consumption. Decomposition in meat is caused by putrefactive bacteria, often accompanied by warmth and moisture.

Sausages comprise various quantities of raw chopped and minced meat, together with fillers and seasoning. Internal mould is a common cause of unfitness. Meat pies may be subject to mould growth and sourness of the meat.

Poultry

Poultry are subject to a wide range of diseases, such as fowl pox, fowl paralysis (big liver disease) and blackhead. When stored under poor conditions and at inadequate temperatures, poultry can rapidly decompose. Larvae (maggots) from certain flies can also infest the carcase.

Canned goods

Distension of the ends of a can indicates the presence of gas within the can caused by decomposition of the contents. This may be due to inadequate processing or the entry of bacteria through defective seams. Cans may leak due to perforation or inadequate sealing, they may exhibit surface rust, which can erode the can (pinholing) or have been subject to damage resulting in denting. Denting may result in damage to the seams allowing decomposition to commence.

Vegetables and fruit

Vegetables of all types rapidly decompose under wet conditions which may be caused by inadequate storage and transport. Soft fruits, such as raspberries and strawberries may be subject to mouldiness and decomposition. Dried fruits can be infested with a wide range of parasites, such as various forms of moth, mite and beetle. Mould growth and fermentation are also a cause of unfitness in dried fruit.

Bakery products

These include various forms of bread and confectionery products. Apart from staleness, various conditions can arise in bread. 'Ropiness' in bread is caused by a specific bacillus which produces a moist slimy mass in the bread. Bread may also be affected by black pin mould. Fresh cream confectionery products may be unfit due to rancidity of the cream.

Fresh fish and shellfish

Decomposition, brought about by bacterial action, is the common cause of unfitness in fish. This is manifested principally by the smell but also by sliminess of the outer surface. Fish are also subject to other bacterial infections, such as furunculosis in salmon, which is indicated by boils and ulcers on the skin. Various roundworms also infest the intestines and flesh of fish, such as *Filaria bicolor*, found in the flesh of cod. Shellfish may be subject to bacterial contamination by sewage.

Milk, dairy products and ice cream

The compulsory heat treatment of milk has largely eliminated many of the early diseases caused by milk, such as tuberculosis. However, milk is an excellent medium for bacterial growth and can sour rapidly. Milk may also display different colorations, and may be infected by yeasts and bacteria. Cream of various types, e.g. single and double cream, rapidly take on moulds and bacterial contamination. Unfit cream has been the cause of many outbreaks of food poisoning. Ice cream can be an ideal medium for bacterial growth, including those causing typhoid and dysentery in man.

Adulteration of food

Bacteria

'Best before' date

Carriers of disease

Contamination

Cross contamination

Danger zone

Diseases transmitted through food

Droplet infection

Eggs and egg products (food hazards)

Fish and shellfish (food hazards)

Food contamination

Food injurious to health

Food poisoning bacteria

Food poisoning (food-borne illnesses)

Food safety risk assessment

Hand contamination of food

Hazard Analysis: Critical Control Point (HACCP)

High risk foods

High risk operations

Ice cream (food hazards)

Infestation prevention and control

Malicious tampering with food

Meat

Meat products (food hazards)

Milk and dairy products (food hazards)

Moulds in food

Reheating of food

Rodent control

'Sell by' date

Smoking hazards

Spoilage of food

Unfitness for human consumption

Food Hazard Warning System

A government system to alert the public and food authorities to national or regional problems concerning food which does not meet food safety requirements. This system is now known as the Food Alerts system.

Food Alerts

Food safety requirements

Food hygiene

The range of practices and procedures involved in ensuring food is safe to eat.

The measures and conditions necessary to control hazards and to ensure fitness for human consumption of a foodstuff taking into account its intended use.

[Regulation (EC) No 852/2004 on the hygiene of foodstuffs]

Food Hygiene (England) Regulations 2006

Regulation (EC) No 852/2004 on the hygiene of foodstuffs

Food Hygiene Audit

A technique for monitoring the hygiene standards in a food premises.

Audit

Food safety management systems

Hazard Analysis: Critical Control Point (HACCP)

Appendix D – Food Hygiene Audit

Food Hygiene (England) Regulations 2006

These Regulations are made under the Food Safety Act 1990 implementing a number of Community instruments dealing with:

a) the hygiene of foodstuffs;

b) specific hygiene rules for food of animal origin;

c) specific rules for the organisation of official controls on products of animal origin intended for human consumption;

d) microbiological criteria for foodstuffs; and

e) official controls for *Trichinella* in meat.

These Regulations:

a) create certain presumptions that, for the purposes of these Regulations, specified food is intended for human consumption; (Regulation 3)

b) provide that the Food Standards Agency is the competent authority for the purposes of the Community Regulations except where it has delegated competences as provided for in the Community Regulations; (Regulation 4)

c) make provision for the execution and enforcement of these Regulations and of the Community Regulations; (Regulation 5)

d) provide for the following enforcement measures to be available in respect of a food business operator:

   i) Hygiene Improvement Notices; (Regulation 6);

   ii) Hygiene Prohibition Orders (Regulation 7);

   iii) Hygiene Emergency Prohibition Notices and Orders (Regulation 8); and

   iv) Remedial Action Notices and Detention Notices (Regulation 9);

e) provide that where the commission of an offence under the Regulations is due to the act or default of some other person that other person is guilty of the offence (Regulation 10);

f) provide that in proceedings for an offence under these Regulations it is a defence for the accused to prove that he took *all reasonable precautions* and exercised *all due diligence* to avoid the commission of the offence (Regulation 11);

g) provide for the procurement and analysis of samples (Regulations 12 and 13);

h) provide powers of entry for authorised officers of an enforcement authority (Regulation 14);

i) create the offence of obstructing an officer (Regulation 15);

j) provide a time limit for bringing prosecutions (Regulation 16);

k) provides that a person who contravenes or fails to comply with the specified provisions of the Community Regulations is guilty of an offence (Regulation 17(1));

l) provide penalties for offences (Regulations 17(2) and (3));

m) provide that a person is considered not to have contravened or failed to comply with a specified provision of Regulation (EC) No 852/2004 (requirement for bulk foodstuffs in liquid, granular or powder form to be transported in receptacles and/or containers/tankers reserved for the transport of foodstuffs) provided the requirements of Schedule 3 are complied with; (Regulation 17(4));

n) provide that where an offence under these Regulations which has been committed by a body corporate is proved to have been committed with the consent or connivance of, or to be attributable to any neglect on the part of, an officer of the body corporate or a person purporting to act as such he as well as the body corporate is deemed to be guilty of that offence and may be proceeded against and punished accordingly (Regulation 18);

o) provide that where an offence under these Regulations which has been committed by a Scottish partnership is proved to have been committed with the consent or connivance of, or to be attributable to any neglect on the part of, a partner he as well as the partnership is deemed to be guilty of that offence and may be proceeded against and punished accordingly (Regulation 19);

p) provide a right of appeal in respect of:

    i) the service of a Hygiene Improvement Notice or a Remedial Action Notice;

    ii) the refusal of an enforcement authority to issue a certificate under specified provisions to the effect that they are satisfied that a food business operator has taken measures to secure that the health risk condition is no longer fulfilled with respect to the food business concerned; and

    iii) the making of a Hygiene Prohibition Order of the making of a Hygiene Emergency Prohibition Order (Regulations 20 to 22).

q) provide for the application, for the purposes of these Regulations, of section 9 of the Food Safety Act 1990, but with a specified modification (Regulation 23);

r) provide for the issue to food authorities by the Secretary of State of codes of recommended practice (Regulation 24);

s) provide for the protection of officers acting in good faith (Regulation 25);

t) provide for the revocation or suspension of the designation or as the case may be appointment of specified officials (Regulation 26);

u) provide that when an authorised officer of an enforcement authority has certified that where any food has not been produced, processed or distributed in compliance with these Regulations and the Community Regulations, it shall be treated for the purposes of section 9 of the Food Safety Act as failing to comply with the food safety requirements (Regulation 27);

v) provide for the service of documents (Regulation 28);

w) provide that the requirements set out in the following Schedules have effect:

    i) Schedule 3 (bulk transport in sea-going vessels of liquid oils or fats and the bulk transport by sea of raw sugar) (Regulation 29);

    ii) Schedule 4 (temperature control requirements) (Regulation 30);

    iii) Schedule 5 (direct supply by the producer of small quantities of meat from poultry or lagomorphs slaughtered on the farm) (Regulation 31);

    iv) Schedule 6 (restrictions on the sale of raw milk intended for human consumption) (Regulation 32);

x)   make consequential amendments to specified instruments; (Regulation 33)

y)   revoke the Food Hygiene (England) Regulations 2005. (Regulation 34)

All reasonable precautions and all due diligence

Appeals against Notices, etc

Appeals to Crown Court

Bulk transport in sea-going vessels of liquid oils, etc

Certificate that there is no longer a risk to health

Chill holding requirements

Community Instruments and Regulations

Corporate offences

Defences

Detention Notices

Direct supply by the producer of small quantities of meat from poultry or lago-morphs slaughtered on the farm

Emergency Prohibition Notices

Emergency Prohibition Orders

Food (definition)

Food business (definition)

Food Condemnation Warning Notice

Health risk condition

Hot holding requirements

Hygiene Emergency Prohibition Notice

Hygiene Emergency Prohibition Order

Hygiene Improvement Notice

Hygiene Prohibition Orders

Improvement Notices

Liquid oils and fats – bulk transport by sea

Obstruction etc of an authorised officer

Premises (definition)

Presumption that food is intended for human consumption

Prohibition Orders

Protection of officers acting in good faith

Raw milk (restrictions on sale)

Food hygiene inspections

A food hygiene inspection is generally taken to mean a scheduled or unscheduled physical inspection of a food premises or part of same by a trained company specialist or an external specialist with a view to assessing current standards of hygiene practice.

Authorised officers undertake hygiene inspections to assess compliance with the FSA and Regulations made thereunder, such as the Food Hygiene (England) Regulations 2006. Statutory Code of Practice No.3 *Inspection Procedures – General* defines 'inspection' as meaning a visit to any food premises which involves one or more of the following activities:

a)   inspection of premises;

b)   inspection of equipment including cleaning and maintenance equipment;

c)   inspection of process or operational procedure;

d)   inspection of the hygiene or practices of personnel;

e)   inspection of food (including ingredients, additives and products at any stage of manufacture) or contact materials;

f)   inspection of labels, labelling requirements and advertising material; and/or

g)   inspection of records.

Statutory Code of Practice No.9 *Food Hygiene Inspections* states that food hygiene inspections have two main purposes.

Firstly, authorised officers should identify contraventions of the Food Safety Act and food hygiene and processing regulations and seek to have them corrected.

Secondly, they should seek to identify potential risks arising from the activities carried on, such as processing, cooking, handling and storage of food.

More specifically, an inspection should include a preliminary assessment of the food safety hazards associated with the business to identify those areas of the processing, distribution, handling, storage and display of food which require closer scrutiny.

[Food Safety Act 1990 Code of Practice No. 9 *Food Hygiene Inspections*]

Internal food hygiene inspections

Operators of food businesses need to undertake food hygiene inspections on a regular basis. Depending upon the size of the business, consideration should be given to the appointment of a trained hygiene officer.

Whilst a food hygiene inspection can cover a number of areas, much depending upon the nature of the premises and processes being undertaken, the following aspects need consideration in the majority of food premises:

Structural Features

All structural features, namely floors, walls, ceilings, doors. etc. should be constructed of such materials and in such a manner as to be impervious and capable of being readily cleansed. They must be maintained and decorated so as to facilitate cleaning and prevent hazards from foreign bodies.

Layout

Food production and storage areas should be designed in such a way as to ensure a continuous flow of products from raw materials entering one part of the premises and finished goods being despatched from another part. Layouts should be designed to eliminate congestion and to facilitate cleaning and house-keeping procedures.

Plant, Machinery and Equipment

These items must be designed and constructed with careful consideration to the type and nature of the foods being prepared or processed. They must be constructed of materials which are impervious and inert to the food in contact with them, and which can be easily cleaned.

Environmental Factors

Appropriate control over temperature, lighting and ventilation is vital in the maintenance of sound hygiene practice.

Food Handlers and Food Handling

All food handlers should be subject to a pre-employment health examination and regular health examinations by an occupational health nurse with a view to assessing their current health state and continuing fitness to handle food.

Training in, and supervision of, food handling operations is essential in preventing contamination of food by food handlers. All staff should receive a basic training course in food hygiene, such as the Foundation Certificate in Food Hygiene course run under the auspices of the Chartered Institute of Environmental Health. Training should be further reinforced by regular discussion on hygiene procedures between supervisors and operators.

Cleaning and Housekeeping Procedures

A formal cleaning schedule, which identifies each item of plant and equipment and specific structural items, the method, materials and equipment to be used, the frequency of cleaning, individual responsibility for ensuring implementation of each cleaning task and any particular precautions necessary, should be operated as a direct means of managing the cleaning process.

Hygiene inspections should monitor the efficiency of implementation of the cleaning schedule.

Prevention of Infestation

Infestation prevention implies the use of structural proofing measures, the maintenance of high levels of cleaning and housekeeping, and the elimination of harbourage for various types of infestation (rodents, crawling and flying insects, birds), with various control measures, such as rodent baiting, as a third line of defence.

Hygiene inspection should be geared to identifying evidence of infestation of all types.

Food and Food Ingredient Control

Inspection should be directed to the examination of incoming raw materials, ingredients and finished products for immediate or ultimate consumption. Particular attention must be paid to the temperature control requirements for a wide range of foods.

Cleaning, disinfection and housekeeping

'Clean place' strategies

Food injurious to health

Any person who renders any food injurious to health by means of any of the following operations, namely:

a)   adding any article or substance to the food;

b)   using any article or substance as an ingredient in the preparation of food;

c)   abstracting any constituent from the food; and

d)   subjecting the food to any other process or treatment,

with intent that it shall be sold for human consumption, shall be guilty of an offence.

In determining for the purposes of this section and section 8(2) (failure to comply with food safety requirements) whether any food is injurious to health, regard shall be had:

a) not only to the probable effect of that food on the health of a person consuming it; but

b) also the probable cumulative effect of food of substantially the same composition on the health of a person consuming it in ordinary quantities.

Injury, in relation to health, includes any impairment, whether permanent or temporary, and *injurious to health* shall be construed accordingly.

[Food Safety Act 1990]

Adulteration of food

All reasonable precautions and all due diligence

Food Safety Act 1990

Food safety requirements

Offences and penalties

Food Labelling Regulations 1996 (as amended)

These regulations are extensive and incorporate many exceptions to same with respect to specific foodstuffs.

The regulations require that labels for most food for human consumption must incorporate the following:

a) name of the food;

b) an ingredients list in weight in descending order;

c) a *best before* date or, in the case of perishable or high risk foods, a *use by* date;

d) any special storage information;

e) the name and address of the manufacturer, supplier or packer; and

f) an indication as to whether the food has been irradiated.

The following foodstuffs are exempted:

a) uncut fresh fruit and vegetables;

b) bread;

c) chewing gum;

d) flour confectionery;

e) sugar, vinegar, cooking and table salt.

These regulations also deal with specific requirements for:

a) vending machines;

b) pre-packed food;

c) alcoholic drinks;

d) raw milk;

e) nutritional claims;

f) medicinal properties;

g) baby food;

h) misleading labels; and

i) the use of certain terms, such as 'cream', 'cheese' and 'wine'.

Certain specific foods are governed by particular regulations, such as:

a) Cocoa and Chocolate Products Regulations 2003

b) Condensed Milk and Dried Milk (England) Regulations 2003;

c) Fruit Juices and Fruit Nectars (England) Regulations 2003;

d) Jam and Similar Products Regulations 2003; and

e) Honey Regulations 2003.

Additives

'Best before' date

Compositional requirements

Date marking

Food Hazard Warning System

High risk foods

'Natural' foods

'Sale' (of food)

'Sell by' date

Shelf life (definition)

Stock control and rotation

'Use by' date

Food poisoning bacteria

All those micro-organisms whose consumption causes food-borne illness.

Bacillus cereus

Bacteria

Bacterial food poisoning

Bacteriology

Bacterial growth curve

Bacteriological standards

Botulism

Campylobacter

Clostridium botulinum (Clostridium welchii)

Clostridium perfringens

Coliforms

Diseases transmitted through food

Dysentery

Enzymes

Escherichia coli (E. coli)

Food contamination

Food poisoning (food-borne illnesses)

Listeria monocytogenes

Norwalk virus

Pathogenic agents (pathogens)

Salmonellae

Spoilage of food

Staphylococcus aureus

Streptococci

Food poisoning (food-borne illnesses)

Food-borne illnesses are defined as diseases, usually either infectious or toxic in nature, caused by agents that enter the body through the ingestion of food. (World Health Organisation)

Consumption of infectious or toxic food most commonly results in food poisoning. Food poisoning is an acute illness of sudden onset caused by the consumption of contaminated food or food which may contain some form of poisonous agent.

The symptoms of food poisoning typically begin several hours after ingestion and, depending on the agent involved, can include one or more of the following body effects:

    a)   nausea;

    b)   abdominal pain;

    c)   vomiting;

    d)   diarrhoea;

    e)   fever;

    f)   headache; or

    g)   tiredness.

Those groups particularly vulnerable are babies, pregnant women, the elderly, the infirm and those with weak immune systems.

Acute food poisoning

Bacterial food poisoning

Bacteriophage (phage) typing

Carriers of disease

Chronic food poisoning

Cooking of food

Core (centre) temperature

Cross contamination

Danger zone

Date marking

Exclusion of food handlers

Excreter

Faecal coliform

Food-borne infection

Freshness and fitness of food

Gastro-enteritis

Hand contamination of food

High risk foods

Incubation period

Indirect contamination

Onset period

Reheating of food

Unfitness for human consumption

Food poisoning incidents

In the investigation of food poisoning incidents, the following matters need consideration:

    a)   the types of bacteria;

    b)   the main sources and vehicles of infection;

    c)   the cause of illness;

    d)   the symptoms;

    e)   the incubation period, i.e. the time between infection and the manifestation of symptoms; and

    f)   the duration of such symptoms.

See cross-references for *Food Poisoning (food-borne illnesses)* above.

Food premises

Any premises, or part of a premises, used for the purposes of a food business.

'Premises' includes any place, any vehicle, stall or moveable structure.

[Food Safety Act 1990]

Food business (definition)

Food business operator

Moveable and temporary structures

Food preparation

Includes manufacture and any form of processing or treatment.

[Food Safety Act 1990]

Food purchase and delivery

This is an essential feature of a food safety management system such as HACCP.

Food should be purchased from well-ordered and run food businesses and delivered in purpose-designed and constructed delivery vehicles.

Operators of food businesses should make regular visits to their suppliers' premises to assess standards of hygiene and hygiene management.

Delivery of food

Food safety management systems

Frozen food

Hazard Analysis: Critical Control Point (HACCP)

Temperature measurement equipment

Food receptacles

Receptacles used for the containment of food.

Conveyances and containers

Regulation (EC) No 852/2004 on the hygiene of foodstuffs

Food rooms

Rooms used for the preparation, processing and storage of food.

Regulation (EC) No 852/2204 on the hygiene of foodstuffs

Structural requirements for food premises

Food safety

All the measures taken to protect human health from harm arising from the consumption of food; the absence of harm to people from food.

Bacterial food poisoning

BS EN ISO 22000: Food Safety Management Systems

'Clean person' strategies

'Clean place' strategies

Codes of Recommended Practice – Food Hygiene (England) Regulations

Contaminant

Contamination

Critical Control Points (CCPs)

Cross contamination

Date marking

Diseases transmitted through food

Environmental Health Officers

European food hygiene legislation

Food Alerts

Food authority

Food-borne infection

Food contamination

Food (definition)

Food Hygiene (England) Regulations 2006

Food poisoning bacteria

Food poisoning (food-borne illnesses)

Food poisoning incidents

Food Safety Act 1990

Food safety provisions

Food safety requirements

Food safety risk assessment

Hazard Analysis: Critical Control Point (HACCP)

Inspection of food premises

Nature, substance or quality

Provisions applicable to foodstuffs

Regulation (EC) No 852/2004 on the hygiene of foodstuffs

Regulations

'Safer Food Better Business'

Food Safety Act 1990

The Food Safety Act 1990 consolidated much of the former legislation dealing with the storage, manufacture and sale of food. Moreover, it affects all sectors of the food distribution chain – farm and grower suppliers, e.g. manufacturers of animal feedstuffs; primary producers, such as farmers; primary food processing activities, e.g. dairies, slaughterhouses, etc.; food manufacturers; wholesalers; retailers and people running catering activities.

The Act applies:

a) in relation to any food which is offered as a prize or reward or given away in connection with any entertainment to which the public are admitted, whether on payment of money or not, as if the food were, or had been, exposed for sale by each person concerned in the organisation of the entertainment;

b) in relation to any food which, for the purpose of advertisement or in furtherance of any trade or business, is offered as a prize or reward or given away, as if the food were, or had been, exposed for sale by the person offering or giving away the food; and

c) in relation to any food which is exposed or deposited in any premises for the purpose of being so offered or given away as mentioned in paragraph (a) or (b) above, as if the food were, or had been, exposed for sale by the occupier of the premises

and in this subsection 'entertainment' includes any social gathering, amusement, exhibition, performance, game, sport or trial of skill.

Consumer protection provisions (Food Safety Act)

Food safety requirements

Defences

Enforcement procedure

Offences and penalties

Food Safety/Hygiene Policy

Organisations should formalise their intentions through a Statement of Food Safety and Hygiene Policy. As with a Statement of Health and Safety Policy, it should incorporate a statement of intent, the organisation and arrangements for implementation of the policy, and the individual responsibilities of everyone concerned. A director or senior manager should be identified as having general responsibility for all food safety operations throughout the organisation.

Such a Statement is the first step in endeavouring to establish the 'all reasonable precautions and all due diligence' defence under the Food Safety Act. However, a clear indication of putting the Policy into practice and monitoring the achievement of the objectives outlined in same will be necessary.

The 'arrangements' element of the policy should incorporate reference to the following elements:

a) clear identification of individual responsibilities of staff at all levels;

b) the procedure for providing information, instruction, training and supervision;

c) quality assurance procedures;

d) specific food contamination hazards and the precautions to be taken by staff;

e) procedures for corrective action;

f) procedures for dealing with consumer complaints;

g) details of registration and licensing under the Act;

h) procedures to be followed in the event of enforcement action;

i) emergency procedures, including product recall arrangements;

j) liaison arrangements with officers of food authorities;

k) cleaning and preventive maintenance arrangements;

l) health surveillance arrangements for food handlers;

m) infestation control procedures;

n) hygiene monitoring arrangements and responsibilities;

o) product labelling and product coding systems;

p) inspection procedures for raw materials, ingredients, packaging materials and intermediate products;

q) waste storage and disposal arrangements; and

r) temperature control systems for high risk products.

All reasonable precautions and all due diligence

BS EN ISO 22000: Food Safety Mmanagement Systems

Cleaning, disinfection and housekeeping

Cleaning schedules

Complaints procedure

Cross contamination

Enforcement procedure

Food handling (practice)

Food hazard

Food safety management objectives

Food safety management systems

Food safety manuals

Hazard Analysis: Critical Control Point (HACCP)

Health surveillance

High risk products

Hygiene inspections

Information, instruction and training

Labelling requirements

Liaison with authorised officers

Personal hygiene

Raw materials

Registration and approval of food premises

Structural requirements for food premises

Temperature control requirements

Training of food handlers

Waste food storage and disposal

Wrapping and packaging of foodstuffs

Food safety management objectives

The principal objectives of a food safety management system are:

a) to produce food products free from physical, chemical and bacteriological contamination;

b) to prevent the sale of unfit food, adulterated food or food which is not of the nature, substance or quality demanded by the purchaser;

c) to ensure compliance with the relevant statutory provisions, namely the Food Safety Act 1990 and regulations made under the Act;

d) to ensure adequate hygiene control of food premises, food vehicles and food importing operations, thereby assisting the quality of products;

e) to ensure products are produced by a well-instructed, informed and trained workforce, adequately supervised at all times;

f) to ensure continuing success of the food business through reduced consumer complaints and the potential for criminal and civil proceedings being brought against the organisation;

g) to ensure a positive and swift response in the event of a food safety incident through the implementation of established management procedures; and

h) to ensure continuing liaison with officers of the food authority in the pursuit of best food safety practices.

All reasonable precautions and all due diligence

Assured Safe Catering (ASC)

BS EN ISO 22000: Food Safety Management Systems

Complaints procedure

Contamination

Food Alerts

Food Hygiene (England) Regulations 2006

Food safety

Food Safety Act 1990

Food Safety/Hygiene Policy

Food safety management systems

Hazard Analysis: Critical Control Point (HACCP)

Information, instruction and training

Liaison with authorised officers

Nature, substance or quality

Product recall systems

Food safety management systems

The implementation of a Food Safety Management System (FSM) should take place in a series of clearly defined stages.

Stage 1 – Formation of the FSM Team

The FSM Team should be headed by a FSM Controller or Leader and include senior and line managers. For the system to have credibility with food processing operators/catering staff, it is essential that these groups are represented on the FSM team.

Stage 2 – Preparation of the Food Safety Policy/Mission Statement

The Food Safety/Hygiene Policy should be prepared by the FSM Team, agreed with senior management and signed and dated by the most senior person in the organisation, e.g. Chief Executive, Managing Director.

Stage 3 – Preparation of Food Safety Manuals and Operating Instructions

Food safety manuals should cover all aspects of a food production or catering process.

Operating instructions for food handlers and other persons who could indirectly contaminate food, such as engineers, should be prepared for all high and medium risk food manufacturing and preparation activities.

Stage 4 – Information, Instruction and Training

It is essential at this stage that everyone is introduced to the FSM system through the provision of information, instruction and training directed at specifying individual responsibilities, risk assessment procedure and the other management systems incorporated in the Food Safety Manual that are relevant to the groups concerned.

Stage 5 – Implementing the Food Safety Management System

Advance publicity and propaganda should be provided specifying a date for the commencement of the FSM system. Line managers will need to ensure that the procedures covered in the previous instruction and training sessions are adhered to and that there is continuing feedback to the FSM Team. The FSM Controller and Team will need to be in attendance at all times in the early stages to ensure procedures are correctly interpreted and understood by all concerned.

Stage 6 – Monitoring the Operation of the System

Recommendations in food safety risk assessments will require regular monitoring by line managers in conjunction with members of the FSM Team.

The FSM Team should also meet on a regular basis to review progress, consider variations and problems identified in the early stages following the introduction of the FSM system.

Stage 7 – Reviewing the Success of the System

The success of the FSM System should be subject to regular review. In the early stages, this should take place on a monthly basis, the time between reviews extending as the system becomes established.

It is recommended that some form of system for recognising and publicising the activities of departments, sections or groups performing well be established at an early stage of the FSM system.

Staff should also be regularly updated on the outcome of reviews, including any modifications necessary.

All reasonable precautions and all due diligence

Assured Safe Catering (ASC)

BS EN ISO 22000: Food Safety Management Systems

Food safety manuals

Food Safety/Hygiene Policy

Food safety management objectives

Food safety risk assessment

Hazard Analysis: Critical Control Point (HACCP)

High risk foods

Food safety manuals

Food safety manuals are an essential element of a food safety management system, such as HACCPs. Such manuals should provide information and advice to both managers and employees on the food safety requirements for various stages of manufacturing and catering processes.

A typical food safety manual should incorporate a series of Codes of Practice including:

a) the organisation's food safety risk assessment procedure;

b) cleaning schedules;

c) planned preventative maintenance system;

d) infestation prevention and control procedures;

e) health surveillance arrangements for food handlers;

f) procedures for providing information, instruction and training;

g) food complaints procedure;

h) hygiene monitoring systems, e.g. hygiene inspections;

i) product recall procedure;

j) supplier monitoring arrangements; and

k) procedures for liaison with food authority officers.

All reasonable precautions and all due diligence

BS EN ISO 22000: Food Safety Management Systems

Food safety management systems

Hazard Analysis Critical Control Point (HACCP)

Food safety provisions

There are two principal offences relating to food safety, namely:

a) rendering food injurious to health; and

b) selling food not complying with the food safety requirements.

Rendering food injurious to health

In the first case, any person who renders any food injurious to health by means of any of the following operations, namely:

a) adding any article or substance to food;

b) using any article or substance as an ingredient in the preparation of food;

c) abstracting any constituent from the food; and

d) subjecting the food to any other process or treatment,

with the intent that it shall be sold for human consumption, shall be guilty of an offence.

In determining whether food is injurious to health, regard shall be had:

a) not only to the probable effect of that food on the health of the consumer; but

b) also the probable cumulative effect of food of substantially the same composition on the health of a person consuming it in ordinary quantities.

[Food Safety Act 1990]

This requirement is not new and is principally concerned with the offence of adding other materials to food, for instance to increase weight, to enhance the flavour of unfit food, or subjecting the food to some form of treatment which improves it in some way.

Food safety requirements

Food shall not be placed on the market if it is unsafe.

Food shall be deemed to be unsafe if it is considered to be:

a) injurious to health;

b) unfit for human consumption.

In determining whether any food is unsafe, regard shall be had:

a) to the normal condition of use of the food by the consumer and at each stage of the production, processing and distribution; and

b) to the information provided to the consumer, including information on the label, or other information generally available to the consumer concerning the avoidance of specific adverse health effects from a particular food or category of foods.

In determining whether any food is injurious to health, regard shall be had:

a) not only to the probable immediate and/or short-term and/or long-term effects of that food on the health of a person consuming it, but also in subsequent generations;

b) to the probable cumulative effects;

c) to the particular health sensitivities of a specific category of consumers where the food is intended for that category of consumers.

In determining whether any food is unfit for human consumption, regard shall be had to whether the food is unacceptable for human consumption according to its intended use, for reasons of contamination, whether by extraneous matter or otherwise, or through putrefaction, deterioration or decay.

Where any food which is unsafe is part of a batch, lot or consignment of food of the same class or description, it shall be presumed that all the food in that batch, lot or consignment is also unsafe, unless following a detailed assessment there is no evidence that the rest of the lot, batch or consignment is unsafe.

Food that complies with specific Community provisions governing food safety shall be deemed safe insofar as the aspects covered by the specific Community provisions are concerned.

Conformity of a food with specific provisions applicable to that food shall not bar the competent authorities from taking appropriate measures to impose restrictions on it being placed on the market or to require its withdrawal from the market where there are reasons to suspect that, despite such conformity, the food is unsafe.

Where there are no specific Community provisions, food shall be deemed to be safe when it conforms to the specific provisions of National Food Law of the Member State in whose territory the food is marketed.

[Food Safety Act 1990 as amended]

Adulteration of food

Consumer protection provisions (Food Safety Act)

Enforcement procedure

Exposing food for sale

Food (definition)

Food Safety Act 1990

Food safety management objectives

Labelling and description offences

Labelling requirements

Malicious tampering with food

Nature, substance or quality

Offences and penalties

Presumption that food is intended for human consumption

Provisions applicable to foodstuffs

Food safety requirements

Food Safety Act 1990

Food safety provisions

Food safety risk assessment

A food safety risk assessment may be defined as:

- an identification of the hazards present in a food manufacturing, processing or catering operation and an estimate of the extent of the risks involved, taking into account whatever precautions are already being taken.

It is essentially a five-stage process:

a) identification of all the food safety hazards;

b) measurement of the risks;

c) evaluation of the risks;

d) implementation of measures to eliminate or control the risks; and

e) monitoring activities to ensure the control measures are maintained.

Approaches to food safety risk assessment

There are different approaches which can be adopted:

a) examination of each operation which could create food hazards, e.g. sandwich preparation, cleaning procedures;

b) examination of hazards and risks in groups, e.g. catering equipment, ingredients, delivery vehicles; and/or

c) examination of specific food production areas, kitchens, serveries.

Principal features of a food safety risk assessment

A food safety risk assessment must:

a) identify all the hazards associated with the food preparation process, equipment or area and evaluate the risks arising from those hazards, taking into account current legal requirements, such as the Food Hygiene (England) Regulations;

b) record the significant findings;

c) identify any part of the process, feature of equipment and part of a premises, as the case may be, where risks could arise;

d) evaluate existing food safety controls, stating whether or not they are satisfactory and, if not, what action should be taken;

e) evaluate the need for the provision of information, instruction, training and supervision of groups of food handlers;

f) judge and record the probability or likelihood of an incident occurring as a result of uncontrolled risk, including the 'worst case' likely outcome;

g) record any circumstances arising from the assessment where significant risks to food safety could arise; and

h) provide an action plan giving information on implementation of additional controls, in order of priority, and with a realistic timescale.

Recording the assessment

The assessment should be recorded and incorporate details of items (a) to (h) above.

Generic assessments

These are assessments produced once only for a given process or type of food processing area. In cases where an organisation has several locations or situations where the same food preparation process is undertaken, such as the preparation of ready-cooked meals or manufacture of a product, then a generic risk assessment could be carried out for each specific process to cover all locations. Similarly, where operators work away from the main location and undertake a specific task, e.g. preparation and service of burgers in food vehicles, a generic assessment should be produced.

For generic assessments to be effective:

a) 'worst case' situations must be considered; and

b) provision should be made on the assessment to monitor implementation of the assessment controls which are/are not relevant at a particular location, and what action needs to be taken to implement the relevant required actions from the assessment.

In certain cases, there may be risks which are specific to one situation only, and these risks may need to be incorporated in a separate part of the generic risk assessment.

Maintaining the risk assessment

The risk assessment should be maintained. This means that any significant change to a process, operation or food preparation area, or the introduction of any new process, equipment or procedure should be subject to risk assessment. If new hazards come to light, then these should also be subject to risk assessment. The risk assessment, furthermore, should be periodically reviewed and updated.

This is best achieved by a suitable combination of hygiene monitoring techniques, which require corrective and/or additional action where the need is identified.

Typical monitoring systems include:

a) preventive maintenance inspections;

b) cleaning efficiency inspections;

c) hygiene audits and inspections;

d) ensuring compliance with food safety specifications to suppliers;

e) inspections to detect the presence of infestation and to monitor the effectiveness of current pest control activities;

f) temperature checks of food commodities;

g) food supplier audits and inspections.

Useful information on checking performance against control standards can also be obtained reactively from the following activities:

a) investigation of food safety incidents;

b) food sampling activities;

c) observation of food handling practices; and

d) health surveillance of food handlers.

Reviewing the risk assessment

The frequency of review depends upon the level of risk in the operation. Further, if a serious food safety incident occurs in the organisation, or elsewhere, but is possible in the organisation, and where a check on the risk assessment shows no assessment or a gap in assessment procedures, then a review is necessary.

Preventing or controlling the risks

Once the food safety hazards have been identified and risks assessed, an operator of a food business must either prevent the risk arising or, alternatively, control same. Much will depend upon the magnitude of the risk in terms of the controls applied. In certain cases, the level of competence of food handlers and others may need to be assessed prior to their undertaking certain work, e.g. preparation of high risk foods.

A range of controls must be considered, including:

a) well-managed cleaning procedures;

b) temperature monitoring of freezers, display units, cold stores and refrigerators and of frozen foods at time of delivery;

c) planned preventive maintenance systems covering, for instance, structural items, processing equipment, hot water supplies and mechanical ventilation systems;

d) effective structural proofing against various forms of infestation, together with monitoring the performance of pest control contractors;

e) food labelling, dating and stock rotation;

f) measures to protect food from risk of contamination and cross contamination;

g) the provision of information, instruction and training for all staff;

h) health surveillance of food handlers in particular, including the use of health questionnaires for newly-appointed food handlers;

i) hygienic storage and disposal of waste, together with strict control over rejected food;

j) checking the quality and fitness of fresh high risk food supplied from external sources, e.g. wholesalers, butchers; and

k) the operation of a formally documented product recall system.

All reasonable precautions and all due diligence

BS EN ISO 22000: Food Safety Management Systems

Food source

Any growing crop or live animal, bird or fish from which food is intended to be derived (whether by harvesting, slaughtering, milking, collecting eggs or otherwise).

[Food Safety Act 1990]

Commercial operations

Food standards

These are the legal requirements covering the quality, composition, labelling, presentation and advertising of food and of materials or articles in contact with food.

Food Standards Act 1999

Food Standards Inspection

Food Standards Act 1999

This statute established the Food Standards Agency and outlined its general functions in relation to food and animal feedstuffs. The Agency has powers, in particular, to make observations with a view to acquiring information and to monitor enforcement action by food authorities.

Food standards

Food Standards Agency

Food Standards Agency

An independent agency set up as a result of the James Report in 1997 to:

a) co-ordinate national food safety policy, including the micro-biological, chemical and nutritional aspects of food;

b) monitor food standards and labelling;

c) develop policy, proposing and drafting legislation;

d) certain food law enforcement; and

e) be responsible for public education and information on food safety and standards.

Food Alerts

Food standards

Food Standards Act 1999

Labelling requirements

Food Standards Committees

These committees, which are composed of technical and legal specialists, advise Ministers on mainly compositional standards in foods, labelling and additives in food.

Food Safety Act 1990

Food standards

Food Standards Inspection

This is defined as 'an inspection carried out in order to establish whether food standards are being met'.

Factors to be considered in a Food Standards Inspection are outlined in Statutory Code No. 8: *Food Standards Inspections and include the following:*

Manufacturing premises

1. Product design and recipe
2. Raw materials
3. The production process
4. Quality systems
5. The completed product
6. Storage and distribution
7. Product labelling
8. Other points as appropriate

Non-manufacturing premises

1. Quality systems
2. Stock rotation

3. Product packaging and labelling

4. Materials and articles in contact with food

5. Other points (as appropriate)

Contact material

Food safety management systems

Food standards

Hazard Analysis: Critical Control Point (HACCP)

Labelling requirements

Raw materials

Regulation (EC) No 852/2004 on the hygiene of foodstuffs

Stock control and rotation

Wrapping and packaging of foodstuffs

Food storage

Most foods will deteriorate if not stored correctly and, in many cases, at the correct temperature. Deterioration may be associated with the food losing its moisture content, as with bread and confectionery products, i.e. the process of staling; food absorbing odours from chemicals, such as disinfectants; or bacterial spoilage resulting in gradual decomposition, particularly in the case of meat, fruit and vegetables.

Food hazards

Foodstuffs – provisions applicable to

Spoilage of food

Stock control and rotation

Temperature control requirements

Foodstuffs – provisions applicable to

Chapter IX of Annex II to Regulation (EC) No 852/2004 on the hygiene of foodstuffs lays down the following provisions applicable to foodstuffs.

1. A food business operator is not to accept raw materials or ingredients, other than live animals, or any other material used in processing products, if they are known to be, or might reasonably be expected to be, contaminated with parasites, pathogenic micro-organisms or toxic,

decomposed or foreign substances to such an extent that, even after the food business operator had hygienically applied normal sorting and/or preparatory or processing procedures, the final product would be unfit for human consumption.

2. Raw materials and all ingredients stored in a food business are to be kept in appropriate conditions designed to prevent harmful deterioration and protect them from contamination.

3. At all stages of production, processing and distribution, food is to be protected against any contamination likely to render the food unfit for human consumption, injurious to health or contaminated in such a way that it would be unreasonable to expect it to be consumed in that state.

4. Adequate procedures are to be in place to control pests. Adequate procedures are also to be in place to prevent domestic animals from having access to places where food is prepared, handled or stored (or, where the competent authority so permits in special cases, to prevent such access from resulting in contamination).

5. Raw materials, ingredients, intermediate products and finished products likely to support the reproduction of pathogenic micro-organisms or the formation of toxins are not to be kept at temperatures that might result in a risk to health. The cold chain is not to be interrupted. However, limited periods outside temperature control are permitted, to accommodate the practicalities of handling during preparation, transport, storage, display and service of food, provided that it does not result in a risk to health. Food businesses manufacturing, handling and wrapping processed foodstuffs are to have suitable rooms, large enough for the separate storage of raw materials from processed material and sufficient refrigerated storage.

6. Where foodstuffs are to be held or served at chilled temperatures they are to be cooled as quickly as possible following the heat-processing stage, or final preparation stage if no heat process is applied, to a temperature which does not result in a risk to health.

7. The thawing of foodstuffs is to be undertaken in such a way as to minimise the risk of growth of pathogenic micro-organisms or the formation of toxins in the foods. During thawing, foods are to be subjected to temperatures that would not result in a risk to health. Where run-off liquid from the thawing process may present a risk to health it is to be adequately drained. Following thawing, food is to be handled in such a manner as to minimise the risk of growth of pathogenic micro-organisms or the formation of toxins.

8. Hazardous and/or inedible substances, including animal feed, are to be adequately labelled and stored in separate and secure containers.

[Regulation (EC) No 852/2004 on the hygiene of foodstuffs]

Chill holding requirements

Cold chain

Contamination

Cooling of food

Cross contamination

Food business (definition)

Food business operator

Food contamination

Food Hygiene (England) Regulations 2006

Food receptacles

Food waste

Infestation prevention and control

Labelling requirements

Packaging

Proofing of buildings

Raw materials

Regulation (EC) No 852/2004 on the hygiene of foodstuffs

Structural requirements for food premises

Thawing of frozen food

Wrapping and packaging of foodstuffs

Food waste

Chapter VI of Annex II to Regulation (EC) No 852/2004 on the hygiene of food-stuffs lays down requirements with respect to food waste thus:

1. Food waste, non-edible by-products and other refuse are to be removed from rooms where food is present as quickly as possible so as to avoid their accumulation.

2. Food waste, non-edible by-products and other refuse are to be deposited in closable containers, unless food business operators can demonstrate to the competent authority that other types of containers

or evacuation systems used are appropriate. These containers are to be of an appropriate construction, kept in sound condition, be easy to clean and, where necessary, to disinfect.

3.   Adequate provision is to be made for the storage and disposal of food waste, non-edible by-products and other refuse. Refuse stores are to be designed and managed in such a way as to enable them to be kept clean and, where necessary, free of animals and pests.

4.   All waste is to be eliminated in a hygienic and environmentally friendly way in accordance with Community legislation applicable to that effect, and is not to constitute a direct or indirect source of contamination.

[Regulation (EC) No 852/2004 on the hygiene of foodstuffs]

Contamination

Infestation prevention and control

Proofing of buildings

Structural requirements for food premises

Waste food storage and disposal

Food which has not been produced, processed or distributed in accordance with the Hygiene Regulations

On an inspection of any food, an authorised officer of an enforcement authority may certify that it has not been produced, processed or distributed in compliance with the Hygiene Regulations.

Where any food is certified as above it shall be treated for the purposes of section 9 of the Act as failing to comply with food safety requirements.

Where any food certified as above is part of a batch, lot or consignment of food of the same class or description, all the food in the batch, lot or consignment shall, until it is proved that it has been produced, processed or distributed in compliance with the Hygiene Regulations, be treated for the purposes of the above paragraph as having been so certified.

[Food Hygiene (General) Regulations 2006]

Batches, lots or consignments of food

Food Hygiene (England) Regulations 2006

Foreign bodies

A foreign body is a form of physical contamination commonly encountered in a wide range of both raw and processed foods. Typical foreign bodies include:

a)   *Raw materials*

Minute stones, stalks, caterpillars and other insects in vegetables in particular.

b)   *Food ingredients*

Numerous forms of physical contamination, including stalks, stones, hair, dead insects and rodent droppings.

c)   *Packaging materials*

Elements of initial packaging materials, such as pieces of plastic, hessian sacking, staples, cardboard and paper.

d)   *Infestation*

Rat, mice and bird droppings, dead caterpillars and adult insects.

e)   *Returnable food containers*

Dirty milk bottle foil caps, chemical contaminants where food containers have been used for storage of a range of chemical substances, soil and dead insects.

f)   *Personal items*

Buttons from clothing, items of jewellery, hair slides and grips, pens, cigarette ends, false finger nails and dentures.

g)   *Processing machinery and plant*

Nuts, bolts, staples, oil and grease, parts of cleaning rags, shreds of conveyor belt, splinters of wood from pallets and flakes of paint.

h)   *Structural elements*

Shards of broken light bulb and fluorescent strip, pieces of brick and wall tile, shreds of rust from overhead steelwork and pipes,

i)   *Cleaning materials*

Scraps of sponge, wipers, rags and paper, string from string mops, brush bristles and cleaning agent deposits.

Foreign body control is an essential element of a food safety management system.

In a very small number of cases, there may be evidence of malicious insertion of foreign bodies into food.

Bird control

'Clean person' strategies

'Clean place' strategies

Cockroach control

Consumer protection provisions (Food Safety Act)

Contamination

Contractors on site

Food contamination

Food hazard

Food safety management objectives

Food safety requirements

Food safety risk assessments

Housekeeping procedures

Infestation prevention and control

Malicious tampering with food

Nature, substance and quality

Proofing of buildings

Raw materials

Rodent control

Structural requirements for food premises

Supplier monitoring

Wall surfaces

Freezer burn

A form of food spoilage arising from the unwarranted or accidental dehydration of food, particularly meat joints, caused by the formation of large ice crystals particularly when food is thawed slightly and then refreezes.

Spoilage of food

Freezers

Chest freezers and upright freezers are a standard feature of both commercial food premises and domestic premises. Two aspects are of significance in the correct and safe use of freezers, namely temperature control and storage requirements.

Temperature control

Freezers operate within a temperature range of -18ºC to -30ºC. It is essential that the temperature is monitored on an on-going basis as part of a food safety management system as, at around -10ºC, spoilage organisms can commence growth.

In the case of frozen food deliveries, items should be checked to ensure correct delivery temperature and then put into freezer storage immediately. Where the delivery temperature is between -12ºC and -18ºC, the food should not be accepted and the supplier notified of the reason for non-acceptance.

Storage requirements

Freezers should be located in a relatively cool area of the premises away from heat sources and not exposed to direct sunlight. Delivered items should be date marked and a system of stock rotation operated.

Meat, fruit and vegetables have a best life of 9 to 12 months, after which they can lose colour, flavour and texture. Other foods should be used within 3 to 6 months. Close attention should be paid to the suppliers' instructions with respect to frozen storage.

Certain open-topped or display freezers have a maximum load line, above which storage should not take place.

Food safety management systems

Hazard Analysis: Critical Control Point (HACCP)

Food Hygiene (England) Regulations 2006

Freezer burn

Frozen food

Quick freezing

Regulation (EC) No 852/2004 on the hygiene of foodstuffs

Temperature control requirements

Thawing of frozen food

Fresh meat

Meat that has not undergone any preserving process other than chilling, freezing or quick freezing, including meat that is vacuum-wrapped or wrapped in a controlled atmosphere.

[Animal By-Products (Identification) Regulations 1995 as amended by the Food Hygiene (General Regulations 2006]

Freshness and fitness of food

All foods, from the initial preparation stage, undergo a process of decomposition due to bacterial growth within the food. The rate of decomposition depends upon many factors, such as the nature of the food, e.g. meat, vegetables, ambient and storage temperature conditions, humidity and structural storage conditions.

Loss of freshness and ultimate unfitness is associated with:

a)   odour, as with decomposing fish and poultry;

b)   appearance, for instance, loss of colour in meat;

c)   break down of texture;

d)   rancidity, in the case of butter;

e)   moulds, yeasts and fungi;

f)   external contamination;

g)   dehydration and staleness; and

h)   various forms of infestation, e.g. bluebottles, resulting in maggot infestation.

The inspection of food should take these factors into account.

Ambient temperature

Bacterial growth curve

Bacteriological standards

'Best before' date

Chilled storage

Cold chain

Contamination

Critical Control Points (CCPs)

Danger zone

Date marking

Delivery of food

Direct contamination

Distribution chain

Examination of food

Fish and shellfish (food hazards)

Food contamination

Food poisoning bacteria

Food safety management systems

Food storage

Foodstuffs, provisions applicable to

Food which has not been produced, processed or distributed in accordance with the Hygiene Regulations

Fungi

High risk foods

Ice cream (food hazards)

Inspection of food

Intrinsic contamination

Meat

Meat products (food hazards)

Milk and dairy products (food hazards)

Moulds in food

Poultry (food hazards)

Rancidity

'Sell by' date

Spoilage of food

'Use by' date

Frozen food

The freezing of food is one of the principal forms of food preservation and a number of techniques are used by food suppliers, such as accelerated freeze drying, blast freezing, cook-freeze, plate freezing and quick freezing.

Freezing stops bacterial growth through reducing the available water in the food commodity. However, it has little effect on toxins and spores.

Accelerated freeze drying

Blast chilling and freezing

Cook-freeze

Freezers

Plate freezing

Quick freezing

Thawing of frozen food

Fumigation

The process of filling a building or part of a building with an aerosol fumigating agent, such as methyl bromide or hydrogen cyanide, with a view to eliminating cockroaches and stored product pests, such as flour beetle and biscuit beetle. Much will depend upon the structure and layout of the building as to the effectiveness of this form of infestation control as re-infestation frequently occurs later. Several fumigation exercises, spaced out at monthly intervals, may, therefore, be necessary to be successful.

Whilst such processes may be partially successful, fumigation must be used in conjunction with other infestation control techniques, such as efficient cleaning and housekeeping techniques, Clean-as-you-go procedures on the part of operators, and regular stock rotation, which creates a 'disturbance' effect and slows down reproduction.

It is standard practice to advise both the local Environmental Health Department and Health and Safety Executive well in advance of any such intended fumigation exercise.

Clean-as-you-go

Cleaning, disinfection and housekeeping

Cockroach control

Flying insect control

Infestation prevention and control

Fungi

Groups of micro-organisms, which include yeasts and moulds, and other organisms, such as mushrooms and toadstools.

Fungicides

Moulds in food

Mushroom toxin

Mycotoxin

Fungicides

Pesticides designed to kill fungal growth in food.

Fungi

Moulds in food

Game

A generic term to include:

a)   wild animals, such as deer;

b)   wild birds, such as pheasant, partridge and grouse;

c)   small wild mammals, such as rabbits and hares.

Game handling establishment

Any establishment in which game and game meat obtained after hunting are prepared for placing on the market and which:

a)   is approved or conditionally approved under Article 31(2) of Regulation 882/2004; or

b)   (although lacking approval or conditional approval that is required under Article 4(3) of Regulation 853/2004) was, on 31st December 2005, operating as a licensed wild game processing facility under the Wild Game Meat (Hygiene and Inspection) Regulations 1995.

[Food Hygiene (England) Regulations 2006]

Gastro-enteritis

An inflammatory condition of the mucous lining of the intestines.

Acute food poisoning

'At risk' groups

Bacterial food poisoning

Chronic food poisoning

Food poisoning (food-borne illnesses)

Gelatine

Gelatine is a glutinous substance injected into, particularly, pork pies to fill the void between the pastry crust and the internal meat content. Gelatine is also used as a glaze for meat pies. As such, it is an ideal medium for bacterial growth, having been involved in numerous *Salmonella* food poisoning incidents in the past.

When in the molten state, it should be maintained at a temperature above 63°C and, after application to meat products, should be rapidly cooled.

Food hazards

Food poisoning incidents

Meat

Meat products (food hazards)

Salmonellae

Temperature control requirements

Gelling agents

Agents, such as pectin (E440) in jam, used to change the consistency of food.

Additives

E-numbers

General requirements for food premises

Chapter 1 Article 1 of Regulation (EC) No 852/2004 on the hygiene of foodstuffs lays down the general hygiene requirements for food premises thus:

1. Food premises are to be kept clean and maintained in good repair and condition.

2. The layout, design, construction, siting and size of food premises are to:

   a) permit adequate maintenance, cleaning and/or disinfection, avoid or minimise air-borne contamination, and provide adequate working space to allow for the hygienic performance of all operations;

   b) be such as to protect against the accumulation of dirt, contact with toxic materials, the shedding of particles into food and the formation of condensation or undesirable mould on surfaces;

   c) permit good food hygiene practices, including protection against contamination and, in particular, pest control; and

   d) where necessary, provide suitable temperature-controlled handling and storage conditions of sufficient capacity for maintaining foodstuffs at appropriate temperatures and designed to allow those temperatures to be monitored and, where necessary, recorded.

3. An adequate number of flush lavatories are to be available connected to an effective drainage system. Lavatories must not open directly into rooms in which food is handled.

4. An adequate number of washbasins is to be available, suitably located and designated for cleaning hands. Washbasins for cleaning hands are to be provided with hot and cold running water, materials for cleaning hands and for hygienic drying. Where necessary, the provisions for washing food are to be separate from the hand-washing facility.

5. There is to be suitable and sufficient means of natural or mechanical ventilation. Mechanical air flow from a contaminated area to a clean area is to be avoided. Ventilation systems are to be so constructed as to enable filters and other parts requiring cleaning or replacement to be readily accessible.

6. Sanitary conveniences are to be provided with adequate natural or mechanical ventilation.

7. Food premises are to have adequate natural and/or artificial lighting.

8. Drainage facilities are to be adequate for the purpose intended. They are to be designed and constructed to avoid the risk of contamination. Where drainage channels are fully or partially open, they are to be so designed as to ensure that waste does not flow from a contaminated area towards or into a clean area, in particular an area where foods likely to present a high risk to the final consumer are handled.

9. Where necessary, adequate changing facilities for personnel are to be provided.

Washing facilities

Welfare amenity provisions

Workplace (Health, Safety and Welfare) Regulations 1992

Genetically modified food sources

A genetically modified food source is one in which any genes or genetic material has been artificially modified or is otherwise derived or inherited by replication from modified genetic material.

Genetically modified organisms (GMOs)

Genetically modified organisms (GMOs)

Genetic modification involves altering a plant, animal or micro-organism's genes, or inserting one from another organism. Genes carry the instructions for all the characteristics that an organism inherits.

Genetically modified food sources

Gerber Test

A laboratory test on milk to determine the fat content.

Milk and dairy products (food hazards)

Germicide

Any chemical agent designed to kill micro-organisms (germs).

Biocide

Giardia lamblia

An enteric protozoon responsible for cases of endemic and epidemic diarrhoea and found in the intestinal tracts of humans and animals. Giardia develops in two stages, an initial free living stage followed by the development of the cyst, a means of survival of the organism and, as such, its infective stage. People become infected after consuming a small number of cysts and, commonly, suffer the effects for 7 to 14 days, developing diarrhoea within 7 days. Other symptoms of the infection include nausea, stomach cramps and flatulence.

Transmission takes place from person to person and, in children, the faecal-oral route is very common. Infection may also arise through contaminated water supplies and whilst the organism is sensitive to chlorination of such supplies, the cysts will survive standard concentrations of chlorine used in waste water treatment plants.

Preventive measures include control over water purity, high standards of personal hygiene on the part of food handlers, increasing the awareness of food handlers of the symptoms and the maintenance of scrupulous levels of structural hygiene in food premises.

Coliforms

Cross contamination

Faecal coliform

Faecal organisms (bacteriological standards)

Food handling (practice)

Information, instruction and training

Parasites

Personal hygiene

Protozoa

Structural requirements for food premises

Water supply

Gram-negative bacteria

In the Gram staining technique, those bacteria that turn a light to medium pink colour, such as *Salmonellae.*

Gram positive bacteria

Gram reaction

Gram staining

Gram-positive bacteria

In the Gram staining technique, those bacteria which stay the violet colour of the dye used, such as *Staphylococci*.

Gram-negative bacteria

Gram reaction

Gram staining

Staphylococcus aureus

Gram reaction

A laboratory test that distinguishes the basic characteristics of bacteria.

Gram-negative bacteria

Gram reaction

Gram staining

Gram staining

This technique was developed by Hans CJ Gram, a Danish physician, to distinguish between various forms of bacteria. The technique entails the use of crystal violet dye, iodine and alcohol (or acetone) to distinguish two groups of bacteria. The Gram stain (or Gram reaction) detects differences in the composition of the cell wall of a bacterium and bacteria are classified as Gram +ve (or Gram (+)) or Gram −ve (or Gram (-)) accordingly.

Some differences exist between Gram-positive and Gram-negative bacteria, such as the structure of the cell wall and the types of toxin produced.

Gram-negative bacteria

Gram-positive bacteria

Gram reaction

Gram staining

Grayanotoxin

A toxic substance (diterpene) which occurs naturally in flowering shrubs, such as rhodedendrons. It can contaminate honey in particular.

Natural toxins

Toxin

Hand contamination of food

The principal source of food contamination is through contact with hands.

Physical soiling

Hands may be physically contaminated through contact with dust, dirt, soil and other items on the skin and under nails in particular. (*Clostridium perfringens*)

Chemical soiling

Certain chemicals, such as cleaning chemicals, can contaminate a food product. Some chemicals may be toxic.

Bacteriological soiling

The principal risks of bacteriological contamination of food by the hands are:

a) failing to wash hands and scrub nails after using the toilet resulting in faecal contamination of the hands (*Salmonellae, Clostridia*);

b) use of a handkerchief to blow the nose (*Staphylococci*);

c) hand to mouth/nose on coughing/sneezing (*Staphylococci*);

d) after smoking, eating, drinking (*Salmonellae*);

e) after handling raw meat, poultry, eggs, semi-cooked food (*Salmonellae*);

f) minor cuts and skin lesions (*Staphylococci*);

g) personal habits, such as nose and ear picking, combing the hair, picking spots (*Staphylococci*);

h) after handling waste food or food refuse;

i) after contact with contaminated surfaces, e.g. blood, on floors, preparation surfaces;

j) from one food to another, e.g. from raw meat to cooked meat (*Salmonellae*).

Hand contamination of food is one of the principal causes of food poisoning. There are many reasons why food can be subjected to this form of contamination but they are largely associated with poor standards of personal hygiene amongst food handlers. These include unsatisfactory practices, such as failing to cover minor cuts and skin lesions, hand to mouth contamination and failing to wash the hands in a variety of situations but, particularly, after using a toilet.

Because of the risk of hand contamination of food, handlers should wear some form of disposable hand covering, such as fine latex gloves, during the preparation of, particularly, high risk foods, such as salads, meat and egg dishes, meat pies of all types, poultry and various forms of semi-cooked foods.

Chemical contamination of food

Clostridium perfringens (Clostridium welchii)

Direct contamination

First aid arrangements

Food handling (practice)

Food poisoning (food-borne illnesses)

Hand washing

Hand washing facilities

High risk foods

Indirect contamination

Personal hygiene

Personal protective clothing

Salmonellae

Staphylococcus aureus

Hand washing

Food handlers are required to wash their hands in a specifically-designated wash basin (not a sink) provided with hot and cold water, or water at a suitably-controlled temperature, soap, nailbrush and hand drying facilities in a range of situations, namely:

a)   before entering a food room and commencing the handling of food;

b)   after using a toilet;

c)   after smoking;

d)   after handling raw food, waste food and/or refuse;

e)   prior to leaving a food room before a break; and

f)   after any other situation where hand contamination could have arisen.

Amenity areas

Hand contamination of food

Hand washing facilities

Personal hygiene

Washing facilities

Welfare amenity provisions

Hand washing facilities

Under Regulation (EC) No 852/2004 on the hygiene of foodstuffs an adequate number of wash basins is to be available in a food premises which are suitably located and designated for cleaning hands. Such wash basins must be provided with hot and cold running water, materials for cleaning hands and for hygienic drying. Where necessary, the facilities for washing food must be separate from the hand washing facility.

Similar provisions apply under the Workplace (Health, Safety and Welfare) Regulations 1992.

Food Hygiene (England) Regulations 2006

Hand contamination of food

Hand washing

Personal hygiene

Regulation (EC) No. 852/2004 on the hygiene of foodstuffs

Welfare amenity provisions

Workplace (Health, Safety and Welfare) Regulations 1992

Hazard

A hazard is generally described as 'something with the potential to cause harm'. Food hazards may be of a physical, chemical or biological nature.

Food hazards

Hazard analysis

This entails the identification of food hazards, the measurement and evaluation of the severity of such hazards and assessment of risk arising from same.

In a typical manufacturing process, hazard analysis entails:

a) identifying and describing all the physical, chemical and microbiological food hazards that could arise at each stage of the process for a particular product; and

b) identifying and describing all the prevention and control measures for the identified hazards.

Hazard analysis further entails assessing the level of risk associated with the identified food hazards. Factors such as the severity of the outcome of such a food hazard must be considered together with the numbers who could be exposed to such a hazard. From this exercise it is normally possible to classify foods as being 'high', 'medium' or 'low' risk foods.

Hazard analysis can be assisted by assessing the probability or likelihood of a food poisoning incident associated with, for example, incorrect preparation, use, reconstitution, temperature control, service or storage of the food, together with the measures necessary to avert such incidents.

Food hazards

Food poisoning incidents

Food safety management systems

Food safety risk assessment

Hazard Analysis: Critical Control Point (HACCP)

Appendix D – Food Hygiene Audit

Hazard Analysis: Critical Control Point (HACCP)

Hazard Analysis: Critical Control Point (HACCP) is recognised as a system for the identification, assessment and control of food hazards in food production and has been defined as 'a systematic approach to the identification and assessment of the microbiological hazards and risks associated with food and the definition of means for their control' (ICMSF).

The central feature of HACCP analysis is the determination of the Critical Control Points (CCPs), those stages in the process which must be controlled to ensure the safety of the product. Once the CCPs have been identified, a monitoring system is established for each CCP to ensure that correct procedures are maintained and actions taken if CCP criteria are not achieved.

What is HACCP?

HACCP is a systematic approach to the control of potential hazards in a food operation. A hazard is anything that could harm the consumer. It may be of a physical, chemical or biological nature. HACCP aims to identify problems before they occur, and establish mechanisms for their control at the stages in production critical to ensuring the safety of food. Control is proactive since:

a)   the identification of potential hazards and preventive measures; and

b)   the establishment of monitoring and remedial actions in advance, means that the hazard does not occur.

Table 1 lists the seven principles of HACCP as set out in the Codex Alimentarius Commision Code (1991).

Table 1 – The Seven Principles of HACCP

1. Identify the potential hazards associated with food production at all stages up to the point of consumption. Assess the likelihood of occurrence of the hazards and identify the preventive measures necessary for their control.

2. Determine the points, procedures and operational steps (critical control points – CCPs) that can be controlled to eliminate the hazards or minimise their likelihood of occurrence. A 'step' means a stage in food production or manufacture, e.g. the receipt or production of raw materials, harvesting, transport, formulation, processing and storage.

3. Establish target levels and tolerances which must be met to ensure the CCP is under control.

4. Establish a monitoring system to ensure control of the CCP by scheduled testing or observation.

5. Establish the corrective action to be taken when monitoring indicates that a particular CCP is not under control.

6. Establish procedures for verification, including supplementary tests and procedures to confirm that HACCP is working effectively.

7. Establish documentation concerning all procedures appropriate to these principles and their application.

In analysing the food operation, consideration must be given to the type of raw materials and ingredients used in the process, the means available to control hazards, the likely use of the product once it is manufactured or served and the population at risk, including any epidemiological evidence relating to the safety of that product.

The HACCP Logic Sequence

This sequence shows the steps required to carry out a HACCP procedure. A team is established comprising technical and non-technical personnel. The product to be analysed is described and its intended use identified. An example would be a chicken product intended for public consumption. The flow chart of its production is developed and then verified by 'walking' the production area. Any alteration can be made at this stage and the flow chart agreed. The potential hazards are then listed against each step, and there may be several different hazards for any one step. Preventive measures can then be listed against each hazard. In the case of chicken a potential hazard would be the survival of *salmonellae* during cooking. The preventive measure would be to ensure thorough cooking and heat penetration of the carcase.

The crux of the HACCP analysis is the determination of the critical control points. By applying the HACCP decision tree, the team can home in on those steps which are critical to the safety of the product, set targets and tolerances for that CCP and determine how, when and by whom the CCP is to be measured and observed. The target level is the value to be achieved at each CCP and the tolerances give the acceptable variation from that target.

The target level for cooking chicken might be to heat until deep parts of the flesh reach 75°C; the tolerance could be -2°C from the target. The variables to be monitored should have a measurable value, preferably one which is quick to assess, such as temperature, time or a visual inspection colour change. In addition, the team needs to develop instructions and procedures for dealing with deviations from the CCP tolerance values, including instructions to reprocess or dispose of the products.

A system for monitoring each CCP should then be established, with appropriate record keeping and documentation.

Evaluation of the HACCP

The traditional approach to food safety has involved the training of food handlers, inspection of premises and end-product testing by microbiological analysis of samples taken from batches or a day's production. Training and inspection are key elements of food safety, and there are new developments to increase their effectiveness.

However there are a number of disadvantages associated with end-product testing:

a)   it is retrospective; the product is already made and test results may not be available for several days;

b)   it may involve product recall if a problem is highlighted; this can only be partly effective and is usually costly;

c)   it may fail to detect contaminated batches, and as it is possible to sample only a small number of units from a batch for economic reasons, unsafe units may be missed leading to the false assumption that the whole batch is safe.

THE HACCP SYSTEM

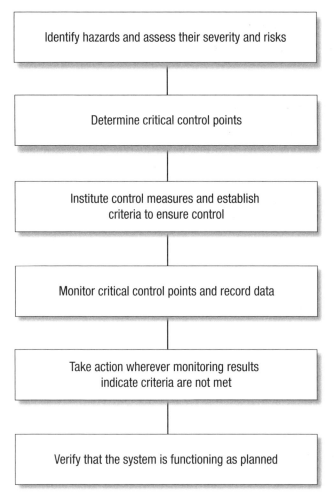

Identify hazards and assess their severity and risks

Determine critical control points

Institute control measures and establish criteria to ensure control

Monitor critical control points and record data

Take action wherever monitoring results indicate criteria are not met

Verify that the system is functioning as planned

All reasonable precautions and all due diligence

Corrective action

Critical Control Points (CCPs)

End product testing

Food hazards

Food safety management systems

Food storage

Product recall systems

Raw materials

Regulation (EC) No 852/2004 on the hygiene of foodstuffs

Stock control and rotation

Appendix A – The HACCP decision tree

Health education

An area of training and education concerned with the education of employees towards healthier modes of living, together with the training of managers and employees in their responsibilities for food safety, personal hygiene, the use of facilities, such as washing facilities, Clean-as-you-go procedures, the reporting of infectious conditions which could prejudice the purity of food and the wearing of personal protective equipment.

Clean-as-you-go

'Clean person' strategies

Food handler

Food handling (practice)

Hand contamination of food

Hand washing facilities

Personal hygiene

Personal protective clothing

Persons suffering from certain medical conditions

Smoking hazards

Training of food handlers

Health records

Records relating to the health status of individuals, particularly food handlers, following health surveillance procedures.

Exclusion of food handlers

Food handler

Health surveillance

Occupational health

Occupational health practitioners

Persons suffering from certain medical conditions

Health risk condition

A term used in connection with the making by a court of a Hygiene Prohibition Order under Food Hygiene (England) Regulations 2006.

The health risk condition is fulfilled with respect to any food business if any of the following involves risk of injury to health (including any impairment, whether permanent or temporary):

a) the use for the purposes of the business of any process or treatment;

b) the construction of any premises used for the purposes of the business, or the use for those purposes of any equipment; and

c) the state or condition of any premises or equipment used for the purposes of the business.

Cleaning, disinfection and housekeeping

Equipment requirements

Food Hygiene (England) Regulations 2006

Hygiene Prohibition Orders

'Imminent risk of injury to health'

Structural requirements for food premises

Health screening documentation

Health screening activities by occupational health practitioners will require the establishment of documentation, such as health questionnaires and health records. These documents may be provided by the occupational health practitioner in some cases.

Specimen documents are produced at Appendix C.

Health records

Health surveillance

Appendix C – Health Screening Documentation

Health supervision

An aspect of health surveillance involving the supervision of the health of, in particular, vulnerable groups at work, such as new and expectant mothers, young persons, disabled persons and those who may have experienced long periods of sickness absence. Those food handlers involved in high risk food preparation and production activities may also need on-going health supervision.

Health surveillance

High risk foods

Health surveillance

Health surveillance, namely the regular monitoring of the health of food handlers and other people who may come into contact with food, such as drivers, porters and cleaners, is an important feature of the prevention of food-borne disease associated with food products.

Health surveillance covers a broad range of activities directed at protecting the health of the operator and the purity of the product. It is most effectively undertaken by occupational health nurses with support, where necessary, from an occupational physician who has a good understanding of the problems of the food industry in this respect.

On this basis, some form of regular health surveillance is essential, together with a firm requirement for food handlers and others to report various diseases and conditions to management immediately and certainly prior to commencing work.

Forms of health surveillance

In the food industry, the following health surveillance procedures are recommended:

a) the completion by those seeking employment of a 'Pre-employment Health Screening Questionnaire' at the job application stage;

b) pre-employment health examinations of all staff with a view to assessing their fitness to handle food;

c) on-going health examinations, e.g. six monthly, annually, of all staff;

d) health examination on return to work following prolonged illness or food-borne infection;

e) examination of staff for the detection of specific conditions, such as dermatitis;

f)   counselling of staff on general health-related issues; and

g)   health supervision of specific groups, such as young persons and disabled persons.

Health surveillance is a significant feature of occupational health practice. In the food industry, health surveillance has a further objective in terms of preventing the spread of food-borne infection, thereby protecting the purity of the product.

Health education

Health screening documentation

Health supervision

Occupational health

Occupational health practitioners

Persons suffering from certain medical conditions

Pre-employment health screening

Appendix C – Health Screening Documentation

Healthy carrier

A healthy person who excretes food poisoning and other organisms without showing the symptoms. Such persons may transmit a range of diseases through food.

Carriers of disease

Excreter

Heat treatment

Milk has traditionally been subject to forms of heat treatment, such as pasteurisation, sterilisation or ultra heat treatment (UHT), all of which destroy pathogenic organisms. Many other foods are also subject to some form of heat treatment.

Regulation (EC) No 852/2004 on the hygiene of foodstuffs lays down the following requirements with respect to heat treatment:

The following requirements apply only to food placed on the market in hermetically sealed containers.

1.   Any heat treatment process used to process an unprocessed product or to process further a processed product is:

a)   to raise every part of the product treated to a given temperature for a given period of time; and

b)   to prevent the product from becoming contaminated during the process.

2.   To ensure that the process employed achieves the desired objectives, food business operators are to check regularly the main relevant parameters (particularly temperature, pressure, sealing and microbiology), including by the use of automatic devices.

3.   The process should conform to an internationally recognised standard (for example, ultra high temperature or sterilisation).

Heat treatment

Pasteurisation

Processing

Regulation (EC) No 882/2004 on the hygiene of foodstuffs

Raw milk (restrictions on sale)

Sterilisation

Temperature control requirements

Ultra Heat Treatment (UHT)

Hepatitis

Inflammation of the liver ascribed to a range of infections.

Hepatitis A

A form of epidemic jaundice spread through human contact or through contaminated food and water supplies.

Cross contamination

Food contamination

Hepatitis

Water-borne infections

Hepatitis B

Also known as 'serum hepatitis', a disease associated with members of the medical and allied professions, particularly those who handle blood and blood products and who work in renal dialysis units. Symptoms of the disease include malaise, muscle pain (myalgia), headache, nausea, vomiting, anorexia and abdominal pain. The patient suffers from jaundice and, in some cases, enlarged liver. Whilst the disease may be relatively mild in most cases, other cases may turn to chronic hepatitis.

Hepatitis

Hermetically sealed container

A container that is designed and intended to be secure against the entry of hazards.

[Regulation (EC) No 852 on the hygiene of foodstuffs]

High risk foods

Those foods, typically with a high moisture and protein content, that are at particular risk of contamination by bacterial spoilage or the action of pathogens. High risk foods will, under favourable conditions, support the growth of pathogenic bacteria.

High risk foods include:

- meat, fish, eggs and prepared products incorporating these foods, together with smoked or cured meat which has been sliced and cured fish
- soft cheeses ripened with moulds or micro-organisms
- smoked and cured fish
- prepared vegetable salads
- fresh cream and artificial cream cakes
- ice cream and frozen desserts
- milk-based desserts
- cooked cereals, such as rice, beans and vegetables
- sandwiches

Strict temperature control is required with respect to these foods. Such foods should be stored at below 8°C or above 63°C.

Bacteria

Bacterial food poisoning

Chilled storage

Chill holding requirements

Chill holding tolerance periods

Cold holding/service

Cooking of food

Cooling of food

Critical Control Points (CCPs)

Cross contamination

Examination of food

Exclusion of food handlers

Fish and shellfish (food hazards)

Food contamination

Food handling (practice)

Food safety risk assessment

Freshness and fitness of food

Hand contamination of food

High risk operations

Hot cabinets

Hot holding requirements

Ice cream (food hazards)

'Imminent risk of injury to health'

Meat

Meat products (food hazards)

Moulds in food

Personal hygiene

Persons suffering from certain medical conditions

Provisions applicable to foodstuffs

Ready-to-eat foods

Reheating of food

Stock control and rotation

Temperature control (premises)

Temperature control requirements

Thawing of frozen food

Training of food handlers

Unfitness for human consumption

High risk operations

Those food processes where strict control over time and temperature is required, such as milk pasteurisation, and the preparation of sandwiches and meat pie fillings.

High risk foods

Meat

Meat products (food hazards)

Pasteurisation

Temperature control requirements

Host

Any organism which supports the growth of a parasite in or on its body.

Definitive (primary) host

Parasites

Hot cabinets

Hot cabinets (or hot cupboards) feature a heated metal cabinet incorporating shelves for keeping food hot prior to service. They are commonly used for the hot storage of high risk foods, such as meat pies, sausage rolls, cooked poultry and jacket potatoes in supermarkets, public houses, cafes, fish and chip shops and other 'take-away' premises.

Food stored in these cabinets should meet the hot holding requirements of the Food Hygiene (England) Regulations and be maintained at above the hot holding temperature of 63°C with the cabinet temperature operating at above 80°C.

Regular temperature checks should be made. Hot cabinets should not be used for reheating food from cold.

Food Hygiene (England) Regulations 2006

High risk foods

Hot holding defences

Hot holding requirements

Reheating of food

Temperature control requirements

Hot holding defences

In any proceedings for an offence consisting of a contravention of paragraph 6 (hot holding requirements), it shall be a defence for the accused to prove that:

a)   a well-founded scientific assessment of the safety of the food at temperatures below 63°C has concluded that there is no risk to health if, after cooking or reheating, the food is held for service or on display for sale:

    i)   at a holding temperature which is below 63°C; and

    ii)   for a period not exceeding any period of time specified in that scientific assessment; and

b)   at the time of the commission of the alleged offence, the food was held in a manner which was justified in the light of that scientific assessment.

In any proceedings for a offence consisting of a contravention of paragraph 6, it shall be a defence for the accused to prove that the food:

a)   had been kept for service or on display for sale for a period of less than two hours; and

b)   had not previously been kept for service or on display for sale by that person.

Food Hygiene (England) Regulations 2006

Hot cabinets

Hot holding requirements

Reheating of food

Hot holding requirements

Any person who in the course of the activities of a food business keeps at or in food premises at a temperature below 63°C any food which:

a)   has been cooked or heated;

b)   is for service or on display for sale; and

c)   needs to be kept at or above 63°C in order to control the growth of pathogenic micro-organisms or the formation of toxins,

shall be guilty of an offence.

[Food Hygiene (England) Regulations 2006]

Food Hygiene (England) Regulations 2006

High risk foods

Hot cabinets

Hot holding defences

Hot holding/service

To ensure the safety of food held on display for service, only as much food as is needed should be prepared and cooked. Batch cooking is ideal for maintaining food temperature and quality. Hot holding equipment that can keep hot foods at 63°C or higher should be used and close attention should be paid to the manufacturer's instructions for the use of such equipment. Hot foods should remain covered when not being served in order to retain heat and prevent contamination.

Internal food temperatures should be measured at least every two hours using a calibrated thermometer.

Foods should be re-heated only in appropriate cooking equipment, such as ovens, steamers, microwave ovens or a stem-jacketed kettle, to at least 63°C within two hours and then transferred to holding equipment. Food should be re-heated only once and any remaining food discarded at the end of service.

Cold holding/service

Food Hygiene (England) Regulations 2006

Hot holding defences

Hot holding requirements

Housekeeping procedures

'Housekeeping' simply implies 'good management of the house', a situation where everything is in the right place at the right time. Inevitably, housekeeping is linked with cleanliness.

Poor housekeeping creates both safety and hygiene hazards. It is commonly associated with the failure to clear spillages immediately, the accumulation of refuse, both internally and externally, slipping and tripping risks created by items left on the floor, inadequate systems and procedures for the removal of scrap items, refuse and waste materials from working areas, or the simple failure to adopt the principle of 'Clean-as-you-go', a basic concept in ensuring a clean and hygienic workplace.

In the majority of cases, poor housekeeping can only be associated with a failure on the part of management to ensure the implementation of cleaning and house-keeping procedures with a view to eliminating the above hazards.

Clean-as-you-go

Cleaning, disinfection and housekeeping

Cleaning schedules

'Clean place' strategies

Food hazards

Waste food storage and disposal

HTST

High temperature short time (HTST) is a technique used in the pasteurisation of milk. In this process, milk is held at a temperature of 72°C for at least 15 seconds, followed by immediate cooling to 10°C.

Heat treatment

Milk and dairy products (food hazards)

Pasteurisation

Raw milk (restrictions on sale)

Hydrogen swell

The build up of hydrogen gas in canned goods arising from internal corrosion of the can and resulting in 'blowing' of one or both ends of a can. Hydrogen swell is particularly common with acidic canned fruits and tomatoes.

Canned goods

Canning processes

Hygiene audit

A systematic critical examination of a food business's hygiene procedures with the principal objective of minimising loss.

Food hygiene inspections

Appendix D – Food hygiene audit

Hygiene Emergency Prohibition Notice

If an authorised officer of an enforcement authority is satisfied that the health risk condition is fulfilled with respect to any food business he may by a notice served on the relevant food business operator (in these Regulations referred to as a 'Hygiene Emergency Prohibition Notice') impose the appropriate prohibition.

[Food Hygiene (England) Regulations 2006]

Authorised officer

Emergency prohibition action

Enforcement procedure

Food Hygiene (England) Regulations 2006

Health risk condition

Hygiene Emergency Prohibition Order

Hygiene Emergency Prohibition Order

If a Magistrates Court is satisfied, on application of an authorised officer, that the health risk condition is fulfilled with respect to any food business, the court shall, by an order (in these Regulations referred to as a 'Hygiene Emergency Prohibition Order'), impose the appropriate prohibition.

[Food Hygiene (England) Regulations 2006]

Authorised officer

Emergency prohibition action

Enforcement procedure

Food Hygiene (England) Regulations 2006

Health risk condition

Hygiene Emergency Prohibition Notice

Hygiene Improvement Notice

If an authorised officer of an enforcement authority has reasonable grounds for believing that a food business operator is failing to comply with the Hygiene Regulations, he may by a notice served on that person (in these Regulations referred to as a 'Hygiene Improvement Notice'):

- a) state the officer's grounds for believing that the food business operator is failing to comply with the Hygiene Regulations;
- b) specify the matters which constitute the food business operator's failure to comply;
- c) specify the measures which, in the officer's opinion, the food business operator must take in order to secure compliance; and
- d) require the food business operator to take those measures, or measures which are at least equivalent to them, within such period (not being less than 14 days) as may be specified in the notice.

Any person who fails to comply with a hygiene improvement notice shall be guilty of an offence.

[Food Hygiene (England) Regulations 2006]

Authorised officer

Food business operator

Enforcement procedure

Improvement Notices

Hygiene inspections

A scheduled or unscheduled inspection or examination of a food premises, or part of same, by a trained person, such as an environmental Health Officer or company hygiene officer, with the principal objectives of identifying food hazards, observing food handling practice and ensuring compliance with food safety/hygiene legislation and internal codes of practice.

Hygiene check lists may be used by supervisors when inspecting areas under their control. Check lists should be regularly reviewed.

Food handling (practice)

Food hazard

Food safety management systems

Hygiene managers/officers

Structural requirements for food premises

Hygiene managers/officers

Managers appointed to organise, manage and ensure hygiene procedures are maintained within an organisation. They are generally responsible for:

a)   overseeing cleaning and housekeeping arrangements;

b)   the preparation and effective implementation of cleaning schedules;

c)   infestation control, including monitoring the performance of external pest control contractors; and

d)   the provision of information, instruction, training and supervision for food handlers.

The role, function and accountability of the hygiene manager/officer should be clearly identified in an organisation's Food Safety/Hygiene Policy.

Cleaning, disinfection and housekeeping

Cleaning schedules

Food Safety/Hygiene Policy

Infestation prevention and control

Information, instruction and training

Pest control contracts

Training of food handlers

Hygiene Prohibition Orders

If:

a) a food business operator is convicted of an offence under the Hygiene Regulations; and

b) the court by or before which he is so convicted is satisfied that the health risk condition is fulfilled with respect to the food business concerned,

the court shall by an order impose the appropriate prohibition.

The health risk condition is fulfilled with respect to any food business if any of the following involves risk of injury to health (including any impairment, whether permanent or temporary), namely:

a) the use for the purposes of the business or any process or treatment;

b) the construction of any premises used for the purposes of the business, or the use for those purposes of any equipment; and

c) the state or condition of any premises or equipment used for the purposes of the business.

[Food Hygiene (England) Regulations 2006]

Enforcement procedure

Equipment requirements

Food business (definition)

Food business operator

Food Hygiene (England) Regulations 2006

Health risk condition

Structural requirements for food premises

Hypochlorites

Chemical substances, which are the salts of hypochlorous acid, commonly used as disinfectants due to their subsequent release of chlorine, which has a bactericidal effect in contact with surfaces, and which is effective against spores. Surfaces should be clean, as soiling may reduce the effectiveness of bactericidal action, and should be rinsed afterwards.

The relative risks associated with hypochlorites should be appreciated, in particular, the hazards arising from mixing same with other cleaning chemicals.

Bactericide

Cleaning, disinfection and housekeeping

Disinfectants

Ice

'Ice' is included within the definition of 'food' and, as such, consideration must be given to the risks, in particular, of salmonellosis, arising from ice which has not been manufactured with clean potable water. Whilst most ice is prepared in specific machines, these should be well-maintained and subject to regular cleaning to avoid risk of contamination.

Cleaning, disinfection and housekeeping

Equipment requirements

Food (definition)

Potable water

Salmonellae

Ice cream (food hazards)

Ice cream is a frozen dessert which includes a range of ingredients including milk, eggs, thickening agents, sugar, fruit, nuts and water and, in many cases, varying amounts of air according to the style of ice cream.

Manufacture of ice cream entails pasteurisation and sterilisation of the ice cream mix. In the storage and service of ice cream under no circumstances should ice cream be re-frozen if it has thawed. The product should generally be stored in a refrigerator operating at -18°C. However, special ice cream refrigerators, operating at -12°C may be adequate for very short-term storage, namely a maximum period of one week.

All pathogenic organisms present in milk may also be present in ice cream. Diseases associated with ice cream in the past, often of an epidemic nature, are typhoid and paratyphoid fevers, scarlet fever, dysentery, septic throat and food poisoning.

Ice cream scoops which, it has been shown in the past, can be infected with a number of micro-organisms, including *Escherichia coli,* should be washed and disinfected between each service.

Bacterial food poisoning

Escherichia coli (E. coli)

Freezers

Frozen food

High risk foods

Milk and dairy products (food hazards)

Pasteurisation

Pathogenic agents (pathogens)

Sterilisation

'Imminent risk of injury to health'

Section 11 of the Food Safety Act enables a Magistrates Court to make a prohibition order:

a) to close down insanitary food premises;

b) to prohibit premises from being used for particular kinds of food businesses;

c) to prevent the use of a piece of equipment for any food business or a particular food business ;

d) to prohibit a particular process; or

e) to prohibit a person from carrying on or managing any food business,

on public health grounds.

Section 11 applies if there is a risk of injury to health and Section 12 if there is *an imminent risk* of injury to health.

The term *imminent* is important before any emergency prohibition action can be considered by an enforcement officer. For example, if the condition of the premises appears to carry a high risk of causing an outbreak of food poisoning within the next few days, then the risk could be said to be *imminent.*

[Food Safety Act 1990]

Enforcement procedure

Equipment requirements

Food business (definition)

Food business operator

Food poisoning (food-borne illnesses)

Food Safety Act 1990

Prohibition action

Prohibition from handling food

Prohibition of a person

Statutory Codes under the Food Safety Act

Structural requirements for food premises

Improvement Notices

The power under the Food Safety Act to serve Improvement Notices to remedy breaches of regulations is similar to that under the Health and Safety at Work etc Act 1974. A person aggrieved may use the appeal provisions under section 30 of the Act.

Procedures covering Improvement Notices are covered in Statutory Code of Practice No 5: *The Use of Improvement Notices*. The issue of an Improvement Notice, however, does not preclude the food authority from pursuing prosecution at the same time for the breaches of the regulations which are the subject of the notice. The Improvement Notice procedure is designed to ensure that the defects are remedied within a relatively short period of time.

Section 10 states that if an authorised officer of an enforcement authority has reasonable grounds for believing that the proprietor of a food business is failing to comply with any regulations to which this section applies, he may, by a notice served on that proprietor (in this Act referred to as an Improvement Notice):

a)   state the officer's grounds for believing that the proprietor is failing to comply with the regulations;

b)   specify the matters which constitute the proprietor's failure so to comply;

c)   specify the measures which, in the officer's opinion, the proprietor must take in order to secure compliance; and

d)   require the proprietor to take those measures, or measures which are at least equivalent to them, within such period (not being less than 14 days) as may be specified in the notice. (Section 10(1))

Section 10(1)(d) makes it clear that *works of equivalent effect* may be carried out to comply with the Improvement Notice. Such alternative works must be agreed between the authorised officer and the proprietor, and the authorised officer must confirm the agreement in writing. It is the responsibility of the food authority to make this fact known to a proprietor.

Any person who fails to comply with an Improvement Notice shall be guilty of an offence. (Section 10(2))

Statutory Code No 5 makes the following points about Improvement Notices.

Service of an Improvement Notice

An Improvement Notice is only served when the authorised officer is satisfied that there has been a contravention of one of the relevant food hygiene or food processing regulations, but that the contravention does not pose an imminent risk to health.

Where there is a breach of a recommendation of some industry guidelines or an industry code of practice an improvement notice cannot be issued if there is no failure to comply with an appropriate regulation.

The notice procedure should be properly used by all authorised officers. The procedure, and particularly their appeal rights, should be properly understood by recipients. The notice may need to be accompanied by a covering letter written in the recipient's own language suggesting that he seek help if he does not fully understand the meaning of the notice, or the notice may need to be explained with the assistance of an interpreter. The issue of a notice should be treated seriously. The person receiving it should understand that he is obliged to comply with the notice and that, save in special circumstances, he will be prosecuted by the authority.

Typical Improvement Notice situations

Guidance is given with the Statutory Code on typical situations where the service of Improvement Notices would be appropriate, thus:

a) where rodent proofing or the provision of flying insect screening is necessary to prevent any risk of infestation;

b) where there are deficiencies in the structure or facilities in the food business, e.g. where structural repairs are required or where additional equipment is necessary to comply with temperature control requirements;

c) where there has been a previous history of obstruction or unwillingness on the part of the food business to conform to legal requirements;

d) where the facilities to wash and prepare food and to wash equipment and utensils are inadequate;

e) where there is inadequate mechanical ventilation in a kitchen area;

f) where there is inadequate artificial lighting in a food room; and

g) where there is a failure to maintain premises in a satisfactory state of cleanliness.

Notice details

The wording of the notice should be clear and easily understood. It should contain detail of the legal provisions contravened and the reason for the opinion of the authorised officer that there has been a contravention.

An Improvement Notice specifies both the measures to be taken and the period of time within which the proprietor must implement those measures. The minimum period which may be specified is 14 days, but specified periods of time for completion of works must be realistic. In most cases the period of time would be agreed with the proprietor although an authorised officer can set a limit without the proprietor's agreement. The following factors should be taken into account before a time limit is set:

a)   the nature of the problem;

b)   the risk to health; and

c)   the availability of solutions.

Service of the Notice

The Food Safety Act requires the notice to be served on the proprietor, and the person responsible for taking action should receive a copy of the notice, especially in cases where the local manager is not the proprietor. (See both section 50(1) of the Act, which covers the service of documents, and section 50(2) which deals with situations where it is not possible to ascertain the name and address of the owner or occupier of the premises.)

An Improvement Notice need not necessarily be served by the authorised officer who signed it and issued it. It should be served by a competent person who would be able to take any required action, for example, explaining the purpose of the notice.

Requests for extension of time

In certain situations a proprietor may request an extension of the time period for complying with an Improvement Notice. In these situations, authorised officers must take the following aspects into account:

a)   the risk associated with the fault if an extension was granted;

b)   the reason for the request;

c)   the remedy involved;

d)   the past record of co-operation of the proprietor; and

e)   any temporary action which the proprietor proposes to take to remedy the defect.

An authorised officer, if he considers a request for an extension of time to be reasonable, may decide not to enforce the notice until a further period of time has elapsed. Requests for time extensions must be made in writing before the expiry date of the notice otherwise, technically, an offence will be committed if there has been failure to comply.

Appeals

The proprietor has a right of appeal against the decision of an authorised officer to serve an Improvement Notice (Section 37) by way of a complaint to the magistrates court. Appeal is made by way of complaint to the Magistrates Court pursuant to section 51 of the Magistrates Courts Act 1980. Although the form of complaint is prescribed by the Magistrates Courts (Forms) Rules 1981, Form 98, the complaint need not be made in writing. It can be made by the complainant personally or by his solicitor or counsel (rule 4 Magistrates Courts Rules 1981). Once the magistrate has judicially considered the complaint, a summons is issued. The hearing of the complaint is governed by the rules in sections 53 – 57 of the Magistrates Courts Act 1980. The procedure in Scotland is to make a summary application to the sheriff.

The time limit for appeals against an Improvement Notice is:

    (a)   one month from the date the notice was served; or

    (b)   the period specified in the Improvement Notice if that is shorter.

The Act sets out the powers of the magistrates on an appeal against an Improvement Notice in section 39(1). The court may cancel, affirm or modify the terms of the notice, for example, to delete or reduce what it deems to be an over vigorous requirement or to extend the time in which the proprietor is required to comply with the notice. However, magistrates must first decide whether or not a notice is valid before they exercise their powers under section 39(1).

Compliance

The Act does not make any provision for the 'signing off' of an Improvement Notice by the food authority, but the Code does recommend such a procedure.

Authorised officers are encouraged to liaise with proprietors while work is being undertaken, ensuring notification to the authority when work is completed. The work should be checked as soon as possible after notification whenever possible by the officer who served the notice.

Food authorities are also recommended to review the frequency of inspection of the premises after the works have been carried out bearing in mind the nature of the risk which led to the issuing of the notice.

Appeals against Notices, etc

Authorised officer

Cleaning, disinfection and housekeeping

Enforcement procedure

Food authority

Food hygiene inspections

Food Hygiene (England) Regulations 2006

Food Safety Act 1990

'Imminent risk of injury to health'

Liaison with authorised officers

Lighting recommendations

Obstruction etc of an authorised officer

Offences and penalties

Proofing of buildings

Prosecution

Service of documents

Statutory Codes under the Food Safety Act

Structural requirements for food premises

Ventilation requirements

Washing of food and food equipment

Incubation period

This is the period of time in between consumption of a contaminated food and the appearance of the first symptoms of illness. The period can range from hours to days depending on the agent and the quantity consumed.

Food-borne infection

Food contamination

Onset period

Indicator organisms

Micro-organisms which indicate the presence of faecal contamination together with poor or inadequate levels of cleaning and disinfection.

Coliforms

Faecal coliform

Faecal organisms (bacteriological standards)

Indirect contamination

Contamination introduced by a vehicle of contamination, that is, any living person, article or substance capable of transferring contamination from one point to another.

Contamination

Cross contamination

Extrinsic contamination

Food contamination

Intrinsic contamination

Infection

The presence in or on the body, and multiplication in or on the body, of a pathogen that causes a disease.

Food poisoning (food-borne illnesses)

Infectious dose

Infective dose

Infectious dose

This is the amount of agent that must be consumed to give rise to symptoms of food-borne illness.

Infective dose

This is the number of micro-organisms needed to produce the symptoms of a disease. The infective dose varies according to the agent and the consumer's age and state of health.

Infestation

'Infestation' means the presence of any one or more of the following:

- Rodents – rats and mice
- Insects
    - flying insects – house flies, bluebottles, wasps, etc.;
    - crawling insects – cockroaches, ants, etc.
- Birds – sparrows, feral pigeons, starlings.

Alphachloralose

Ant control

Bird control

Cleaning, disinfection and housekeeping

Cockroach control

Eradication (infestation)

Flour mite

Flying insect control

Fumigation

Infestation prevention and control

Insecticides

Larva

Pest

Pesticides

Prohibition action

Proofing of buildings

Residual insecticide

Rodent control

Stored product pest

Infestation prevention and control

Infestation prevention and control is based on three areas of action.

Structural proofing

'Proofing' implies any steps taken to deny pests access to buildings and the abolition, as far as possible, of harbourage areas. Proofing is the first line of defence in infestation control. Proofing measures include specific treatments to external doors, ducts, cavity walls and pipe and conduit runs passing through walls, together with the screening of structural openings, such as windows, to prevent ingress by pests.

Housekeeping practices

Housekeeping practices are the second line of defence and are a field of unlimited scope. Such measures should ensure:

a) denial of food and water, together with opportunities for breeding;

b) early detection of the existence of infestation by regular inspection of all areas; and

c) reduction of the risk of contamination of food to a minimum.

These principles will only be achieved by:

a) a correct attitude on the part of all staff towards the dangers of infestation;

b) a high standard of cleanliness of yards, production and storage areas, machinery, plant and equipment; the operation of cleaning schedules is essential;

c) a daily inspection system, supported by a staff notification procedure;

d) examination of incoming deliveries of food and raw materials;

e) the storage of all commodities in such a way as to assist cleaning and inspection procedures;

f) regular rotation of stored ingredients, finished products and packaging materials; the 'disturbance factor' is significant here; and

g) storage of food so that, in the event of infestation, the risk of contamination is reduced to a minimum.

Eradication

This is the third line of defence in preventing infestation. This can be under-taken using trained staff in a company-operated pest control scheme or by the use of a commercial pest control company.

In the latter case, it is essential that the terms of the Contract of Service with a pest control contractor are fully understood by management, and that the performance of the contractor is monitored continuously.

Ant control

Bird control

Cleaning, disinfection and housekeeping

Cockroach control

Eradication (infestation)

Flour mite

Flying insect control

Food Hygiene (England) Regulations 2006

Infestation

Pest

Pesticide

Proofing of buildings

Residual insecticide

Rodent control

Stock control and rotation

Informal enforcement procedures

The current procedure of authorised officers giving advice orally, sending advi-sory letters and informal warnings is well-established and is accepted and understood by the food trade. For instance, many food authorities use an informal type of notice, ('Minded to' Notice) which confirms details of contraventions of regulations identified particularly during the inspection of a food premises. Autho-rised officers may use these informal procedures as long as they believe that such procedures will be as effective as those allowed for under the statutory system.

In some cases, a food business operator may be advised of the outcome of an inspection by letter. It is important that letters sent by authorised officers distin-guish between actual legal requirements and what is considered good hygiene practice.

Authorised officer

Enforcement procedure

Food authority

Food hygiene inspections

Food Standards Inspections

Liaison with authorised officers

'Minded to' Notice

Information, instruction and training

All employees should be informed and instructed at induction, and on a regular basis, of food hygiene and safety requirements and procedures.

Evidence of staff having received formal training is crucial, and many organisations achieve this requirement by running courses accredited through, for example, the Chartered Institute of Environmental Health (CIEH), Royal Society for the Promotion of Health (RSH) and the Royal Institute of Public Health (RIPH). Most local environmental health departments run these courses on a phased or in-company basis, together with commercial training providers approved by the CIEH, RSH and RIPH.

Food handling (practice)

Food Hygiene (England) Regulations 2006

Training of food handlers

Training records

Insecticides

Chemical compounds designed to kill both crawling and flying insect pests.

Infestation

Infestation prevention and control

Pest

Pesticides

Residual insecticide

Inspection (definition)

Statutory Code of Practice No 3 – *Inspection procedures – General* defines *inspection* as a visit to any food premises which involves one or more of the following activities:

a) inspection of premises;

b) inspection of equipment including cleaning and maintenance equipment;

c) inspection of process or operational procedure;

d) inspection of hygiene or practices of personnel;

e) inspection of food (including ingredients, additives and products at any stage of manufacture) or contact materials;

f) inspection of labels, labelling requirements and advertising material; and/or

g) inspection of records.

The taking of appropriate samples and their subsequent analysis and/or examination often forms an integral part of inspection, particularly the inspection of factories.

The term 'inspection' does *not* cover the following, unless, as will often be the case, they are combined with one or more of the above activities:

a) visits *solely* to deal with complaints;

b) visits responding to requests for advice from traders;

c) visits *solely* to take samples;

d) visits for purposes such as ensuring compliance with Improvement Notices or checking circumstances prior to prosecution; and

e) visits conducted as part of a survey.

Equipment requirements

Food handling (practice)

Food hazard

Food hygiene inspections

Food Standards Inspection

Improvement Notices

Inspection of food

Inspection of food premises

Labelling requirements

Samples, procurement of

Sampling and analysis

Statutory Codes under the Food Safety Act

Structural requirements for food premises

Training records

Inspection of food

Section 9(1) of the Food Safety Act empowers an authorised officer of a food authority at all reasonable times to inspect any food intended for human consumption which:

a)   has been sold or is offered or exposed for sale;

b)   is in the possession of, or has been deposited with or consigned to, any person for the purpose of sale or preparation for sale.

Subsections (3) to (9) shall apply where, on such inspection, it appears to the authorised officer that any food fails to comply with the food safety requirements.

The term *inspect* is not defined in the Act, but is related to the requirements of the Council Directive 89/337/EEC on the official control of foodstuffs in relation to inspection procedures. Statutory Code of Practice No. 3 *Inspection Procedures – General* advises food authorities on procedures for undertaking inspections, including programmed inspection, notice of inspection, co-ordination of inspection visits, operating in other areas and post inspection procedures.

For the purposes of this Code of Practice and, when not otherwise stated, for the purpose of other codes issued under the Act, *inspection* means – a visit to any food premises which involves one or more of the following activities:

a)   inspection of premises;

b)   inspection of equipment including cleaning and maintenance equipment;

c)   inspection of a process or operational procedures;

d)   inspection of the hygiene or practices of personnel;

e)   inspection of food (including ingredients, additives and products at any stage of manufacture) or contact materials;

f)   inspection of labels, labelling requirements and advertising material; and/or

g)   inspection of records.

The taking of appropriate samples and their subsequent analysis and/or examination often forms an integral part of inspection, particularly the inspection of factories.

Generally, authorised officers visit premises in two broad circumstances. Firstly, they may visit in response to a particular complaint, to take samples and to check compliance with an enforcement notice, such as an Improvement Notice. Statutory Code of Practice No.2: *Legal Matters* outlines the procedures to be followed. Secondly, an authorised officer may visit a premises to undertake one or both of two types of inspection, a Food Standards Inspection and/or a food hygiene inspection. Procedures to be followed by authorised officers are detailed in Statutory Code of Practice No.8: *Food Standards Inspections* and Statutory Code of Practice No.9: *Food Hygiene Inspections*.

In the case of unfit food, once the authorised officer has carried out the inspection he has two choices in dealing with such food. He can detain the food in question or seize it.

Taking action without inspection

Similar powers are given where it appears that food may cause food poisoning or a disease communicable to human beings in circumstances not arising from actual inspection of the food. (Section 9(2)) Statutory Code of Practice No.4: *Inspection, Detention and Seizure of Suspect Food* advises authorised officers that section 9(2) may apply equally to food which has not been inspected. This would occur when it appears to the officer that the food is so contaminated or that it is likely to cause food poisoning or any disease communicable to human beings. In such cases the authorised officer may act to seize or detain the food without an inspection if, for instance, information is received from another reliable source, e.g. other food authorities, public health laboratory service, central government, etc. that the food may be contaminated or cause food poisoning or any communicable disease. In such circumstances, inspection is not required by law, but it may be necessary to inspect the food if only for identification purposes.

In the non-metropolitan counties, this provision should only be used by authorised officers of the district councils.

Cleaning, disinfection and housekeeping

Complaints procedure

Cross contamination

Detention or seizure of food

Detention Notices

Inspection of food premises

Authorised officers of the enforcement authority have a statutory power of entry to inspect premises with a view to assessing levels of food safety and hygiene. The procedures for inspections are covered in Statutory Codes of Practice No.8 *Food Standards Inspections* and No. 9: *Food Hygiene Inspections*.

Food business operators should also ensure a system is in place for regular inspections by an appropriate person, such as a designated hygiene manager, hygiene officer or external consultant.

Supervisors should also be involved in the inspection process, perhaps through the use of a check list, supported by appropriate training in the use of the check list and the system for ensuring recommendations arising from the inspection are dealt with promptly.

Food hygiene inspections

Food Standards Inspection

Hygiene inspections

Hygiene managers/officers

Powers of entry

Statutory Codes under the Food Safety Act

Appendix D – Food Hygiene Audit

Integrated Pest Management

A form of pest control management based on co-operation between a commercial pest control company and the operator of a food business. Emphasis is placed on preventive measures, such as structural proofing together with cleaning and housekeeping measures, with eradication as a third line of defence against infestation.

Cleaning, disinfection and housekeeping

Cleaning schedules

Eradication (infestation)

Food business operator

Infestation

Infestation prevention and control

Pest control contracts

Proofing of buildings

Regulation (EC) No. 852/2004 on the hygiene of foodstuffs

Intermediate (secondary) host

The host in which the larval stages of endoparasites develop.

Endoparasite

Host

Parasites

Intoxication

The process in the body of dealing with poisons, including the symptoms of poisoning.

Bacterial food poisoning

Bacterial toxin

Food poisoning bacteria

Food poisoning (food-borne illnesses)

Natural toxins

Toxin

Intrinsic contamination

Contamination which is associated with the food itself and not through other causes of contamination.

Contamination

Food contamination

Spoilage of food

Intrinsic factor

Any inherent factors, such as nutrients available, pH, A_w and temperature, that have an effect on the survival, growth and multiplication of micro-organisms.

Acidity

Alkalinity

A_w (water activity)

Bacterial growth curve

pH

Iodophors

Iodophors are sanitising agents containing iodine used, in some cases, by dairies in CIP systems and which are particularly effective.

Cleaning, disinfection and housekeeping

Cleaning-in-Place (CIP) systems

Irradiation

Exposure to gamma radiation to destroy spoilage and pathogenic organisms in food is commonly used for a range of fruits, potatoes, vegetables, cereals and poultry. However, in the UK irradiation is approved for use at specified doses for a narrow range of food products, such as spices and herbs, and any irradiated food must be clearly labelled as such.

The irradiation of food entails exposure of specified foods to energy in the form of ionising rays, such as Gamma rays, X-rays, microwaves and ultra violet radiation which have strong penetrating capabilities. Non-spore forming bacteria, mould spores and yeasts are eliminated at much lower doses of radiation than spore forming bacteria.

Irradiation has many benefits in the treatment of solid and packaged foods, in particular the prevention of recontamination of the product. However, irradiation can result in loss of colour, variations in taste and smell and, following high dose levels, a change in structure or texture of the food.

Labelling requirements

Moulds in food

Yeast

Jewellery

The possibility of items of jewellery, such as pendants, rings, earrings, nose studs and bracelets contaminating food products must be considered. Apart from the personal loss to the food handler concerned, such items can carry contamination and be dangerous if consumed by customers.

Most organisations ban the wearing of any form of jewellery during food preparation and processing other than a simple plain wedding ring.

Contamination

Food handling (practice)

Food Safety/Hygiene Policy

Foreign bodies

Personal hygiene

Personal protective clothing

Labelling and description offences

These offences are covered in section 15 of the Food Safety Act with respect to falsely describing or labelling food.

False or misleading descriptions and information

Food Safety Act 1990

Labelling requirements

Labelling requirements

It is illegal to label, describe, advertise or present food in such a manner that it is likely to mislead the average person.

Specific requirements for the labelling of food are dealt with in the Food Labelling Regulations 1996 (as amended) and specific regulations, such as the Fish Labelling Regulations 2003.

'Best before' date

Food Labelling Regulations 1996 (as amended)

Inspection (definition)

Inspection of food

Labelling and description offences

'Use by' date

Lag phase

The first stage of bacterial growth in which an organism adapts to its surroundings and does not reproduce.

Bacterial food poisoning

Bacterial growth curve

Larva

The immature stage of an insect undergoing the process of metamorphosis. Metamorphosis takes four stages, namely the egg, larva, pupa and adult stages.

Infestation prevention and control

Insecticides

Pest

Pesticides

Layout of food premises

The term 'layout' refers to the space available for people working in a particular room or area and the situation of plant, machinery and equipment, etc in relation to the operator and the tasks performed. Well-designed layouts in food manufacturing and catering premises contribute significantly to the avoidance of various forms of contamination. Ideally, raw materials are introduced at one end of the premises and finished products leave at the other end, with the intermediate stages of storage, preparation, production/cooking and assembly taking place in a sequential flow between these two points.

An efficient layout should make a material contribution to preventing or reducing overcrowding, minimising the effort required to perform operations, expediting the process in an orderly and sequential flow, and ensuring maximum hygiene and safety standards throughout, together with facilitating the cleaning process. Above all, the working areas should be large enough for the processes carried out, a problem encountered with many restaurant kitchens, for example.

Contamination

Cross contamination

European food hygiene legislation

Food hazard

Food Hygiene (England) Regulations 2006

Regulation (EC) No 852/2004 on the hygiene of foodstuffs

Structural requirements for food premises

Workplace (Health, Safety and Welfare) Regulations 1992

Liaison with authorised officers

The Food Safety Act and Food Hygiene (England) Regulations provide extensive enforcement powers for authorised officers of the food authorities, i.e. Environmental Health Officers and Trading Standards Officers.

Whilst their role is principally that of enforcement, it is vital that managers in the food manufacturing and catering industries establish a sound working relationship with officers of the enforcement authority.

This liaison may be established in a number of ways:

a) by seeking guidance, particularly at the design stage of new projects, on matters such as legal requirements relating to, for instance, structural finishes;

b) by discussing matters such as the formulation of cleaning schedules, preventive maintenance schedules, sampling procedures, temperature control systems, infestation control procedures, prior to their implementation;

c) by agreeing training needs for individual groups prior to running food safety training programmes;

d) by agreeing complaints procedures and product recall systems;

e) by seeking agreement on the contents of food safety manuals, operating procedures, labels, etc. prior to publication;

f) by reviewing corrective action reporting procedures in the light of past experience; and

g) prior to the introduction of formal food safety management systems, such as Hazard Analysis: Critical Control Points (HACCP).

Authorised officer

Cleaning schedules

Complaints procedure

Corrective action

Enforcement procedure

Food Hygiene (England) Regulations 2006

Food Safety Act 1990

Food safety manuals

Hazard Analysis: Critical Control Point (HACCP)

Infestation prevention and control

Information, instruction and training

Labelling requirements

Preventive maintenance

Product recall systems

Sampling and analysis

Structural requirements for food premises

Training of food handlers

Licensing and registration of food premises

Food premises are subject to two specific regimes with respect to their premises and business activities.

Licensing Act 2003

A licence, issued by the local authority, is required for the following activities:

a)   to sell alcohol by retail;

b)   as a qualifying club, to supply alcohol to a club member or to a guest of a club member;

c)   to provide regulated entertainment; and

d)   to sell late night refreshment, i,e, selling hot food or drink between 11 pm and 5 am for consumption on or off the premises, unless the premises are a hotel, staff canteen or camp site.

Food Premises (Registration) Regulations 1991

Most food premises are required to register with the local authority under these regulations.

Regulation (EC) No. 852/2004 on the hygiene of foodstuffs

Food business operators must register their establishments, i.e. each separate unit of their food business, with the local authority, except establishments which:

a)   are subject to approval by the authority under Regulation (EC) No. 853/2004; or

b)   fall outside the scope of Regulation (EC) No. 852/2004.

Food businesses include market stalls, delivery vehicles and mobile food vendors.

Responsibility rests with food authorities for recording and maintaining details of the food business establishments which have been registered with them under Regulation (EC) No. 852/2004. These food business establishments do not include those engaged only in primary production activities.

Where a person uses, or intends to use, any premises for the purpose of a food business on five or more days (whether consecutive or not) in any period of five consecutive weeks, he must apply to register with the local authority at least 28 days before the first day of such use.

Business

Community Instruments and Regulations

Food authority

Food business (definition)

Primary products

Registration and approval of food premises

Regulation (EC) No. 852/2004 on the hygiene of foodstuffs

Lighting recommendations

Current HSE recommendations for lighting (illuminance) levels in food premises are shown in the Table below:

Average Illuminance (Lux)	Minimum Measured (Lux) Illuminance	
50	20	Loading bays, storage areas, bottling and canning plants
100	50	Kitchens, food manufacture
200	100	High risk areas, laboratories

Average illuminances and minimum measured illuminances (lighting)

Regulation (EC) No 852 on the hygiene of foodstuffs

Workplace (Health, Safety and Welfare) Regulations 1992

Linear flow

This is the production flow, during a food manufacturing or catering process, from raw materials to the finished product.

Linear flow generally takes the following series of operations:

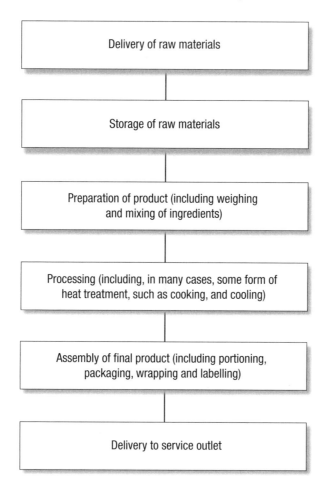

Delivery of raw materials

Storage of raw materials

Preparation of product (including weighing and mixing of ingredients)

Processing (including, in many cases, some form of heat treatment, such as cooking, and cooling)

Assembly of final product (including portioning, packaging, wrapping and labelling)

Delivery to service outlet

Food safety risk assessment procedures and management systems should endeavour to ascertain the potential for contamination at each stage of the linear flow.

Assured Safe Catering (ASC)

Food purchase and delivery

Food safety management systems

Food safety risk assessment

Hazard Analysis: Critical Control Point (HACCP)

Stock control and rotation

Liquid oils and fats – bulk transport by sea

Regulation 29 and Schedule 3 to the Food Hygiene (England) Regulations 2006 lay down requirements for the bulk transport in sea-going vessels of liquid oils or fats and the bulk transport by sea of raw sugar.

A person who contravenes or fails to comply with any of the requirements of the Schedule shall be guilty of an offence.

Food Hygiene (England) Regulations 2006

Offences and penalties

Listeria monocytogenes

This bacterium has been found in most farm animals, poultry and domestic pets, wild birds, insects, soil, sewage and decaying vegetable matter. The more vulnerable members of society, e.g. young children, pregnant mothers, the elderly and the sick are most at risk of contracting the disease known as Listeriosis. As such, *Listeria* is resistant to heat, drying and freezing, and is capable of growth in a refrigerator if the temperature consistently exceeds 5°C.

Listeriosis has been associated with a range of foods, such as raw and smoked fish, milk, ice cream, pates, cooked meats, full-fat soft cheeses, such as Camembert and Brie, prepared salads and sandwiches.

Measures to prevent listerial growth include:

- thorough reheating of foods to a core temperature of at least 70°C
- ensuring cook-chill products are consumed well within the 'use by' date
- frequent defrosting of refrigerators
- washing of salad foods.

Generally, evidence of *Listeria* in foods is an indication of poor hygiene practices.

Bacteria

Bacterial food poisoning

Cook-chill

Dehydration

Fish and shellfish (food hazards)

Food handling (practice)

Ice cream (food hazards)

Milk and dairy products (food hazards)

Refrigerators

Reheating of food

'Use by' date

Washing of food and food equipment

Log (logarithmic) phase

A stage of fast bacterial multiplication.

Bacterial growth curve

Lag phase

Stationary phase

Machinery and work equipment

All food processing machinery and equipment must be maintained in a hygienic condition and subject to regular cleaning and maintenance.

Cleaning, disinfection and housekeeping

Cleaning schedules

Equipment requirements

Food Hygiene (England) Regulations 2006

Provision and Use of Work Equipment Regulations 1998

Regulation (EC) No 852/2004 on the hygiene of foodstuffs

Magistrates Court

This is the lowest of the courts in England and Wales and deals mainly with summary offences, principally criminal offences, including breaches of food safety legislation brought by enforcement authorities. The jurisdiction of the Magistrates Court is limited in terms of the sentences that can be imposed. Lay Justices of the Peace (JPs) determine and sentence for many of the less serious offences.

Magistrates also hold preliminary examinations into other offences to ascertain whether the prosecution can show a prima facie case on which the accused may be committed for trial at a higher court, such as the Crown Court.

The Sheriff Court performs a parallel function in Scotland, although procedures differ from those of the Magistrates Courts.

Criminal offences

Enforcement procedure

Prosecution

Mail order food

Food supplied by mail order is subject to the temperature control requirements of the Food Hygiene (England) Regulations.

No person shall supply by mail order any food which:

a) is likely to support the growth of pathogenic micro-organisms or the formation of toxins; and

b) is being or has been conveyed by post or by a private or common carrier to the final consumer;

at a temperature which has given rise or is likely to give rise to a risk to health.

Chill holding requirements

Food Hygiene (England) Regulations 2006

Pathogenic agents (pathogens)

Temperature control requirements

Malicious tampering with food

The intentional contamination, interference with and insertion of foreign bodies in food.

Food Safety Act 1990

Foreign bodies

Nature, substance or quality

Meat

All forms of meat – beef, pork, mutton, lamb and poultry – have a high protein content and, when cooked, must be classed as high risk foods due to the risk of bacterial contamination.

Raw meat should always be stored in a refrigerator prior to cooking and, as far as possible, separated from other food commodities to prevent cross-contamination, particularly from blood dripping on to food items below. Ideally, raw meat should be stored in a separate refrigerator designated for this purpose.

Evidence of unfitness in meat may be associated with:

a) decomposition

b) abnormal colour

c) abnormal odour

d) surface slime

d) phosphorescence

e) fat discolouration and rancidity

f) parasitic infestations, e.g. roundworms, flatworms.

Cestoda

Contamination

Cross contamination

Cysticerci

Flatworms

Food hazard

Meat

Meat products (food hazards)

Nematodes

Parasites

Phosphorescence

Rancidity

Spoilage of food

Unfitness for human consumption

Meat products (food hazards)

All meat products, such as sausages, salami, meat pies, rissoles, faggots, tripe and black pudding, undergo some form of processing prior to sale. This may entail various forms of heat treatment and the incorporation of a range of food additives, such as preservative, seasonings, spices and colouring agents.

As such, they represent a serious risk to food safety if not stored correctly in refrigerators or chilled display cabinets. Those engaged in slicing and service of meat products must maintain high standards of personal hygiene.

Additives

Chilled storage

Colours

Food handling (practice)

Food hazard

Food Labelling Regulations 1996 (as amended)

Meat

Meat products (food hazards)

Personal hygiene

Preservatives

Processed products

Refrigerators

Smoked foods

Spoilage of food

Temperature control (premises)

Temperature control requirements

Unfitness for human consumption

Meat thermometer

A specific form of thermometer used for measuring the core temperature of meat joints and poultry, such as turkeys, during cooking. Core temperature measurement, or probing, is the most effective means of ensuring that the core or centre has reached a minimum of 70°C in order to destroy bacteria. The thermometer should be washed and disinfected to prevent cross contamination.

Cooking of food

Core (centre) temperature

Temperature control requirements

Temperature measurement equipment

Mesophile

A micro-organism preferring the temperature range 10°C to 55°C.

Micro-organisms (Microbes)

Thermophile

Methylene blue test

A standard indirect method used for estimating bacterial numbers in milk, cream and ice cream. The test is based on the fact that methylene blue, a dye, remains blue in the presence of oxygen and colourless in the absence of same. The rate at which bacteria in milk use up available oxygen, indicated by loss of colour in the dye, is an indication of the degree of bacterial contamination.

Bacteriological control systems

Bacteriological standards

Detection methods

Milk and dairy products (food hazards)

Microbe

An alternative term used for micro-organisms.

Micro-organisms (Microbes)

Microbiological criteria

The Microbiological Criteria for Foodstuffs Regulations 2005 complement the EU food hygiene legislation as part of a risk-based approach to food safety. The microbiological criteria can be used by food businesses to validate and verify their food safety management procedures and when assessing the acceptability of foodstuffs, or their manufacturing, handling and distribution processes.

The legislation is structured so it can be applied flexibly in all food businesses, regardless of their type or size. Microbiological criteria should be applied within the framework of procedures based on HACCP principles.

For some products, the regulations set out specific sampling and testing requirements but, in most cases, producers are able to set the frequency and volume of testing according to the type of product and the nature and size of the business.

The regulations support Regulation (EC) No. 852/2004 on the hygiene of foodstuffs with particular reference to the operation of food safety management systems, such as Hazard Analysis Critical Control Point (HACCP).

Assured Safe Catering (ASC)

Business (definition)

End product testing

Food business (definition)

Food safety management objectives

Food safety management systems

Food safety risk assessment

Food Standards Inspection

Hazard Analysis: Critical Control Point (HACCP)

Microbiological criteria

Microbiological hazards

Regulation (EC) No. 852/2004 on the hygiene of foodstuffs

Sampling and analysis

Microbiological hazards

These are the hazards associated with pathogenic and spoilage bacteria, together with viruses, parasites and fungi.

Bacteria

Bacterial food poisoning

Bacterial growth curve

Fungi

Parasites

Spoilage of food

Viruses

Microbiology

The science involving the study of microbes (micro-organisms).

Bacteria

Micro-organisms (Microbes)

Micro-organisms (Microbes)

Any form of organism that is so small that it can be viewed only through the use of a microscope.

Microbiology

Microwave ovens

Microwave ovens are extensively used in the home, in retail premises such as fish and chip shops, cafeterias, restaurants and workplaces. These ovens operate on the principle that, when food is contained inside the metal-lined oven with a sealed door, microwave energy cannot penetrate the metal lining and, subsequently, is reflected back towards the food which absorbs this energy. As a result the heat can undertake a number of functions, from thawing frozen food to the actual cooking or simple re-heating of food commodities.

Whilst, from a general safety viewpoint, it is recognised that microwave ovens can be dangerous, important considerations in the use of microwave ovens from a food safety viewpoint include:

a) attention to the manufacturer's instructions with respect to:

   i) standing time prior to removal from the cabinet;

   ii) temperature during cooking; and

   iii) duration of cooking;

b) during the standing time a temperature of at least 70°C should be attained; and

c) limiting the size of solid food items, such as meat joints and poultry, due to uncertainty as to achieving complete cooking.

Cooking of food

Temperature control requirements

Thawing of frozen food

Milk and dairy products (food hazards)

Milk

Milk contains approximately:

87.25%	Water
3.8%	Fats
4.7%	Carbohydrates
3.5%	Proteins
0.75%	Ash

Milk also contains enzymes, vitamins and other trace elements. Variations in fat content are associated with the particular breed of cow, intervals between milking and the actual period during lactation.

Milk is an excellent medium for bacterial growth, particularly those lactic acid bacteria associated with fermentation. Such bacteria attack the milk sugar (lactose) converting small amounts of it to lactic acid. This gives the milk a sour smell and taste and will eventually result in coagulation of the milk.

Poor standards of milking parlour hygiene on the farm can result not only in poor keeping quality but also a range of changes in the milk colour and consistency caused by the action of bacteria, such as:

a)   *Gassy milk* caused by yeasts, such as *Torula cremoris*;

b)   *Red milk* caused by pigment-producing bacteria, including *Bacillus prodigiosus*;

c)   *Sweet curdling* where the milk is coagulated by bacteria which secrete a rennet-like enzyme such as *Streptococcus liquefaciens*.

None of these changes occur until the milk has been allowed to stand for a few hours.

Abnormal or 'off' flavours in milk are associated with food fed to cows, such as turnips, the absorption of odours from the atmosphere, the heat treatment process or the addition of foreign materials, such as taints from bottles.

Dairy products

Dairy products include butter, cream, dried milk, ice cream and cheese.

Butter

Butter may be contaminated by extraneous materials (foreign bodies), excessive salt, packing materials, contaminated water supply, utensils and food handlers. Common faults are:

a)   *Sourness* due to excessive rancidity;

b)   *Bitterness* due to feeding stuffs or ripening cream at too low a temperature;

c)   *Food taints* due to an excess of certain foods in animal feeds, such as roots, silage and highly flavoured concentrates;

d)   *Staleness* found, particularly, in hot weather and due to poor quality cream and excessive storage periods;

e)   *Rancidity*, which is the final stage of staleness, closely allied to action by moulds, and indicates advanced deterioration of the product;

f)   *Insipid taste*, caused by insufficient ripening of the cream; and

g)   *Tallowiness*, due to the presence of copper salts in cream, over-ripening of the cream and exposure of the cream to sunlight.

Cream

Cream can be subject to many of the forms of pathogenic and non-pathogenic action associated with milk.

Cheese

Cheese can be roughly classified thus:

a) *Hard cheeses,* such as Cheddar, Cheshire, Gloucester and Gruyere varieties;

b) *Blue-veined cheeses,* such as Stilton, Gorgonzola, Danish Blue and Roquefort varieties;

c) *Soft cheeses,* such as Brie, Camembert and Limburger varieties; and

d) *Special cheeses,* such as various cream cheeses, processed cheeses.

Cheese is liable to a range of abnormalities but, in particular, to:

a) the effects of mould growth on cut and external surfaces; and

b) the effects of infestation by cheese mite and cheese flies which result in crumbling and wastage of cheese.

Cheese may be regarded as unsound if the mouldiness and odour are excessive or if it contains large numbers of maggots or mites, infestation by mites giving the external surface a dusty appearance. With many soft cheeses, they can decompose to such a state where the texture has broken down and odour is offensive.

Cheese in storage readily absorbs foreign flavours and odours from volatile substances.

Ice cream

This is a particularly high risk product and the ingredients vary considerably to include milk, sugar, eggs, water and thickening agents. Many ice cream products contain a substantial amount of air. The final product should be stored at a temperature of – 18°C.

Ice cream is subject to similar bacterial action as milk and cream.

Bacteria

Bacterial growth curve

Enzymes

Foreign bodies

Ice cream (food hazards)

Infestation prevention and control

Larva

Moulds in food

Pasteurisation

Sterilisation

Rancidity

Yeast

'Minded to' Notice

An informal type of notice served by an authorised officer on the operator of a food business advising that person that, unless immediate action, for example, within 14 days, is taken to remedy a breach of food safety law, a formal Improvement Notice will be served.

Authorised officer

Food business operator

Improvement Notices

Ministerial Directions

Emergency Control Orders and Ministerial Directions

Mission Statement

A formal statement of intention by an organisation to manufacture food products, or provide catering services, to the highest possible food safety and hygiene standards and seeking the co-operation of all employees in the attainment of specified objectives.

Food Safety/Hygiene Policy

Food safety management objectives

Modified atmosphere packing

A process of food preservation whereby the chemical composition of the air in hermetically-sealed packaging is regulated.

Preservation of food

Modified food sources

Genetically modified food sources

Monitoring

The observation and/or measurement at a critical control point of the factors or criteria which allow corrective action to be taken.

Corrective action

Critical Control Point (CCPs)

Hazard Analysis: Critical Control Point (HACCP)

Moulds in food

Moulds are, fundamentally, aerobic fungi, frequently appearing as white or blue colony growths on the surface of, for example, fruit, vegetables, cheese and bakery products, such as bread, biscuits and cakes. Moulds reproduce rapidly by the production and release of spores, particularly where atmospheres are moist and warm. They will, however, continue to develop at temperatures below 0°C. Moulds are responsive to water activity and some species tolerate low levels of water activity at below A_w 6.0

They are responsible for food spoilage of a wide range of food products, in particular dry foods with low levels of water activity, such as cheese, biscuits and nuts.

Some species of mould produce toxins (mycotoxins).

Aerobe

A_w (water activity)

Fungi

Meat

Meat products (food hazards)

Milk and dairy products (food hazards)

Mycotoxin

Spoilage of food

Moveable and temporary structures

Chapter III to Annex II of Regulation (EC) No 852/2004 on the hygiene of food-stuffs lays down requirements for moveable and/or temporary premises (such as marquees, market stalls, mobile sales vehicles), premises used primarily as a private dwelling house but where foods are regularly prepared for placing on the market and vending machines thus:

1. Premises and vending machines are, so far as is reasonably practicable, to be sited, designed, constructed and kept clean and maintained in good repair and condition, as to avoid the risk of contamination, in particular, by animals and pests.

2. In particular, where necessary:

   a) appropriate facilities are to be available to maintain adequate personal hygiene (including facilities for the hygienic washing and drying of hands, hygienic sanitary arrangements and changing facilities);

   b) surfaces in contact with food are to be in sound condition and be easy to clean and, where necessary, disinfect. This will require the use of smooth, washable, corrosion-resistant and non-toxic materials, unless food business operators can satisfy the competent authority that other materials used are appropriate;

   c) adequate provision is to be made for the cleaning and, where necessary, disinfecting of working utensils and equipment;

   d) where foodstuffs are cleaned as part of the food business' operations, adequate provision must be made for this to be undertaken hygienically;

   e) an adequate supply of hot and/or cold potable water is to be available;

   f) adequate arrangements and/or facilities for the hygienic storage and disposal of hazardous and/or inedible substances and waste (whether liquid or solid) are to be available;

g)   adequate facilities and/or arrangements for maintaining and monitoring suitable food temperature conditions are to be available;

h)   foodstuffs are to be so placed as to avoid the risk of contamination so far as is reasonably practicable.

Changing facilities

Cleaning, disinfection and housekeeping

Equipment requirements

Food business operator

Hand washing

Hand washing facilities

Infestation prevention and control

Machinery and work equipment

Personal hygiene

Potable water

Regulation (EC) No. 852/2004 on the hygiene of foodstuffs

Structural requirements for food premises

Temperature control (premises)

Temperature control requirements

Vending machines

Washing of food and food equipment

Waste food storage and disposal

Water supply

Multiplication

The means by which microbial reproduction takes place, for example, by binary fission in the case of bacteria and budding in yeasts.

Bacterial growth curve

Binary fission

Microbe

Yeast

Mushroom toxin

Some mushrooms (and toadstools) produce natural toxins which can cause food poisoning. These toxins are not destroyed by cooking, freezing or other food processing activities and consumption can cause extremely variable symptoms, such as hallucinations, convulsions, nausea, vomiting, diarrhoea and death.

The Death Cap mushroom produces a toxin, amatoxin, which can cause heart, liver and kidney damage, resulting in death in several days.

Frozen food

Fungi

Fungicides

Natural toxins

Toxin

Mycotoxin

A mycotoxin is a form of poison produced by some moulds and yeasts and which accumulate in food animals. Mycotoxins are capable of surviving conditions in which bacteria would not normally survive. They are associated with products with a low pH, such as fruit juices, and relatively dry products such as cereal products, dried beans, nuts, coffee and cocoa beans, soya beans and various cured meats, such as ham. They can tolerate low water activity down to 0.80 A_w, and are resistant to heat, such as that produced during heat treatment processes. They are generally present in all areas of the food chain.

Mycotoxins thrive within the temperature range – 7°C to 35°C and their evidence at the lower end of this scale is seen in cold stores where black patches form on damp surfaces and in areas where cleaning has not been effective.

Mycotoxins are highly resistant to preservation techniques and any measures to control same must be concentrated at source by preventing or controlling their formation on farms, supported by quick-drying after the harvesting process. Their control is further assisted by storage of products at temperatures as low as -20°C and maintaining pH at above 6.5 or below 3.0.

Exposure to mycotoxins can cause mycotoxicosis, an illness caused by the toxins produced by some fungi.

Aflatoxin

A_w (water activity)

Dehydration

Fungi

Moulds in food

Mushroom toxin

Natural toxins

pH

Stock control and rotation

Yeast

N

Natural foods

These are foods which do not generally need any form of food processing prior to consumption other than, for instance, boiling. They include fruit, vegetables, nuts and cereals, such as oats.

Natural toxins

Toxic substances which are naturally present in a food product.

Aflatoxin

Biotoxin

Ciguatera poisoning

Endotoxin

Fungi

Moulds in food

Mushroom toxin

Neurotoxin

Red kidney bean poisoning

Scombrotoxin

Toxin

Nature, substance or quality

This is an important requirement of the consumer protection provisions of the Food Safety Act making it an offence to sell food that is not of the 'nature' or not of the 'substance' or not of the 'quality' demanded by the purchaser.

Nature

'Not of the nature' covers the typical 'passing off' offence whereby an inferior product is intentionally supplied by the operator of a food business, such as sirloin steak instead of rump steak, or cod instead of haddock.

Substance

'Not of the substance' implies that a substance may have been contaminated by the addition of an adulterant, such as the addition of water to milk, the presence of antibiotic residues in milk and the presence of a foreign body in food.

Quality

'Not of the quality' involves situations where a food falls short of its expected quality or does not meet some regulatory standard relating to composition. A foreign body in food can render the food not of the quality demanded. *Quality* means the commercial quality of the article sold and not merely its description.

Consumer protection provisions (Food Safety Act)

Food Safety Act 1990

Food safety management objectives

'Passing off' offence

Offences and penalties

Nematodes

These are small worms which may infest the organs and systems of food animals, including *Ascaris lumbricoides* found in the small intestines and bile ducts of pigs, various types of *Strongyli,* such as *Strongylus micurus,* found in the lungs and bronchi of young cattle, and *Trichinella spiralis,* the larvae of a small round worm which invades the muscles of man (trichinosis), pigs and rats.

Ascaris lumbricoides

Cestoda

Parasites

Trichinella spiralis

Neurotoxin

A toxic substance which attacks the central nervous system and the most dangerous biotoxin known. They are produced by several organisms. Common neurotoxins are exotoxins produced by *Staphylococci, Clostridium botulinum* and ciguatoxin (*Ciguatera)* from dinoflagellates.

Biotoxins

Ciguatera poisoning

Clostridium botulinum (Clostridium welchii)

Endotoxin

Exotoxins

Natural toxins

Staphylococcus aureus

Toxin

Neutral

A term implying a pH of 7.0.

Acidity

Alkalinity

pH value

Nitrates and nitrites

Various combinations of nitrates and nitrites are used in the preservation of meat and in salting and pickling processes, in order to retain the original colour of the meat.

High concentrations of nitrates in canned goods can result in damage to the can lacquer thereby allowing metallic tin to leach into the canned food.

Careful control over concentrations of these chemicals is essential as residues in food may cause acute responses from consumers including prostration, cyanosis, paralysis of the respiratory system and reduced blood pressure.

Brining

Canned goods

Chemical contamination of food

Nitrosamine

Pickling

Nitrosamine

These are chemical compounds formed where nitrates or nitrites used in the curing of meat react with compounds, such as amines. This can cause a particular form of food poisoning. There is evidence that many nitrosamines may be carcinogenic.

Meat that is fresh will normally withstand the actions of nitrosamine as part of the curing process.

Curing of food

Freshness and fitness of food

Meat

Meat products (food hazards)

Nitrates and nitrites

Norwalk virus

Infection with this virus, commonly via the faecal-oral route, causes a mild form of gastro-enteritis. It is commonly associated with shellfish and salad foods which have become contaminated through preparation in infected water. There is a 1 to 2 day incubation period and the symptoms may last for 1 to 3 days. Symptoms include abdominal cramps, diarrhoea, vomiting and nausea.

Control of the virus infection is through strict levels of personal hygiene, ensuring the purity of irrigation water and purchase of seafood products from reliable suppliers.

Faecal coliform

Faecal organisms (bacteriological standards)

Fish and shellfish (food hazards)

Food poisoning (food-borne illnesses)

Gastro-enteritis

Incubation period

Viruses

Washing of food and food equipment

Notices

Authorised officers of local authorities are empowered to serve a range of notices on proprietors of food businesses under both the Food Safety Act and the Food Hygiene (England) Regulations.

Appeals against Notices, etc

Detention Notices

Emergency Prohibition Notices

Emergency Prohibition Orders

Hygiene Emergency Prohibition Notice

Hygiene Improvement Notice

Improvement Notices

'Minded to' Notice

Offences and penalties

Remedial Action Notices

Statutory Codes under the Food Safety Act

Novel food (definition)

Any food which has not previously been used for human consumption in Great Britain or has only been used to a very limited extent.

[Food Safety Act 1990]

Obstruction etc of an authorised officer

Obstruction may take place in a number of ways, the most common being refusal of entry by an authorised officer to a food premises. In such cases an authorised officer may make an application for a warrant to enter the premises under section 32(2) of the Food Safety Act.

Reasonable force may be used to enter premises with a warrant. Such a warrant continues in force for a period of one month. The officer may also ask for police assistance, for example, a police escort.

[Food Safety Act 1990, Section 32(2)]

Similar provisions apply in the case of the Food Hygiene (England) Regulations, thus:

Any person who:

a)   intentionally obstructs any person acting in the execution of the Hygiene Regulations; or

b)   without reasonable cause, fails to give any person acting in the execution of the Hygiene Regulations any assistance or information which that person may reasonably require of him for the performance of his functions under the Hygiene Regulations, shall be guilty of an offence.

Any person who, in purported compliance with any such requirement mentioned in (b) above:

a)   furnishes information which he knows to be false or misleading in a material particular; or

b)   recklessly furnishes information which is false or misleading in a material particular, shall be guilty of an offence.

Food Hygiene (England) Regulations 2006

Food Safety Act 1990

Offences and penalties

Powers of entry

Occupational health

Occupational health is a branch of preventive medicine which is concerned with:

a) the relationship of work to health, and

b) the effects of work on the worker.

Health surveillance

Occupational health practitioners

Occupational health practitioners

Occupational health practitioners have a significant role in the food industry. The various responsibilities of occupational health practitioners are outlined below.

Occupational health nurses

Normally an occupational health nurse would hold a general nursing qualification, e.g. SRN or RGN, together with a separate qualification in occupational health nursing, such as the Certificate in Occupational Health Nursing of the Royal College of Nursing.

The occupational health nurse's role consists of eight main elements:

a) health surveillance/supervision;

b) health education;

c) environmental monitoring and occupational safety;

d) counselling;

e) treatment services;

f) rehabilitation and resettlement;

g) unit administration and record systems; and

h) liaison with other agencies, e.g. employment medical advisers of the Employment Medical Advisory Service, Health and Safety Executive.

The Royal College of Nursing lists the following duties which could be undertaken by a fully trained occupational health nurse:

a) health assessment in relation to the individual worker and the job to be performed;

b) noting normal standards of health and fitness and any departures or variations from these standards;

c) referring to the occupational physician or doctor such cases which, in the opinion of the nurse, require further investigation and medical, as distinct from nursing, assessment;

d) health supervision of vulnerable groups, e.g. young persons, high risk food handlers;

e) routine visits to and surveys of the working environment, and informing, as necessary, the appropriate expert when a particular problem requires further specialised investigation;

f) employee health counselling;

g) health education activities in relation to groups of workers, e.g. avoiding hand and other contamination of products;

h) the assessment of injuries or illness occurring at work and treatment or referral as appropriate;

i) responsibility for the organisation and administration of occupational health services, and the control and safe-keeping of non-statutory personal health records; and

j) a teaching role in respect of the training of first aid personnel and the organisation of emergency services.

Occupational physicians

An occupational physician is a registered medical practitioner and should preferably hold additional qualifications in occupational medicine, such as membership of a Faculty of Occupational Medicine or other appropriate organisation.

The British Medical Association has identified the role of the occupational physician as encompassing the following:

1. The effect of health on the capacity to work, which includes:

   a) provision of advice to employees on all health matters relating to their working capacity;

   b) examination of applicants for employment and advice as to their placement;

   c) immediate treatment of surgical and medical emergencies occurring at the place of employment;

   d) examination and continued observation of persons returning to work after illness or accident and advice on suitable work; and

   e) health surveillance/supervision of all employees with special reference to young persons, pregnant women, elderly persons and disabled persons.

2. The effects of work on health, which includes:

   a) responsibility for nursing and first aid services;

   b) study of the work and working environment and how they affect the health of employees;

   c) periodical examination of employees exposed to special hazards in respect of their employment;

   d) advising management regarding:

      i) the working environment in relation to health;

      ii) occurrence and significance of hazards;

      iii) accident prevention; and

      iv) statutory requirements in relation to health;

   e) medical supervision of the health and hygiene of staff and facilities, with particular reference to canteens, kitchens, etc and those working in the production of food or drugs for sale to the public;

   f) arranging and carrying out such education work in respect of the health, fitness and hygiene of employees as may be desirable and practicable; and

   g) advising those committees within the organisation which are responsible for the health, safety and welfare of employees.

Exclusion of food handlers

Food handler

Food handling (practice)

Hand contamination of food

Health supervision

Health surveillance

Liaison with authorised officers

Occupational health

Persons suffering from certain medical conditions

Pre-employment health screening

Training of food handlers

Welfare amenity provisions

Appendix C – Health screening documentation

Occupier

Any person carrying on the business of producing or handling raw cows' milk or his duly authorised representative.

[Food Hygiene (England) Regulations 2006]

Ochratoxin

A mycotoxin produced by the genus *Aspergillus*.

Aspergillus

Mycotoxin

Offences and penalties

Operators of food businesses may be guilty of a range of offences under the Food Safety Act and Regulations made under the Act. Offences and penalties are outlined below:

Food Safety Act 1990

A person guilty of an offence under section 33(1) (obstruction etc of officers) shall be liable on summary conviction to a fine not exceeding level 5 on the standard scale or to imprisonment for a term not exceeding three months or to both.

A person guilty of any other offence under the Food Safety Act shall be liable:

a) on conviction on indictment, to a fine or to imprisonment for a term not exceeding two years or to both;

b) on summary conviction, to a fine not exceeding the relevant amount or to imprisonment for a term not exceeding six months or both.

Food Hygiene (England) Regulations 2006

Subject to paragraph 4, any person who contravenes or fails to comply with any of the specified Community provisions shall be guilty of an offence.

Subject to paragraph 3, a person guilty of an offence under these Regulations shall be liable:

a) on summary conviction to a fine not exceeding the statutory maximum; or

b) on conviction on indictment to imprisonment for a term not exceeding two years, to a fine or to both.

A person guilty of an offence under regulation 15 (obstruction etc of officers) shall be liable on summary conviction to a fine not exceeding level 5 on the standard scale or to imprisonment for a term not exceeding three months or to both.

A person shall be considered not to have contravened or failed to comply with Article 4(2) of Regulation 852/2004 as read with paragraph 4 of Chapter IV of Annex II to that Regulation (bulk foodstuffs in liquid, granulate or powder form to be transported in receptacles and/or containers/tankers reserved for the transport of foodstuffs) provided the requirements of Schedule 3 are complied with.

[Food Hygiene (England) Regulations 2006]

Business (definition)

Community Instruments and Regulations

Consumer protection provisions (Food Safety Act)

Food business operator

Food receptacles

Food safety requirements

Food Hygiene (England) Regulations 2006

Food Safety Act 1990

Magistrates Court

Obstruction etc of an authorised officer

Regulation (EC) No 852/2004 on the hygiene of foodstuffs

Offences by bodies corporate

Where an offence under both the Food Safety Act and Food Hygiene (England) Regulations which has been committed by a body corporate is proved to have been committed with the consent or connivance of, or to be attributable to any neglect on the part of:

a) any director, manager, secretary or similar officer of the body corporate; or

b) any person who was purporting to act in any such capacity,

he as well as the body corporate shall be deemed to be guilty of that offence and shall be liable to be proceeded against and punished accordingly.

'Director', in relation to any body corporate established by or under any enactment for the purpose of carrying on under national ownership any industry or part of an industry or undertaking, being a body corporate whose affairs are managed by its members, means a member of that body corporate.

[Food Safety Act 1990]

[Food Hygiene (England) Regulations 2006]

Food Hygiene (England) Regulations 2006
Food Safety Act 1990
Offences and penalties

Offences by Scottish partnerships

Where an offence under the Regulations which has been committed by a Scottish partnership is proved to have been committed with the consent or connivance of, or to be attributable to any neglect on the part of, a partner, he, as well as the partnership shall be deemed to be guilty of that offence and liable to be proceeded against and punished accordingly.

[Food Hygiene (England) Regulations 2006]

Offences and penalties

Official Feed and Food Controls (England) Regulations 2006

These regulations apply to the EU Official Feed and Food Controls Regulation in England. This EU Regulation sets out general requirements for competent authorities that are responsible for checking that businesses comply with feed and food legislation, together with animal health and welfare rules.

The Regulation also sets out the role of the Commission's Food and Veterinary Office.

European food hygiene legislation

Onset period

The period of time in between consumption of a contaminated food and the initial symptoms of illness, also known as 'incubation period'.

Incubation period

Orders

The criminal courts and the Minister have specific powers with respect to the making of Orders under food safety legislation.

Emergency Control Orders and Ministerial Directions

Emergency Prohibition Orders

Enforcement procedure

Hygiene Emergency Prohibition Order

Hygiene Prohibition Orders

Prohibition Orders

Statutory codes under the Food Safety Act

Organism

An independent form of life.

Micro-organisms (Microbes)

Packaging

The placing of one or more wrapped foodstuffs in a second container and the latter container itself.

[Regulation (EC) No 852/2004 on the hygiene of foodstuffs]

Food receptacles

Wrapping and packaging of foodstuffs

Paralytic shellfish poisoning

A form of food poisoning associated with shellfish which have become temporarily toxic following seasonal consumption of toxic plankton.

Food poisoning (food-borne illnesses)

Parasites

Parasites are animals, plants and micro-organisms that derive sustenance and shelter in or on other organisms, thriving on their body substance or metabolites.

Parasites need a living host which enables their development in a series of stages from the egg stage to the mature adult. This may entail one or more intermediate hosts which could be various food sources, such as live animals.

Ant control

Bacterial food poisoning

Cestoda

Cysticerci

Fasciola hepatica

Flatworms

Freshness and fitness of food

Host

Microbe

Micro-organisms (Microbes)

Protozoa

Rodent control

Taenia saginata

Taenia solium

Tapeworms (Cestodes)

Trichinella spiralis

Yersinia enterocolitica

Zoonoses

Particular foods

Section 18 of the Food Safety Act makes special provisions for particular foods.

The Ministers may by regulations make provision:

a)   for prohibiting the carrying out of commercial operations with respect to novel foods, or food sources from which such foods are intended to be derived, of any class specified in the regulations;

b)   for prohibiting the carrying out of such operations with respect to genetically modified food sources, or foods derived from such food sources, of any class so specified; or

c)   for prohibiting the importation of any food of a class so specified,

and (in each case) for excluding from the prohibition any food or food source which is of a description specified by or under the regulations and, in the case of a prohibition on importation, is imported at an authorised place of entry.

Food Safety Act 1990

Genetically modified food sources

Novel foods (definition)

'Passing off' offence

This term is commonly used to describe the unsatisfactory practice of intentionally supplying to a purchaser a food commodity which is not of the nature demanded by the purchaser.

Examples of 'passing off' offences include supplying cod when haddock had specifically been requested, or sirloin steak in place of rump steak.

Food Safety Act 1990

Nature, substance or quality

Pasteurisation

A method of heat treatment of, particularly, milk, that destroys tuberculous pathogens and reduces other pathogen levels to acceptable safe levels for humans.

Heat treatment

Sterilisation

Ultra Heat Treatment (UHT)

Pathogenic agents (pathogens)

Organisms which can cause disease.

Micro-organisms (Microbes)

Organism

Penalties

Failure to comply with the requirements of the Food Safety Act and Regulations made under the Act can result in a range of penalties being imposed on a food business operator.

Food business operator

Food Hygiene (England) Regulations 2006

Food Safety Act 1990

Offences and penalties

Regulation (EC) No 852/2004 on the hygiene of foodstuffs

Perfumes and toiletries

Food handlers should be banned from the use of perfumes and strong-smelling toiletries, such as after-shave, due to the potential for the tainting of certain products, such as milk and milk products. Many products are particularly susceptible to this form of chemical contamination.

Food contamination

Food handler

Food handling (practice)

Indirect contamination

Personal hygiene

Chapter VIII of Regulation (EC) No 852/2004 on the hygiene of foodstuffs lays down the following requirements with respect to personal hygiene:

1. Every person working in a food handling area is to maintain a high degree of personal cleanliness and is to wear suitable, clean and, where necessary, protective clothing.

2. No person suffering from, or being a carrier of a disease likely to be transmitted through food or afflicted, for example, with infected wounds, skin infections, sores or diarrhoea is to be permitted to handle food or enter any food handling area in any capacity if there is any likelihood of direct or indirect contamination. Any person so affected and employed in a food business and who is likely to come into contact with food is to report immediately the illness or symptoms, and if possible their causes, to the food business operator.

Principles of personal hygiene

Basic principles of personal hygiene for food handlers are as follows:

1. Hands must be kept clean and nails kept clipped if they are handling food.

2. They must not smoke, spit, eat or drink whilst handling food or in a food room.

3. Any skin lesion or wound must be securely covered with a waterproof dressing.

4. They must not wear jewellery (a plain wedding ring is generally permitted) or false nails that may expose food to a risk of contamination.

5. They must wear any protective clothing, i.e. coats, tunic, aprons, hats and hair nets, etc. correctly, changing that protective clothing in the event of soiling. The use of safety shoes is recommended for all food handlers.

Visitors to food premises should be required to wear an appropriate protective coat, hat and hair net.

The practice of food handling staff travelling to work in their protective clothing should be discouraged, particularly if they travel by public transport, due to the risk of soiling.

Carriers of disease

Changing facilities

Personal protective clothing

All forms of protective clothing, such as head coverings, snoods, hair nets, gloves, overalls, aprons and footwear designed to prevent the transfer of bacteria from food handlers to food.

Personal Protective Equipment at Work Regulations 1992

These Regulations are made under the Health and Safety at Work etc Act 1974 and cover all aspects of the provision, maintenance and use of personal protective equipment (PPE) other than those outlined in more specific legislation such as the Control of Substances Hazardous to Health (COSHH) Regulations.

Personal protective equipment means all equipment (including clothing affording protection against the weather) which is intended to be worn or held by a person at work and which protects him against one or more risks to his health and safety, and any addition or accessory designed to meet this objective.

Provision of personal protective equipment (PPE)

1. Every employer shall ensure that suitable PPE is provided to his employees who may be exposed to a risk to their health and safety while at work except where and to the extent that such risk has been adequately controlled by other means which are equally or more effective.

2. Similar provisions as above apply in the case of self-employed persons.

3. PPE shall not be suitable unless:

   a) it is appropriate for the risk or risks involved and the conditions at the place where exposure to the risk may occur, and the period for which it is worn;

   b) it takes account of ergonomic requirements and the state of health of the person or persons who may wear it, and the characteristics of the workstation of each such person;

   c) it is capable of fitting the wearer correctly, if necessary after adjustments within the range for which it is designed; and

   d) so far as is practicable, it is effective to prevent or adequately control the risk or risks involved without increasing overall risk.

4. Where it is necessary to ensure that PPE is hygienic and otherwise free of risk to health, every employer and every self-employed person shall ensure that PPE provided under this regulation is provided to a person for use only by him.

Compatibility of personal protective equipment

1. Every employer shall ensure that where the presence of more than one risk to health or safety makes it necessary for his employee to wear or use simultaneously more than one item of PPE, such equipment is compatible and continues to be effective against the risk or risks in question.

2. Similar provisions apply in the case of self-employed persons.

3. PPE shall not be suitable unless:

   a) it is appropriate for the risk or risks involved, the conditions at the place where exposure to the risk may occur, and the period for which it is worn;

   b) it takes account of ergonomic requirements and the state of health of the person or persons who may wear it, and of the characteristics of the workstation of each such person;

c) it is capable of fitting the wearer correctly, if necessary after adjustments within the range for which it is designed;

d) so far as is practicable, it is effective to prevent or adequately control the risk or risks involved without increasing overall risk;

e) it complies with any enactment (whether in Act or instrument) which implements in Great Britain any provision on design or manufacture with respect to health or safety of any of the relevant Community directives listed in Schedule 1 which is applicable to that item of PPE.

4. Where it is necessary to ensure that PPE is hygienic and otherwise free of risk to health, every employer and every self-employed person shall ensure that PPE provided under this regulation is provided to a person for use only by him.

Assessment of personal protective equipment

1. Before choosing any personal protective equipment which he is required to provide, an employer or self-employed person shall make an assessment to determine whether the PPE he intends to provide is suitable.

2. The assessment shall comprise:

a) an assessment of any risk or risks which have not been avoided by other means;

b) the definition of the characteristics which PPE must have in order to be effective against the risks referred to above, taking into account any risks which the equipment itself may create;

c) comparison of the characteristics of the PPE available with the characteristics referred to in (b) above; and

d) an assessment as to whether the PPE is compatible with other PPE which is in use and which an employee would be required to wear simultaneously.

The assessment shall be reviewed forthwith if:

a) there is reason to suspect that any element of the assessment is no longer valid; or

b) there has been a significant change in the work to which the assessment relates;

and where, as a result of the review, changes in the assessment are required, these changes shall be made.

Maintenance and replacement of personal protective equipment

Every employer and every self-employed person shall ensure that any PPE provided by them is maintained in relation to any matter which it is reasonably foreseeable will affect the health and safety of any person in an efficient state, in efficient working order, in good repair and in hygienic condition.

Accommodation for personal protective equipment

Every employer and every self-employed person shall ensure that appropriate accommodation is provided for PPE when it is not being used.

Information, instruction and training

Where an employer is required to provide PPE to an employee, the employer shall provide that employee with such information, instruction and training as is adequate and appropriate to enable the employee to know:

a)   the risk or risks which the PPE will avoid or limit;

b)   the purpose for which and the manner in which the PPE is to be used; and

c)   any action to be taken by the employee to ensure that the PPE remains in an efficient state, in efficient working order, in good repair and in hygienic condition, and shall ensure that such information is kept available to employees.

Without prejudice to the generality of paragraph 1, the employer shall, where appropriate, and at suitable intervals, organise demonstrations in the wearing of PPE.

Use of personal protective equipment

1.   Every employer who provides any PPE shall take all reasonable steps to ensure that it is properly used.

2.   Every employee and self-employed person who has been provided with PPE shall:

a)   make full and proper use of the PPE; and

b)   take all reasonable steps to ensure it is returned to the accommodation provided for it after use.

Reporting loss or defect

Every employee who has been provided with PPE by his employer shall forth-with report to his employer any loss of or obvious defect in that PPE.

Guidance on the Regulations

Detailed HSE guidance is provided on the requirements of the Regulations.

Changing facilities

Information, instruction and training

Personal hygiene

Personal protective clothing

Persons suffering from certain medical conditions

Food business operators must make special provisions for persons suffering from certain medical conditions. In certain cases, such persons must be prohibited from handling food or entering a food room.

Exclusion of food handlers

Food Hygiene (England) Regulations 2006

Personal hygiene

Prohibition from handling food

Regulation (EC) No 852/2004 on the hygiene of foodstuffs

Pest

Any living creature, e.g. rodents, crawling and flying insects, and birds, capable of contaminating food by direct or indirect contact.

Bird control

Cockroach control

Confused flour beetle (Tribolium confusum)

Eradication (infestation)

Flour mite

Flying insect control

Fumigation

Housekeeping procedures

Infestation prevention and control

Insecticides

Integrated Pest Management

Pest control contracts

Pesticide

Proofing of buildings

Residual insecticide

Rodent control

Pest control contracts

Commercial pest control contractors operate in all sectors of the food industry. Reputable contractors should provide a contract incorporating the following elements:

a) the pests covered in the contract, e.g. rats, mice, crawling insects, stored product insects, flying insects, birds, e.g. feral pigeons, starlings and sparrows;

b) pests not covered in the contract but which can be exterminated by separate arrangement, e.g wasps nests, bluebottles;

c) the frequency of service visits;

d) arrangements for supervision of servicemen by the contractor;

e) emergency visiting arrangements following, for example, serious rodent, flying insect or bird infestation;

f) baiting equipment and materials to be used, including closed equipment in food rooms and storage areas;

g) additional materials and equipment to be used in specific circumstances or for specific purposes, e.g. external wasp baits, cockroach detectors, tracking dusts in the case of rodent infestation, baiting of drainage systems;

h) inspection and surface treatments in the case of stored product pests;

i) any additional services, such as fumigation of storage areas, proofing of buildings and training of hygiene staff in elementary pest recognition;

j) the system for reporting infestation and control methods used;

k) telephone number, e-mail address and emergency telephone number; and

l) health and safety-related information with respect to pesticides used, including health risk assessments under the Control of Substances Hazardous to Health Regulations and the Control of Pesticides Regulations.

Cockroach control

Critical Control Points (CCPs)

Drainage of food premises

Flying insect control

Food Hygiene (England) Regulations 2006

Fumigation

Infestation prevention and control

Integrated Pest Management

Regulation (EC) No 852/2004 on the hygiene of foodstuffs

Pest

Pesticides

Proofing of buildings

Structural requirements for food premises

Training of food handlers

Pesticides

Several groups of chemical compounds designed to kill a wide range of pests, including crawling and flying insects, birds, rodents, weeds in growing crops, mites, moulds and fungi.

Pesticides may be present in foods as a result of contamination of natural water supplies and soil following their application to growing crops.

Alphachloralose

Ant control

Bird control

Cockroach control

Flour mites

Flying insect control

Infestation prevention and control

Fungi

Integrated Pest Management

Residual insecticide

Phage typing

A method used in the identification of bacteria by using specific viruses that attack certain strains of bacteria.

Bacteriological control systems

Bacteriophage (phage) typing

Phosphorescence

A deleterious post-mortem change in the surface of meat which, when viewed in a dark room, appears luminous. This change is caused by the growth of specific bacteria on the surface of the meat.

Meat

Meat products (food hazards)

pH value

The logarithm to the base 10 of the hydrogen ion concentration of a substance and, fundamentally, the degree of acidity or alkalinity of a substance. pH values below 7 are acidic, above 7 alkaline, with a pH of 7 representing neutrality.

Most foods support bacterial multiplication and the relative acidity or alkalinity of a food is an intrinsic factor in the growth of bacteria. Most bacteria grow best at or near a neutral pH and, to this extent, high or low pH can have a serious effect on such growth. Bacterial spores, on the other hand, can survive at any level, but germination will only take place at a pH of 4.5 and above.

The way a food is manufactured, processed and stored can have the effect of lowering the pH, thereby inhibiting bacterial growth except in the case of certain moulds which thrive at low pH values.

Acidity

Alkalinity

Bacterial growth curve

Food preparation

Stock control and rotation

Physical contamination

Most forms of foreign body found in food, such as metal staples, nuts, bolts, screws, string, pieces of packing material and plastic items. In many cases, this represents inadequate control of certain operations, such as unpacking of containers, routine maintenance of plant and equipment, housekeeping procedures and waste storage.

In certain cases, there may be evidence of malicious tampering with food.

Extrinsic contamination

Food hazard

Foreign bodies

Malicious tampering with food

Nature, substance or quality

Pickling

A well-established method of food preservation which can take a number of forms:

a)   immersion of certain vegetables, such as onions and cabbage, in a weak solution of acetic acid, i.e. vinegar; or

b)   immersion of pork sides in brine tanks for a specified period, or the injection of brine into the flesh.

Brining

Curing of food

Preservation of food

Plate freezing

A method of freezing relatively uniform and flat packages of food, such as beef burgers, between pressure plates containing a circulating refrigerant for a specified period of time.

Frozen food

Port health authority

Means:

a) in relation to the London port health district (within the meaning given to that phrase for the purposes of the Public Health (Control of Disease) Act 1984 by section 7(1) of that Act), the Common Council of the City of London; and

b) in relation to any port health district constituted by order under section 2(3) of the Public Health (Control of Disease) Act 1984, a port health authority for that district constituted by order under section 2(4) of that Act.

Food Hygiene (England) Regulations 2006

Post-incident strategies

Despite the measures taken to prevent food safety incidents, it is essential for organisations to have a post-incident procedure aimed at reducing the impact of the incident and improving the situation quickly and efficiently.

1. Emergency Procedure

The need for a plan to cover the aftermath of a food safety incident must be considered, in particular reporting and recording procedures, liaison with the enforcement agencies and the Public Health Laboratory Service, submission of samples, bacteriological examination of surfaces, plant and equipment, and health screening of staff.

2. Improvement Strategies

These strategies are concerned with learning from the mistakes made with a view to preventing a recurrence. They may include staff training, supplier monitoring, product recall systems and the use of propaganda aimed at raising the awareness of staff.

3. Feedback Strategies

Feedback is essential in improving performance and preventing the recurrence of incidents. It includes the interpretation and use of statistical information and the identification of deficiencies in areas such as training, supervision, health surveillance and bacteriological control

Hazard Analysis: Critical Control Point (HACCP)

Bacteriological control systems

Disposal and destruction of food

Food safety management systems

Food safety risk assessment

Health surveillance

Hygiene Emergency Prohibition Notice

Hygiene Emergency Prohibition Order

Liaison with authorised officers

Product recall systems

Prohibition action

Prohibition Orders

Prosecution

Traceability requirements

Voluntary closure

Voluntary surrender

Potable water

Water meeting the minimum requirements laid down in Council Directive 98/83/EC of 3 November 1998 on the quality of water intended for human consumption.

[Regulation (EC) No 852/2004 on the hygiene of foodstuffs]

Regulation (EC) No 852/2004 on the hygiene of foodstuffs

Water-borne infections

Water supply

Poultry (food hazards)

Poultry or lagomorphs

Where a producer supplies small quantities of meat from poultry or lagomorphs (rabbits, hares) that have been slaughtered on the farm to the final consumer or to a local retail establishment directly supplying such meat to the final consumer, the producer shall:

a)   keep a record in adequate form to show the number of birds and the number of lagomorphs received into, and the amount of fresh meat despatched from, his premises during each week;

b)   retain the record for a period of one year; and

c)   make the record available to an authorised officer on request.

A producer who fails to comply with any of these requirements shall be guilty of an offence.

[Food Hygiene (England) Regulations 2006]

Authorised officer

Food Hygiene (England) Regulations 2006

Meat

Offences and penalties

Powers of entry

Authorised officers of the food authority have powers of entry to premises under both the Food Safety Act and the Food Hygiene (England) Regulations thus:

An authorised officer of an enforcement authority shall, on producing, if so required, some duly authenticated document showing his authority, have a right at all reasonable hours:

a)   to enter any premises within the authority's area for the purpose of ascertaining whether there is or has been on the premises any contravention of the provisions of this Act, or of regulations or orders made under it; and

b)   to enter any business premises, whether within or outside his authority's area, for the purpose of ascertaining whether there is on the premises any evidence of any contravention within that area of any of such provisions; and

c)   in the case of an authorised officer of a food authority, to enter any premises for the purpose of the performance by the authority of their functions under this Act;

but admission to any premises used only as a private dwelling house shall not be demanded as of right unless 24 hours' notice of intended entry has been given to the occupier.

[Food Safety Act 1990]

An authorised officer of a food authority shall, on producing, if so required, some duly authenticated document showing his authority, have a right at all reasonable hours:

a)   to enter any premises within the authority's area for the purpose of ascertaining whether there is or has been on the premises any contravention of the provisions of the Hygiene Regulations;

b)   to enter any premises, whether within or outside the authority's area, for the purpose of ascertaining whether there is on the premises any evidence of any such contravention within that area; and

c)   to enter any premises for the purpose of the performance by the authority of their functions under the Hygiene Regulations,

but admission to any premises used only as a private dwelling house shall not be demanded as of right unless 24 hours' notice of the intended entry has been given to the occupier.

An authorised officer of the Food Standards Agency has identical powers of entry.

[Food Hygiene (England) Regulations 2006]

Authorised officer

Food authority

Food Hygiene (England) Regulations 2006

Food hygiene inspections

Food Safety Act 1990

Food Standards Agency

Food Standards Inspection

Pre-employment health screening

An area of health surveillance common in the food industry whereby all new employees are screened through the use of a pre-employment health question-naire and health interview by an occupational health practitioner, such as an occupational health nurse.

'Clean person' strategies

Exclusion of food handlers

Health supervision

Health surveillance

Health screening documentation

Persons suffering from certain medical conditions

Appendix C – Health Screening documentation

Pre-incident strategies

An incident can be an isolated case of food poisoning or an outbreak, affecting many people, which can have serious repercussions for an organisation.

It is essential, therefore, that pre-incident strategies be devised with a view to preventing such incidents arising. These can be classified as 'Clean place' and 'Clean person' strategies.

'Clean place' strategies

'Clean person' strategies

Food poisoning incidents

Food safety management systems

Premises (definition)

Includes any place, any vehicle, stall or moveable structure.

[Food Safety Act 1990]

Includes any establishment, any place, vehicle, stall or moveable structure and any ship or aircraft.

[Food Hygiene (England) Regulations 2006]

Moveable and temporary structures

Structural requirements for food premises

Preservation of food

The process of applying a method of treatment to a food to preserve its quality and prevent decomposition. Preservation may be by the application of a particular chemical substance (preservative), dehydration, heat treatment, chilling or freezing.

Accelerated freeze drying

Additives

Air drying

Blast chilling and freezing

Canned goods

Canning processes

Chilled storage

Cold store

Cook-chill

Cook-freeze

Cryogenic freezing

Fluidised bed freezing

Freezers

Frozen food

Heat treatment

Irradiation

Pasteurisation

Preservatives

Processing

Refrigerators

Ultra Heat Treatment (UHT)

Preservatives

A chemical substance added to a food to delay the natural process of decomposition and to extend the length of time during which the food remains fit for human consumption. In the case of dried fruit, for example, it is often treated with sulphur dioxide (E220) in order to prevent mould or bacterial growth. Bacon, ham, corned beef and other cured meats are often treated with nitrite and nitrate (E249 to E252) during the curing process.

More traditional preservatives, such as vinegar, salt and sugar are commonly used to preserve food.

Most food with a long shelf life is likely to contain preservatives, unless another method of preservation has been used.

Additives

E-numbers

Preservation of food

Presumption that food is intended for human consumption

Any food commonly used for human consumption shall, if placed on the market or offered, exposed or kept for placing on the market, be presumed until the contrary is proved, to have been placed on the market or, as the case may be, to have been or to be intended for placing on the market for human consumption.

The following, namely:

a) any food commonly used for human consumption which is found on the premises used for the preparation, storage or placing on the market of that food; and

b) any article or substance commonly used in the manufacture of food for human consumption which is found on premises used for the preparation, storage or placing on the market of that food, shall be presumed, until the contrary is proved, to be intended for placing on the market, or for manufacturing food for placing on the market, for human consumption.

Any article or substance capable of being used in the composition or preparation of any food commonly used for human consumption which is found on premises on which that food is prepared shall, until the contrary is proved, be presumed to be intended for such use.

[Food Safety Act 1990]

[Food Hygiene (England) Regulations 2006]

'Act or default of another person'

Adulteration of food

All reasonable precautions and all due diligence

Enforcement procedure

Preventive maintenance

The courts regularly deal with complaints of foreign bodies in food. Many of these foreign bodies – nuts, bolts, screws, traces of grease, wood splinters, staples, etc are due to nothing else but poor plant maintenance and the absence of a formal planned preventive maintenance programme or schedule.

A planned preventive maintenance programme, which identifies:

 a) each item of equipment by number and identified in a Plant Register;

 b) the maintenance procedure for each item of equipment;

 c) frequency of maintenance;

 d) precautions necessary; and

 e) individual responsibility for ensuring that maintenance operation takes place,

should be established and operated.

Under the Provision and Use of Work Equipment Regulations 1998, there is an absolute duty to maintain work equipment in an efficient state, in efficient working order and in good repair.

Primary products

Products of primary production including products of the soil, of stock farming, of hunting and fishing.

[Regulation (EC) No 852/2004 on the hygiene of foodstuffs]

Prions

'Prion' means 'proteinaceous infectious particle', an unusual or 'rogue' form of animal protein found, for example, in the brain. The term came to light in the study of certain diseases of animals and man, such as bovine spongiform encephalopathy (BSE) in cattle, scrapie in sheep and variant Creutzfeldt-Jakob disease (vCJD) in man, where prions are one of the principal suspects in terms of causation.

Zoonoses

Processed products

These are foodstuffs resulting from the processing of unprocessed products. They may contain ingredients that are necessary for their manufacture or to give them specific characteristics.

[Regulation (EC) No 852/2004 on the hygiene of foodstuffs]

Additives

Food preparation

Raw materials

Regulation (EC) No 852/2004 on the hygiene of foodstuffs

Processing

Any action that substantially alters the initial product, including heating, smoking, curing, maturing, drying, marinating, extraction, extrusion or a combination of those processes.

[Regulation (EC) No 852/2004 on the hygiene of foodstuffs]

Curing of food

Equipment requirements

Dehydration

Food preparation

Food safety requirements

Heat treatment

Regulation (EC) No 852/2004 on the hygiene of foodstuffs

Temperature control requirements

Production holding

Premises at which milk-producing cows are kept.

[Food Hygiene (England) Regulations 2006]

Milk and dairy products (food hazards)
Raw milk (restrictions on sale)

Product recall systems

A serious situation can arise which could result in a need to recall certain products from the market place. How to recover the product from the market place quickly, quietly and efficiently, without attracting the attention of the media, is a subject which has been pursued by the food industry at great lengths over the last decade, largely as a result of various food sabotage incidents and national food safety scares.

There should be a formal product recall procedure, with an identified senior manager responsible for implementing the various levels of recall, both nationally and locally.

Food safety management systems
Foreign bodies
Hazard Analysis: Critical Control Point (HACCP)
Post-incident strategies

Product specification

This is the detailed description of the composition, content and intended use of a food product.

Consumer protection provisions (Food Safety Act)

Labelling requirements

Nature, substance and quality

Prohibition action

The service of a Prohibition Notice, Emergency Prohibition Notice or the making of an Emergency Prohibition Order in accordance with the requirements of the Food Safety Act and Food Hygiene (England) Regulations.

Appeals against Notices, etc

Appeals to Crown Court

Emergency Prohibition Notices

Emergency Prohibition Orders

Enforcement procedure

Hygiene Emergency Prohibition Notice

Hygiene Emergency Prohibition Order

Prohibition of a person

Prohibition Orders

Prohibition procedures

Statutory Codes under the Food Safety Act

Voluntary closure

Prohibition from handling food

No person suffering from, or being a carrier of a disease likely to be transmitted through food or afflicted, for example, with infected wounds, skin infections, sores or diarrhoea is to be permitted to handle food or enter any food-handling area in any capacity if there is any likelihood of direct or indirect contamination.

[Regulation (EC) No 852/2004 of the European Parliament and of the Council on the Hygiene of Foodstuffs]

Food poisoning (food-borne illnesses)

Persons suffering from certain medical conditions

Prohibition action

Prohibition of a person

Regulation (EC) No 852/2004 on the hygiene of foodstuffs

Reporting of diseases (food handlers)

Prohibition of a person

The service of a Prohibition Notice, Emergency Prohibition Notice or the making of an Emergency Prohibition Order prohibiting a named person from coming into contact with food and/or working in a food business.

Food Hygiene (England) Regulations 2006

Food Safety Act 1990

Prohibition action

Prohibition from handling food

Prohibition Orders

Prohibition procedures

Prohibition Orders

Section 11 (Prohibition Orders) apply to any regulations under this part of the Act which make provision:

    a)   for requiring, prohibiting or regulating the use of any process or treatment in the preparation of food; and

    b)   for securing the observance of hygienic conditions and practices in connection with the carrying out of commercial operations with respect to food or food sources.

Section 11 deals with the circumstances surrounding, and procedures to be followed in respect of, the making of Prohibition Orders by a magistrates court. Section 12, on the other hand, covers the powers of an authorised officer to serve an Emergency Prohibition Notice where there is imminent risk of injury to health in respect of premises, equipment or process, and for a court to make an Emergency Prohibition Order. Procedures covering these aspects of enforcement are dealt with in Statutory Code of Practice No.6: *Prohibition Procedures.*

Where an authorised officer is of the opinion that there is risk or injury to health (the health risk condition) associated with a premises, process or equipment, or through the state or condition of a food premises, he may instigate proceedings against the proprietor of the food business under the Food Hygiene (England) Regulations 2006.

Power to impose the prohibition

Where the proprietor is convicted of an offence under any regulations to which this section applies, (Section 11(1)(a)) and the court by or before which he is so convicted is satisfied that the health risk condition is fulfilled with respect to that business, (Section 11(1)(b)), the court shall by an order impose the appropriate prohibition.

The health risk condition

The health risk condition is fulfilled with respect to any food business if any of the following involves risk of injury to health, namely –

a)   the use for the purposes of the business of any process or treatment;

b)   the construction of any premises used for the purposes of the business, or the use for those purposes of any equipment; and

c)   the state or condition of any premises or equipment used for the purpose of the business. (Section 11(2))

The appropriate prohibition

These extensive powers allow a court, where convinced that the health risk condition is fulfilled, to apply the appropriate prohibition. The appropriate prohibition is:

a)   in a case falling within paragraph (a) of subsection (2) above, a prohibition on the use of the process or treatment for the purpose of the business;

b)   in a case falling within paragraph (b) of that subsection, a prohibition on the use of the premises or equipment for the purposes of the business or any other food business of the same class or description;

c)   in a case falling within paragraph (c) of that subsection, a prohibition on the use of the premises or equipment for the purposes of any food business. (Section 11(3))

The imposition of the Prohibition Order

Section 11(4) deals with the imposition by the court of the Prohibition Order. If the proprietor of a food business is convicted of an offence under any regulations to which this section applies by virtue of section 10(3)(b) and the court by or before which he is so convicted thinks it proper to do so in all the circumstances of the case, the court may, by an order, impose a prohibition on the proprietor participating in the management of any food business, or any food business of a class or description specified in the order.

Service and affixing a copy of the Prohibition Order

As soon as practicable after the making of a Prohibition Order under subsection (1) or (4) above, the enforcement authority must:

a) serve a copy of the order on the proprietor of the business; and

b) in the case of an order under subsection (1), affix a copy of the order in a conspicuous position on such premises used for the purposes of the business as they consider appropriate;

and any person who knowingly contravenes such an order shall be guilty of an offence. (Section 11(5))

Duration of the Prohibition Order

A Prohibition Order shall cease to have effect:

a) in the case of an order under subsection (1) above, on the issue by the enforcement authority of a certificate to the effect that they are satisfied that the proprietor has taken sufficient measures to secure that the health risk condition is no longer fulfilled with respect to the business;

b) in the case of an order under subsection (4) above, on the giving by the court of a direction to that effect. (Section 11(6))

The enforcement authority shall issue a certificate under paragraph (a) of subsection (6) above within three days of their being satisfied as mentioned in that paragraph; and on application by the proprietor for such a certificate, the authority shall:

a) determine, as soon as is reasonably practicable and in any event within 14 days, whether or not they are so satisfied; and

b) if they determine they are not so satisfied, give notice to the proprietor of the reasons for that determination. (Section 11(7))

Appeals

Section 37(1)(b) allows an appeal to the magistrates court by way of complaint against the refusal to issue a certificate under section 11(6). The period within which such an appeal may be brought is one month from the date on which notice of the decision was served on the person desiring to appeal.

A person who is aggrieved by any dismissal by a magistrates court of such an appeal may appeal to the Crown Court. (Section 38(b)) An appeal by an aggrieved person lies to the Crown Court against the decision of magistrates to make a Prohibition Order. The local authority has no right to appeal to the Crown Court where magistrates refuse to make an order.

Direction by a court

The court shall give a direction under subsection (6)(b) above if, on application by a proprietor, the courts thinks it proper to do so having regard to all the circumstances of the case, including in particular the conduct of the proprietor since the making of the order, but no such application shall be entertained if it is made:

a) within six months after the making of the prohibition order; or

b) within three months after the making by the proprietor of a previous application for such a direction. (Section 11(8))

Effect of an Emergency Prohibition Order

Where a magistrates court or, in Scotland, the sheriff makes an order under section 12(2) (Emergency Prohibition Order) with respect to any food business, subsection (1) above shall apply as if the proprietor of the business had been convicted by the court or sheriff of an offence under regulations to which this subsection applies. (Section 11(9))

Application to the manager of a food business

Subsection (4) above shall apply in relation to a manager of a food business as it applies to the proprietor of such a business; and any reference in subsection (5) or (8) above to the proprietor of the business, or to the proprietor, shall be construed accordingly. (Section 11(10))

In subsection (10) above *manager*, in relation to a food business, means any person who is entrusted by the proprietor with the day to day running of the business, or any part of the business. (Section 11(11))

Prosecution of the proprietor

The first step in the procedure under section 11 is for the food authority to successfully prosecute the proprietor of a food business for a breach of hygiene or processing regulations (or orders that may amend or replace them). In some cases the proprietor may have been issued with an Improvement Notice which he has failed to comply with. If the court then considers that the premises, equipment or process put public health at risk it must impose the Prohibition Order. The court also has discretion to ban the proprietor or manager of the business from managing any food business. (Section 11(4) and (8)) The food authority has the power to lift the Prohibition Order on premises, equipment or a process. However, the court must lift the prohibition on the proprietor or manager.

Knowingly contravening a Prohibition Order is an offence triable either way.

Appeals to Crown Court

Authorised officer

Business (definition)

Commercial operation

Emergency Prohibition Orders

Enforcement authority

Equipment requirements

Food business operator

Food hazard

Food Hygiene (England) Regulations 2006

Food Safety Act 1990

Health risk condition

Magistrates Court

Prohibition of a person

Prohibition procedures

Prosecution

Statutory Codes under the Food Safety Act

Structural requirements for food premises

Prohibition procedures

Prohibition procedures hinge around the term *risk and imminent risk of injury to health*.

Section 11 of the Food Safety Act applies if there is a *risk* of injury to health. Section 12, on the other hand, applies if such a risk is *imminent*.

According to Statutory Code of Practice No. 6 *Prohibition procedures*, in applying for an Emergency Prohibition Order, and prior to serving an Emergency Prohibition Notice, the authorised officer must be very certain that the risk is truly 'imminent', e.g. that an outbreak of food poisoning, for instance, could result if action is not taken immediately. Authorised officers must, at all times, bear in mind the risk of a claim for compensation arising before exercising these very extreme powers. On this basis the code provides guidance with regard to possible prohibition action.

Consideration of prohibition action

Guidance in the Code lists a series of situations involving conditions where prohibition of premises, equipment and processes may be appropriate.

1. Conditions when prohibition of PREMISES may be appropriate

Serious infestations by rats, mice, cockroaches or other vermin (including birds) or a combination of these infestations resulting in actual food contamination or a real risk of food contamination. [Example of breach of health risk condition 11(2)(c)]

Very poor structural condition and poor equipment and/or poor maintenance of routine cleaning and/or serious accumulation of refuse, filth or other extraneous matter resulting in a real risk of food contamination. [Example of breach of health risk condition 11(2)(b) and (c)]

Serious drainage defects or flooding of the premises leading to actual contamination or a real risk of food contamination. [Example of breach of health risk condition 11(2)(c)]

Premises or practices which seriously contravene the Food Safety (General Food Hygiene) Regulations 1995 and have been the cause of, or are involved with, an outbreak of food poisoning. [Example of breach of health risk condition 11(2)(c)]

Any combination of the above situations or the cumulative effect of contraventions which together represent an imminent risk of injury to health.

2. Conditions where prohibition of EQUIPMENT may be appropriate

In addition to the above, the following circumstances may be in existence.

Use of defective equipment, for example, a pasteuriser incapable of achieving the required pasteurisation temperature. [Example of breach of health risk condition 11(2)(c)]

Use of equipment involving high risk foods which have been inadequately cleaned or disinfected or which is obviously grossly contaminated and can no longer be properly cleaned. [Example of breach of health risk condition 11(2)(c)]

3. Conditions where prohibition of a PROCESS may be appropriate

In addition to conditions involving prohibition of a premises, the following circumstances may be in existence.

Serious risk of cross contamination. [Example of breach of health risk condition 11(2)(b) or (c)]

Inadequate temperature control, for example, failure to achieve sufficiently high cooking temperatures. [Example of breach of health risk condition 11(2)(a)]

Operation outside critical control criteria, for example, incorrect pH of a product which might allow *Clostridium botulinum* to multiply. [Example of breach of health risk condition 11(2)(a)]

The use of a process for a product which is inappropriate. [Example of breach of health risk condition 11(2)(a)]

Food authorities are encouraged to consider the use of outside experts where the process or treatment under consideration involves specialist knowledge or qualification.

Authorised officer

Clostridium botulinum (Clostridium welchii)

Contamination

Cooking of food

Critical Control Points (CCPs)

Cross contamination

Drainage of food premises

Emergency Prohibition Notices

Emergency Prohibition Orders

Equipment requirements

Food authority

Food contamination

Food Hygiene (England) Regulations 2006

Food poisoning (food-borne illnesses)

Hazard Analysis: Critical Control Point (HACCP)

Health risk condition

Heat treatment

High risk foods

'Imminent risk of injury to health'

Infestation

pH value

Processing

Prohibition action

Statutory Codes under the Food Safety Act

Structural requirements for food premises

Temperature control requirements

Proofing of buildings

Structural proofing is the first line of defence in preventing infestation. All buildings used for the storage, preparation and despatch of raw materials and finished food products should be efficiently proofed against infestation by rodents, crawling and flying insects and birds.

Structural proofing should incorporate the following features:

a) ensuring the closure of all external doors when not in use by the installation of self-closing door gear and ensuring their sound fit to frames and floor; external doors should be fitted with kicking plates of 20 gauge hard metal 6' to 12' high with a maximum 0.25' floor clearance;

b) sealing with cement mortar (1:4 mix) or expanded metal (0.25' mesh: 24 gauge) all openings in external walls, including those created by the placing together of corrugated metal or asbestos cement sheets, together with adequate sealing around ducts, pipes and cables passing through external walls; and

c) the covering of all ventilation openings with 10 mesh 24 S.W.G. wire or 19 x 24 meshes per inch monofilament nylon mesh.

Specific Points

Drainage Systems

Keep in a good state of repair; regular inspection and testing; disused branches filled in; regular checks of inspection chambers, soil pipe/drain connections and fresh air inlets to drainage systems.

Structural Features

Keep in a good state of repair – wood, brickwork, mortar joints, cladding panels; replace defective items immediately; fill in design gaps, e.g. gaps at the base of corrugated asbestos wall cladding and roof edges with profiled filling material.

Cable, Ducting and Pipe Entry Points

Examine the finishing of contractors' work; seal any gaps created with mortar or expanded metal mesh.

Ventilators

Screen air bricks and mechanical ventilation openings with 0.25' mesh.

Windows

Screen in open food areas with wire or nylon mesh; mount nylon mesh on to screw-on metal frames with Velcro strip – the whole unit can then be removed in the winter, washed and stored.

Roof

Seal with mortar, expanded metal mesh or profiled filler junctions formed at eaves and roof apex. Wire balloons should be fitted to the tops of rain water pipes.

Doors

Doors should be kept closed. Where doors must be kept open, an inner fly screen door should be installed where practicable or an air curtain provided.

Hollow Floors

The junction between the wall and the underside of the floor boards should be protected by 0.5' metal mesh, taken up 6' behind the skirting board.

Bird control

Cockroach control

Doors

Drainage of food premises

Flying insect control

Infestation

Infestation prevention and control

Provisions applicable to foodstuffs

Rodent control

Structural requirements for food premises

Windows

Prosecution

Statutory Code of Practice No2 *Legal Matters* provides guidance to food authorities on prosecution issues.

In deciding whether to prosecute, food authorities are advised to consider a
number of factors, which may include the following:

a)   the seriousness of the alleged offence;

b)   the previous history of the party concerned;

c)   the likelihood of the defendant being able to establish a due diligence
     defence;

d)   the ability of any important witnesses and their willingness to co-operate;

e)   the willingness of the party to prevent a recurrence of the problem;

f)   the probable public benefit of a prosecution and the importance of the
     case, e.g. whether it might establish legal precedent in other companies
     or in other geographical areas;

g)   whether other action, such as issuing a formal caution in accordance
     with Home Office Circular 59/1990 or an Improvement Notice or imposing
     a prohibition, would be more appropriate or effective. (It is possible in
     exceptional circumstances to prosecute as well as issuing a notice; failure
     to comply with a notice would be an additional offence.)

h)   any explanation offered by the affected company.

Protection of officers acting in good faith

An officer of a food authority is not personally liable in respect of any act done by him:

a)   in the execution or purported execution of this Act; and

b)   within the scope of his employment,

if he did that act in the honest belief that his duty under this Act required or entitled him to do it.

Nothing in the above paragraph shall be construed as relieving any food authority from any liability in respect of the acts of their officers.

Where an action has been brought against an officer of a food authority in respect of an act done by him:

a)   in the execution or purported execution of this Act; but

b)   outside the scope of his employment,

the authority may indemnify him against the whole or part of any damages which he has been ordered to pay or any costs which he may have incurred if they are satisfied that he honestly believed that the act complained of was within the scope of his employment.

A public analyst appointed by a food authority shall be treated for the purposes of this section as being an officer of the authority, whether or not his appointment is a full-time appointment.

[Food Safety Act 1990]

Identical provisions apply under the Food Hygiene (England) Regulations 2006.

Authorised officer

Enforcement authorities

Enforcement procedure

Environmental Health Officers

Food authority

Food Hygiene (England) Regulations 2006

Powers of entry

Prosecution

Protozoa

These are single celled organisms, some of which are pathogenic, such as *Entamoeba hystolytica*.

Several forms of protozoa can form cysts which can survive without food. Protozoa also have a range of mechanisms, or highly developed organs, to assist in movement, such as flagella, undulating membranes and lashes.

Cryptosporidia

Giardia lamblia

Parasites

Pathogenic agents (pathogens)

Provision and Use of Work Equipment Regulations 1998

These Regulations apply to all work equipment, defined as 'any machinery, appliance, apparatus, tool or installation for use at work, (whether exclusively or not)'. *Use* in relation to work equipment means ' any activity involving work equipment and includes starting, stopping, programming, setting, transporting, repairing, modifying, maintaining, servicing and cleaning'.

Important general provisions include:

Suitability of work equipment

Work equipment must be so constructed or adapted as to be suitable for the purpose for which it is used or provided.

Maintenance

Work equipment must be maintained in an efficient state, in efficient working order and in good repair.

Inspection

Where the safety of work equipment depends upon the installation conditions, employers must ensure that it is inspected:

a) after installation and before being put into service for the first time; and

b) after assembly at a new site or in a new location.

Part II of the Regulations further deals with specific risks, information and instruction, training, conformity with Community requirements, dangerous parts of machinery, protection against specified hazards, high or very low temperature, controls for starting or making a significant change in operating conditions, stop controls, emergency stop controls, controls, control systems, isolation from sources of energy, stability, lighting, maintenance operations, markings and warnings. Part III covers mobile work equipment, such as lift trucks, and Part IV, power presses.

The Regulations are accompanied by an Approved Code of Practice issued by the Health and Safety Commission and HSE Guidance.

Equipment requirements

Foreign bodies

Preventive maintenance

Provisions applicable to foodstuffs

Chapter IX of Regulation (EC) No 852/2004 on the hygiene of foodstuffs lays down the following provisions applicable to foodstuffs:

1. A food business operator is not to accept raw materials or ingredients, other than live animals, or any other material used in processing products, if they are known to be, or might reasonably be expected to be, contaminated with parasites, pathogenic micro-organisms or toxic, decomposed or foreign substances to such an extent that, even after the food business operator has hygienically applied normal sorting and/or preparatory processing procedures, the final product would be unfit for human consumption.

2. Raw materials and all ingredients stored in a food business are to be kept in appropriate conditions designed to prevent harmful deterioration and protect them from contamination.

3. At all stages of production, processing and distribution, food is to be protected against any contamination likely to render the food unfit for human consumption, injurious to health or contaminated in such a way that it would be unreasonable to expect it to be consumed in that state.

4. Adequate procedures are to be in place to control pests. Adequate procedures are also to be in place to prevent domestic animals from having access to places where food is prepared, handled or stored (or, where the competent authority so permits in special cases, to prevent such access from resulting in contamination).

5. Raw materials, ingredients, intermediate products and finished products likely to support the reproduction of pathogenic micro-organisms or the formation of toxins are not to be kept at temperatures that might result in a risk to health. The cold chain is not to be interrupted. However, limited periods outside temperature control are permitted, to accommodate the practicalities of handling during preparation, transport, storage, display and service of food, provided that it does not result in a risk to health. Food businesses manufacturing, handling and wrapping processed foodstuffs are to have suitable rooms, large enough for the separate storage of raw materials from processed material and sufficient separate refrigerated storage.

6. Where foodstuffs are to be held or served at chilled temperatures, they are to be cooled as quickly as possible following the heat-processing stage, or final preparation stage if no heat process is applied, to a temperature which does not result in a risk to health.

7. The thawing of foodstuffs is to be undertaken in such a way as to minimise the risk of growth of pathogenic micro-organisms or the formation of toxins in the foods. During thawing, foods are to be subjected to temperatures that would not result in a risk to health. Where run-off liquid from the thawing process may present a risk to health it is to be adequately drained. Following thawing, food is to be handled in such a manner as to minimise the risk of growth of pathogenic micro-organisms or the formation of toxins.

8. Hazardous and/or inedible substances, including animal feed, are to be adequately labelled and stored in separate and secure containers.

[Regulation No EC 852/2004 on the hygiene of foodstuffs]

Business (definition)

Chill control

Cold chain

Contamination

Cooling of food

Cross contamination

Food business operator

Food contamination

Food handling (practice)

Foreign bodies

Infestation prevention and control

Micro-organisms (Microbes)

Packaging

Parasites

Pathogenic agents (pathogens)

Processing

Raw materials

Thawing of frozen food

Toxin

Unfitness for human consumption

Upward variation of the 8°C temperature by manufacturers, etc

Wrapping and packaging of foodstuffs

Psychrophile

An organism which flourishes at temperatures between – 5°C and 20°C.

Psychrotroph

Psychrotroph

An organism which flourishes at temperatures between 0°C and 35°C.

Psychrophile

Publication in the course of a business

In proceedings for an offence under any of the preceding provisions of this Part consisting of the advertisement for sale of any food, it shall be a defence for that person to prove:

a) that he is a person whose business it is to publish or arrange for the publication of advertisements; and

b) that he received the advertisement in the ordinary course of business and did not know and had no reason to suspect that its publication would amount to an offence under that provision.

[Food Safety Act 1990]

This defence corresponds with that provided in section 25 of the Trade Descriptions Act 1968. Fundamentally this defence is aimed at protecting an individual who has published material, such as a label, or an advertisement, on a bona fide basis, which is illegal.

This defence should be read in conjunction with section 15 of the Act (falsely describing or presenting food) with regard to labels which may falsely describe the food or mislead as to the nature or the substance or quality of a particular food.

Advertising food for sale

False or misleading descriptions and information

Labelling requirements

Nature, substance or quality

Quality Assurance

Quality Assurance covers all those features of a process or operation which ensure the continuance of a defined quality standard in a product.

Assured Safe Catering (ASC)

Food safety management systems

Hazard Analysis: Critical Control Point (HACCP)

Quarternary ammonium compounds

These are a form of bactericide which are relatively safe, non-corrosive, stable and taint-free and incorporate detergent characteristics. Such compounds have a narrow range of use and are generally less effective than hypochlorites against Gram-negative bacteria.

Bactericide

Detergents

Hypochlorites

Quick freezing

A freezing process which causes ice to form as small crystals within the cells of a food product.

Blast chilling and freezing

Chilled storage

Frozen food

Plate freezing

R

Rancidity

Rancidity is a cause of unfitness in fatty foods, such as dairy products and oils. It is associated with the formation of substances causing odours and off-flavours in the products concerned, such as butter.

Freshness and fitness of food

Milk and dairy products (food hazards)

Raw foods

Foods which have not undergone a process of cooking, heat treatment or freezing.

Blast chilling

Canned goods

Chilled storage

Contamination

Controlled atmosphere packing

Cross contamination

Food contamination

Food safety management systems

High risk foods

Quick freezing

Temperature control requirements

Raw materials

Raw milk

Milk which has not been heat treated by pasteurisation, sterilisation or other means to destroy pathogenic micro-organisms.

Pasteurisation

Raw milk (restrictions on sale)

Sterilisation

Ultra Heat Treatment (UHT)

Raw milk (restrictions on sale)

Raw milk is milk which has not been subjected to a process of heat treatment, namely pasteurisation, UHT or sterilisation, or other means in order to destroy pathogenic organisms. In the past, the consumption of raw milk has been responsible for diseases including tuberculosis and brucellosis, together with food poisoning associated with *Staphylococcus, Campylobacter and Salmonella* species.

Any person who sells raw milk intended for direct human consumption in contravention of paragraph 5 shall be guilty of an offence.

1. If any person other than the occupier of a production holding or a distributor sells raw cows' milk intended for direct human consumption he shall be guilty of an offence.

2. If the occupier of a production holding sells raw cows' milk intended for direct human consumption in contravention of paragraph 3 he shall be guilty of an offence.

3. If a distributor sells raw cows' milk intended for direct human consumption in contravention of paragraph 4 he shall be guilty of an offence.

The occupier of a production holding may only sell raw cows' milk intended for direct human consumption:

a) at or from the farm premises where the animals from which the milk has been obtained are maintained; and

b) to:

   i)   the final consumer for consumption other than those at farm premises;

   ii) a temporary guest or visitor to those farm premises as or as part of a meal or refreshment; or

   iii) a distributor.

A distributor may only sell raw cows' milk intended for direct human consumption:

a) which he has bought pursuant to sub-paragraph (b)(iii) of paragraph 3;

b) in the containers in which he receives the milk, with the fastenings of the containers unbroken;

c) from a vehicle which is lawfully used as a shop premises; and

d) direct to the final consumer.

The raw milk shall meet the following standards:

Plate count at 30°C (cfu per ml)	< 20,000
Coliforms (cfu per ml)	< 100

In the case where farm premises are being used for the sale of raw cows' milk intended for direct human consumption pursuant to sub-paragraph (a) of paragraph 3, the Agency shall carry out such sampling, analysis and examination of the milk as it considers necessary to ensure that it meets the standards specified in paragraph 5.

In any case where the Agency carries out sampling, analysis and examination of raw cows' milk in accordance with paragraph 6, there shall be due to the Agency from the occupier of the production holding who is selling the milk a fee of £63, which is payable by the occupier to the Agency on demand.

[Food Hygiene (England) Regulations 2006]

Bacteriological control systems

Campylobacter

Coliforms

Distributor

Farm premises

Food Hygiene (England) Regulations 2006

Occupier

Pasteurisation

Production holding

Salmonellae

Shop premises

Staphylococcus aureus

Sterilisation

Ready-to-eat foods

A term generally taken to mean food produced for immediate consumption without further treatment or processing except, in some cases, heating.

Chill holding requirements

Chilled storage

Cold holding/service

Freshness and fitness of food

Temperature control requirements

Record keeping

Responsible record keeping is an essential feature of a food safety management system. Depending upon the nature of the food business, the following records are recommended:

a) cleaning schedules;

b) planned preventive maintenance schedules;

c) recent hygiene audits and inspections;

d) sampling and analysis of foods during and following manufacture;

e) temperature monitoring of processes and foods during production and preparation;

f) individual pre-employment health screening questionnaires;

g) individual health examinations;

h) individual medical enquiries to doctors;

i) inspection reports from pest control contractors and rodent baiting charts;

j) food hygiene risk assessments;

k) food hygiene incidents;

l) HACCP verification activities;

m) glass and blades registers;

n) hygiene training of employees;

o) supplier audits; and

p) records of inspection by authorised officers of the food authority.

All reasonable precautions and all due diligence

Chilled storage

Cleaning schedules

Corrective action

Critical Control Points (CCPs)

Exclusion of food handlers

Food Hygiene Audit

Food hygiene inspections

Food safety management systems

Hazard Analysis: Critical Control Point (HACCP)

Sampling and analysis

Stock control and rotation

Supplier monitoring

Training of food handlers

Red kidney bean poisoning

Red kidney beans contain a toxic substance (phytohaemagglutin or lectin). Where beans are inadequately cooked, this substance affects certain people causing vomiting, nausea and other symptoms within approximately 6 hours of consumption.

The toxin is destroyed by rapid boiling for 10 – 12 minutes. However, slow cooking may not reach the temperature required to destroy the toxin. Beans should be soaked for 2 – 3 hours and the soaking water discarded prior to rapid boiling.

Natural toxins

Refrigerators

Refrigerators are used for the chilled storage of principally high risk fresh foods at a temperature between 1°C and 4°C. Whilst storage at this temperature does not kill pathogenic bacteria, such bacteria remain dormant and spoilage organisms are slow in multiplying.

A number of points must be considered in the safe use of refrigerators:

a) correct placement of foods should ensure free circulation of air around these foods;

b) any hot food should be properly cooled before being placed in a refrigerator;

c) containers for open food should be food grade and fitted with covers;

d) refrigerators should be sited away from any source of heat, such as radiators or ovens;

e) under no circumstances should food be stored in the original opened cans;

f) in catering and other commercial food premises the provision of separate refrigerators for cooked and uncooked foods is recommended;

g) raw meat should be stored below cooked foods to prevent cross-contamination from dripping blood;

h) defrosting should be undertaken on a scheduled basis;

i) daily temperature recording should be carried out; and

j) the refrigerator should be cleaned regularly with particular attention to the door seals.

Canned goods

Chilled storage

Cooling of food

Cross contamination

Refuse storage and disposal

Poor standards of refuse storage and disposal are one of the principal causes of contamination of food and infestation by rodents, birds, crawling and flying insects.

Depending on the size of the food premises and scale of operations, refuse storage areas should take the form of specifically designated compounds. The compound should incorporate a hard standing, with a permanent water supply to enable regular hosing down, access to a drainage system and clearly designated food waste and non-food waste refuse containers.

Cleaning of the area should be incorporated in a cleaning schedule for the premises and regular inspections of this area should be undertaken.

Cleaning schedules

'Clean place' strategies

Disposal and destruction of food

Infestation prevention and control

Food Hygiene (England) Regulations 2006

Waste food storage and disposal

Registration and approval of food premises

Under Article 31(1)(a) of Regulation (EC) No 852/2004 food business operators are required to register all of their premises with the local authority. Registration is free and cannot be refused by the local authority. Once registered, no further action is required other than notification of a change of proprietor or a change in the nature of the business.

Food business operators whose establishments are required to be registered should approach the relevant local authority ideally before they open (or before starting to use new premises).

The premises for certain types of businesses need to be approved, rather than registered, including those producing the following foods:

  a)   meat and meat products;

  b)   eggs;

  c)   milk and dairy products; and

  d)   fish and fish products.

Eggs and egg products (food hazards)

Fish and shellfish (food hazards)

Food business operator

Meat

Meat products (food hazards)

Milk and dairy products (food hazards)

Regulation (EC) No. 852/2004 on the hygiene of foodstuffs

Regulation (EC) No 852/2004 on the hygiene of foodstuffs

Council Directive 93/43/EEC of 14 June 1993 on the hygiene of foodstuffs laid down the general rules of hygiene for foodstuffs and the procedures for verification of compliance with these rules.

With regard to public health, these rules and procedures contain common principles, in particular, in relation to the manufacturers' and competent authorities' responsibilities, structural, operational and hygiene requirements for establishments, procedures for the approval of establishments, requirements for storage and transport and health marks.

The principal objective of the general and specific hygiene rules is to ensure a high level of consumer protection with regard to food safety.

The Regulation incorporates the following Chapters and Annexes:

Chapters

1. General provisions

2. Food business operators' obligations

3. Guides to good practice

4. Imports and exports

5. Final provisions

Annexes

1. Primary production
   - Part A: General hygiene provisions for primary production and associated operations
   - Part B: Recommendations for guides to good hygiene practice

2. General hygiene requirements for all food business operators (except when Annex 1 applies)

Food Hygiene (England) Regulations 2006

Regulations

Most statutes, such as the Food Safety Act, enable the Minister or Secretary of State to make Regulations.

Regulations lay down more detailed requirements with respect to a particular area of food safety, such as food hygiene, food labelling, food processing, slaughtering of animals and the compositional aspects of certain foods.

[Regulations are subject to the process of Regulatory Impact Assessment.]

Food Hygiene (England) Regulations 2006

Food Labelling Regulations 1996 (as amended)

Food Safety Act 1990

Regulatory Impact Assessments

Statutory Codes under the Food Safety Act

Regulatory Impact Assessments

Assessments produced by the Food Standards Agency of particular legislation's requirements, the impact on industry, on enforcement authorities and other sectors and of the costs and benefits.

Regulations

Reheating of food

Many foods are cooked, cooled, or frozen, and then re-heated prior to consumption. This practice can have dangers and, generally, a chilled or frozen food should only be re-heated once, to at least 63°C, in order to avoid bacterial growth.

Cold holding/service

Cook-chill

Cooking of food

Frozen food

Hot holding requirements

Thawing of frozen food

Remedial Action Notices

Where it appears to an authorised officer of an enforcement authority that in respect of an establishment subject to approval under Article 4(2) of Regulation 853/2004:

a) any of the requirements of the Hygiene Regulations is being breached; or

b) inspection under the Hygiene Regulations is being hampered, he may, by a notice in writing (in these Regulations referred to as a 'Remedial Action Notice) served on the relevant food business operator or his duly authorised representative:

c) prohibit the use of any equipment or any part of the establishment specified in the notice;

d) impose conditions upon or prohibit the carrying out of any process; or

e) require the rate of operation to be reduced to such extent as is specified in the notice, or to be stopped completely.

[Food Hygiene (England) Regulations 2006]

Authorised officer

Enforcement procedure

Equipment requirements

Food business operator

Food Hygiene (England) Regulations 2006

Food hygiene inspections

Prohibition action

Reporting of diseases (food handlers)

Any person suffering from, or being a carrier of a disease likely to be transmitted through food, employed in a food business and who is likely to come into contact with food is to report immediately the illness or symptoms, and if possible their causes, to the food business operator.

[Regulation (EC) No 852/2004 on the hygiene of foodstuffs]

Food handler

Persons suffering from certain medical conditions

Prohibition of a person

Regulation (EC) No. 852 on the hygiene of foodstuffs

Reservoir of infection

A common location in the body where a pathogen may always be found in considerable numbers. Examples are:

a)   nose, mouth, throat – *Staphylococci*

b)   intestines – *Salmonellae, Clostridia, E. coli*

Clostridium botulinum (Clostridium welchii)

Clostridium perfringens

Escherichia coli (E. coli)

Pathogenic agents (pathogens)

Salmonellae

Staphylococcus aureus

Streptococci

Residual insecticide

An insecticide which, when applied to a surface, remains active for a considerable period of time.

Ant control

Cockroach control

Flour mite

Flying insect control

Infestation prevention and control

Insecticides

Responsibilities for food: food business operators

If a food business operator considers or has reason to believe that a food which he has imported, produced, processed, manufactured or distributed is not in compliance with the food safety requirements, it shall immediately initiate procedures to withdraw the food in question from the market where the food has left the immediate control of that initial food business operator and inform the competent authorities thereof. Where the product may have reached the consumer, the operator shall effectively and accurately inform the consumers of the reason for its withdrawal and, if necessary, recall from consumers products already supplied to them when other measures are not sufficient to achieve a high level of health protection.

A food business operator responsible for retail or distribution activities which do not affect the packaging, labelling, safety or integrity of the food shall, within the limits of its respective activities, initiate procedures to withdraw from the market products not in compliance with the food safety requirements and shall participate in contributing to the safety of the food by passing on relevant information necessary to trace food, co-operating in the action taken by producers, processors, manufacturers and/or the competent authorities.

A food business operator shall immediately inform the competent authorities if it considers or has reason to believe that a food that it has placed on the market may be injurious to health. Operators shall inform the competent authorities of the action taken to prevent risks to the final consumer and shall not prevent or discourage any person from co-operating, in accordance with National Law and legal practice, with the competent authorities, where this may prevent, reduce or eliminate a risk arising from a food.

Food business operators shall collaborate with the competent authorities on action taken to avoid or reduce risks posed by a food that they supply or have supplied.

[Food Safety Act 1990 as amended]

Competent authority

Food business (definition)

Food business operator

Food safety requirements

Product recall systems

Regulation (EC) No 852/2004 on the hygiene of foodstuffs

Rest facilities

Under the Workplace (Health, Safety and Welfare) Regulations 1992, employers are required to provide suitable and sufficient rest facilities at readily accessible places.

Rest facilities provided shall:

a) where necessary, for reasons of health or safety include, in the case of a new workplace, extension or conversion, rest facilities provided in one or more rest rooms, or, in other cases, in rest rooms or rest areas;

b) include suitable facilities to eat meals where food eaten in the workplace would otherwise be likely to become contaminated.

Suitable facilities must be provided for any person at work who is a pregnant woman or nursing mother to rest.

Workplace (Health, Safety and Welfare) Regulations 1992

Retailers

The last part of the distribution chain, retailers are taken as those who sell food in small quantities directly to the consumer.

Distribution chain

Risk assessment

The identification of hazards, the measurement and evaluation of the risks arising from hazards, and the implementation of preventive and protective measures to prevent or control exposure to those hazards.

Food safety risk assessment

Rodent control

Rodent control entails the practical procedures directed at denying access to rodents, exterminating rats and mice who may have entered food premises and denying food and shelter. These procedures include:

a) the laying of rodenticide baits;

b) the use of rat and mouse traps;

c) structural proofing of premises;

d) strict standards of hygiene and cleaning, including the removal of all food waste;

e) good housekeeping, including regular stock rotation, thereby denying harbourage; (the 'disturbance factor' in terms of denying facilities for breeding, is important here) and maintenance of refuse storage areas and refuse containers in a scrupulously clean and tidy condition;

f) employee training to recognise evidence of rodent infestation; and

g) planned preventive maintenance procedures directed at maintaining the integrity of structures, doors, windows and other means of access for rodents.

Pest control contractors should be monitored on a regular basis to ensure effective contract compliance.

Cleaning, disinfection and housekeeping

Housekeeping procedures

Infestation prevention and control

Pest control contracts

Preventive maintenance

Proofing of buildings

Stock control and rotation

Structural requirements for food premises

Training of food handlers

Waste food storage and disposal

Rooms where foodstuffs are prepared

Chapter II of Annex 2 to Regulation (EC) No 852/2004 on the hygiene of foodstuffs lays down specific requirements in rooms where foodstuffs are prepared, treated or processed (excluding dining areas and those premises specified in Chapter III), thus:

1. In rooms where food is prepared, treated or processed (excluding dining areas and those premises specified in Chapter III, but including rooms contained in means of transport) the design and layout are to permit good food hygiene practices, including protection against contamination between and during operations. In particular:

    a) floor surfaces are to be maintained in a sound condition and be easy to clean and, where necessary, disinfect. This will require the use of impervious, non-absorbent, washable and non-toxic materials, unless food business operators can satisfy the competent authority that other materials used are appropriate. Where appropriate, floors are to allow adequate surface drainage;

b) wall surfaces are to be maintained in a sound condition and easy to clean and, where necessary, disinfect. This will require the use of impervious, non-absorbent, washable and non-toxic materials and require a smooth surface up to a height appropriate for operations, unless food business operators can satisfy the competent authority that other materials used are appropriate;

c) ceilings (or, where there are no ceilings, the interior surface of the roof) and overhead fixtures are to be constructed and finished so as to prevent the accumulation of dirt and reduce condensation, the growth of undesirable moulds and the shedding of particles;

d) windows and other openings are to be constructed to prevent the accumulation of dirt. Those which can be opened to the outside environment are, where necessary, to be fitted with insect-proof screens which can easily be removed for cleaning. Where open windows would result in the contamination of foodstuffs, windows must remain closed and fixed during production;

e) doors are to be easy to clean and, where necessary, to disinfect. This will require the use of smooth and non-absorbent surfaces, unless food business operators can satisfy the competent authority that other materials used are appropriate; and

f) surfaces (including surfaces of equipment) in areas where foodstuffs are handled and in particular those in contact with food are to be maintained in a sound condition and be easy to clean and, where necessary, to disinfect. This will require the use of smooth, washable, corrosion-resistant and non-toxic materials, unless food business operators can satisfy the competent authority that other materials used are appropriate.

2. Adequate facilities are to be provided, where necessary, for the cleaning, disinfecting and storage of work tools and equipment. These facilities are to be constructed of corrosion-resistant materials, be easy to clean and have an adequate supply of hot and cold water.

3. Adequate provision is to be made, where necessary, for washing of food. Every sink or other such facility provided for the washing of food is to have an adequate supply of hot and/or cold potable water consistent with the requirements of Chapter VII and be kept clean and where necessary, disinfected.

Ceilings in food premises

Cleaning, disinfection and housekeeping

Contamination

Cross contamination

Equipment requirements

Floor surfaces

Food contamination

Food rooms

Layout of food premises

Proofing of buildings

Regulation (EC) No. 852/2004 on the hygiene of foodstuffs

Structural requirements for food premises

Wall surfaces

Washing of food and food equipment

Rotaviruses

This type of virus is responsible for several forms of gastro-enteritis, particularly in young children, resulting in severe diarrhoea, vomiting, fever and dehydration. Man is the source, together with sewage-contaminated water. Onset is within one to three days and the duration, four to eight days. Foods commonly associated with Rotavirus are salad, vegetables and raw shellfish.

Fish and shellfish (food hazards)

Gastro-enteritis

Viruses

Water supply

S

'Safer Food Better Business'

The Food Standards Agency has developed several food safety management packs to help businesses to comply with regulations.

Specific guidance is provided for small retail businesses that sell food, including any food that needs to be kept cold to keep it safe, such as milk. These include small convenience stores, corner shops and confectioners, tobacconists and newsagents. This pack covers:

a) cross-contamination;

b) cleaning;

c) chilling;

d) management;

e) cooking and preparation; and

f) diary (documentation suggestions).

Chill control

Chilled storage

Chill holding requirements

Chill holding tolerance periods

Cleaning, disinfection and housekeeping

Cleaning schedules

Cooking of food

Cooling of food

Cross contamination

Food Hygiene (England) Regulations 2006

Food safety management systems

Hazard Analysis: Critical Control Point (HACCP)

'Sale' (of food)

Under section 2 of the Food Safety Act, *sale* has an extended meaning, and for the purposes of the Act:

a) the supply of food, otherwise than on sale, in the course of a business; and

b) any other thing which is done with respect to food and is specified in an order made by the Ministers, shall be deemed to be the sale of food and references to purchasers and purchasing shall be construed accordingly.

The Act, from an enforcement viewpoint, has two principal themes, namely ensuring the safety of the food people eat and, secondly, protecting the consumer in various ways, for instance, from false descriptions.

Consumer protection provisions (Food Safety Act)

Food Safety Act 1990

Food safety management objectives

Food safety provisions

Salmonellae

Salmonella is a Gram-negative, non-spore forming, short rod-shaped bacterium which is widely distributed in humans and animals. Their effects can vary widely and there are nearly 3,000 known serotypes.

Salmonellae can be classified into three principal groups:

a) those that infect only people and which can be transmitted through food, e.g.*Salmonella Typhi* and *Salmonella Paratyphi*;

b) host-adapted strains, some of which are human pathogens and which can be transmitted by food, e.g. *Salmonella Dublin*; and

c) certain strains which do not have a particular host, but which may have pathogenic effects on people and animals.

The most common causes of food poisoning are those associated with *Salmonella Typhimurium* and *Salmonella Enteriditis* which result in the condition known as 'salmonellosis' The symptoms include sickness, fever, diarrhoea and severe abdominal pain lasting as long as seven days in some cases. A person suffering from salmonellosis excretes the bacteria in the faeces and may transmit the disease to others.

Salmonellae multiply quickly at a temperature between $7^{O}C$ and $45^{O}C$ and the route of infection is through raw animal products, such as milk, poultry, eggs and egg-based products and raw meat. They can also be carried on insects, rodents, birds and animal pets, together with water and sewage.

Prevention of infection is based on the maintenance of high standards of personal hygiene, thorough cleaning and disinfection of food processing areas, prevention of cross contamination, strict control of the time-temperature relationship in the preparation of high risk foods and effective pest control procedures.

Bacteria

Bacterial food poisoning

Samples, analysis of

An authorised officer of an enforcement authority who has procured a sample under regulation 12 shall:

a)   if he considers that the sample should be analysed, submit it to be analysed:

i)   by the public analyst for the area in which the sample was procured; or

ii)   by the public analyst for the area which consists of or includes the area of the authority; and

b)   if he considers that the sample should be examined, submit it to be examined by a food examiner.

A person, other than such an officer, who has purchased any food, or any substance capable of being used in the preparation of food, may submit a sample of it:

a)   to be analysed by the public analyst for the area in which the purchase was made: or

b)   to be examined by a food examiner.

[Food Hygiene (England) Regulations 2006]

Samples, procurement of

An authorised officer of an enforcement authority may:

a) purchase a sample of any food, or any substance capable of being used in the preparation of food;

b) take a sample of any food, or any such substance, which:

i) appears to him to be intended for placing on the market or to have been placed on the market, for human consumption; or

ii) is found by him on or in any premises which he is authorised to enter by or under regulation 14;

c) take a sample from any food source, or a sample of any contact material, which is found by him on or in any such premises; and

d) take a sample of any article or substance which is found by him on or in any such premises and which he has reason to believe may be required as evidence in proceedings under any of the provisions of this Act or regulations made under it.

Statutory Code of Practice No. 7 *Sampling for Analysis or Examination* covers the procedures to be followed by food authorities with respect to sampling and analysis.

[Food Safety Act 1990]

[Food Hygiene (England) Regulations 2006]

Food Hygiene (England) Regulations 2006
Food Safety Act 1990
Samples, analysis of
Sampling and analysis

Sampling and analysis

Authorised officers of local authorities, namely environmental health officers and trading standards officers, are charged with the regular sampling of a wide range of foodstuffs with a view to ascertaining compliance with quality and compositional requirements. Samples may be taken on a formal or informal basis, and it is quite common for such officers to operate a sampling programme over a period of time.

With an informal sample, the food is simply purchased and submitted to a public analyst for both bacteriological and compositional analysis. Where an informal sample indicates a possible breach of food safety legislation, a formal sample will subsequently be taken.

Formal sampling involves a set procedure of:

a) purchasing a sample of the food in question;

b) making a statutory declaration to the vendor that the food has been purchased for analysis by a public analyst;

c) dividing the sample into three equal portions in the presence of the vendor;

d) sealing and labelling the three portions of the sample;

e) handing the first portion to the vendor and obtaining a receipt for same;

f) submitting a second portion to the public analyst; and

g) retaining the third portion for analysis by the government analyst in the event of discrepancy in the results produced by the public analyst and those of the vendor's analyst.

Where there are breaches of the Food Safety Act, the vendor may be prosecuted.

Adulteration of food

Advertising food for sale

All reasonable precautions and all due diligence

Compositional requirements

Consumer protection provisions (Food Safety Act)

Defences

False or misleading descriptions and information

Fault of another person (defence)

Food Safety Act 1990

Labelling and description offences

Nature, substance or quality

Penalties

Prosecution

Statutory Codes under the Food Safety Act

Time limit for prosecutions

Sanitary conveniences

1. Suitable and sufficient sanitary conveniences shall be provided at readily accessible places.

2. Sanitary conveniences shall not be suitable unless:

    a) the rooms containing them are adequately ventilated and lit;

    b) they and the rooms containing them are kept in a clean and orderly condition; and

    c) separate rooms containing conveniences are provided for men and women, except where and so far as each convenience is in a separate room the door of which can be secured from inside.

[Workplace (Health, Safety and Welfare) Regulations 1992

An adequate number of flush lavatories are to be available and connected to an effective drainage system. Lavatories are not to open directly into rooms in which food is handled.

[Regulation (EC) No. 852/2004 on the hygiene of foodstuffs]

Amenity areas

Food Hygiene (England) Regulations 2006

Regulation (EC) No. 852/2004 on the hygiene of foodstuffs

Welfare amenity provisions

Workplace (Health, Safety and Welfare) Regulations 1992

Sanitiser

A chemical compound used in cleaning and disinfecting equipment and surfaces.

Cleaning, disinfection and housekeeping

Cleaning schedules

Detergents

Detergent-sanitisers

Scombrotoxin

A histamine-like substance which causes the symptoms of scombroid food poisoning. This type of food poisoning is associated with the consumption of certain species of fish, such as salmon, pilchards, anchovies and sardines. The substance has also been identified in some Swiss cheeses.

Natural toxins

Toxin

Scottish partnerships (offences by)

Offences by Scottish partnerships

'Sell by' date

An obsolete form of date coding of food indicating the last possible date for sale of the specific food. This method has now been replaced by 'best before' and 'use by' dates.

'Best before' date

Date marking

Food Labelling Regulations 1996 (as amended)

Labelling requirements

'Use by' date

Separation

Separation is one of the basic principles of food protection. It implies the physical separation of food against bacterial and other forms of contamination. It can include:

a) separation of food and utensil washing sinks from wash hand basins;

b) separating utensils for the preparation of different food products;

c) separating raw food from processed or cooked food; and

d) separating 'dirty areas', where initial preparation takes place, from 'clean areas' where the final product is assembled and packed.

'Clean place' strategies

Food hazard

Indirect contamination

Raw foods

Sequestrants

Sequestrants are chemicals that counteract or suppress the effects of other chemical substances. They are incorporated in detergents principally as water-softening agents, thereby preventing or reducing the formation of lime scale and hard soap deposits on surfaces.

Detergents

Serotyping

A method of identifying bacteria through specific antigen or antibody reactions.

Antibody

Antigen

Bacteriological standards

Bacteriology

Service of documents

Any document which is required or authorised under the Hygiene Regulations to be served on a food business operator may be served:

a)   by delivering it to that person;

b)   in the case of an incorporated company or body, by delivering it to their secretary at their registered or principal office, or by sending it in a prepaid letter addressed to him at that office; or

c)   in the case of any other food business operator, by leaving it or sending it in a prepaid letter addressed to him at his usual or last known residence.

Where a document is to be served on a food business operator under the Hygiene Regulations and it is not reasonably practicable to ascertain the name and address of the person on whom it should be served, or the premises of the food business operator are unoccupied, the document may be served by addressing it to the food business operator concerned in the capacity of occupier of those premises (naming them), and

a)   by delivering it to some other person at the premises; and

b)   if there is no other person at the premises to whom it can be delivered, by affixing it or a copy of it to some conspicuous part of the premises.

[Food Hygiene (England) Regulations 2006]

Similar provisions apply under the Food Safety Act 1990.

Food Hygiene (England) Regulations 1990

Food Safety Act 1990

Hygiene Emergency Prohibition Notice

Hygiene Emergency Prohibition Order

Hygiene Improvement Notice

Hygiene Prohibition Order

Improvement Notices

Prohibition action

Prohibition Orders

Prohibition procedures

Remedial Action Notices

Shelf life (definition)

The period within which food is both at its best quality and safe for human consumption.

Shelf life means:

a) in relation to food with respect to which an indication of maximum durability is required in accordance with regulation 20 of the Food Labelling Regulations 1996 (form of indication of minimum durability), the period up to and including the date required to be included in that indication;

b) in relation to food with respect to which a 'use by' date is assigned in the form required in accordance with regulation 21 of the Food Labelling Regulations 1996 (form of indication of 'use by' date), the period up to and including that date; and

c) in relation to food which is not required to bear an indication of minimum durability or a 'use by' date, the period for which the food can be expected to remain fit for sale if it is kept in a manner which is consistent with food safety.

[Food Hygiene (England) Regulations 2006]

'Best before' date

Date marking

Food Labelling Regulations 1996 (as amended)

'Use by' date

Shellfish

A term used to cover:

    a)   univalves – whelks and winkles;

    b)   bivalves – mussels, cockles, oysters; and

    c)   crustacea – lobsters, crabs, prawns, shrimps.

Fish and shellfish (food hazards)

Shellfish toxin

Shellfish toxin

Where mussels and other shellfish have fed on contaminated or poisonous plankton they, in turn, can become contaminated by a neurotoxin. Consumption of contaminated shellfish can result in paralytic shellfish poisoning, commencing immediately with tingling or numbness of the mouth, spreading to the arms and legs within four to six hours. Death, due to respiratory paralysis, may follow in two to twelve hours. This neurotoxin can withstand cooking and is difficult to detect in affected shellfish.

Fish and shellfish (food hazards)

Food poisoning (food-borne illnesses)

Natural toxins

Neurotoxin

Shigella

A group of Gram-negative non-sporing bacteria found in the intestine of man and other animals, responsible for bacillary dysentery or shigellosis. Shigellosis is common in many tropical countries, being associated with sewage-polluted water supplies, and is commonly known as 'Delhi belly' and 'gyppy tummy'.

The disease has an incubation period of 12 to 48 hours and symptoms include diarrhoea, vomiting, fever, abdominal pain and cramps. Severe cases may manifest pus and blood in the faeces.

Bacteria

Bacterial food poisoning

Dysentery

Incubation period

Water supply

Shop premises

Premises from which any food is sold to the final consumer.

[Food Hygiene (England) Regulations 2006]

Business (definition)

Food business operator

Food Hygiene (England) Regulations 2006

Structural requirements for food premises

Sinks

Large basins, with supplies of hot and cold water and incorporating an outlet, for the washing of food and food equipment.

Regulation (EC) No. 852/2004 on the hygiene of foodstuffs

Washing of food and food equipment

Slaughterhouse

An establishment used for slaughtering and dressing animals, the meat of which is intended for human consumption and which:

a) is approved or conditionally approved under Article 31 (2) of Regulation 882/2004; or

b) (although lacking the approval or conditional approval that is required under Article 4(3) of Regulation 853/2004) was, on 31st December 2005, operating as a licensed slaughterhouse under the Fresh Meat (Hygiene) Regulations 1995 or the Poultry Meat (Hygiene and Inspection) Regulations 1995 or the Poultry Meat, Farmed Game Bird and Rabbit Meat (Hygiene and Inspection) Regulations 1995.

[Food Hygiene (England) Regulations 2006]

Smoked foods

Food produced using a smoking process to preserve fitness and impart a particular flavour to that food, e.g. kippers.

Curing of food

Smoking hazards

It is an offence for a food handler to smoke while engaged in the handling of food or in a food room.

The principal hygiene risk is that of hand-to-mouth contamination being passed to high risk foods during preparation.

Food handling (practice)

Food Hygiene (England) Regulations 2006

High risk foods

Personal hygiene

Regulation (EC) No. 852/2004 on the hygiene of foodstuffs

Sources of law

Sources of law with respect to food safety include:

- Statutes, such as the Food Safety Act 1990;
- Regulations, such as the Food Hygiene (England) Regulations 2006;
- Statutory Codes of Practice under the Food Safety Act; and
- Case law, namely precedents established in the criminal and civil courts and recorded in official Reports, such as the All England Reports.

Food Hygiene (England) Regulations 2006

Food Safety Act 1990

Regulations

Statutory Codes under the Food Safety Act

Sous vide

A French term meaning 'under vacuum' and used to describe a specific inter-rupted catering process in which lightly cooked food is heat-sealed in plastic pouches in vacuum conditions.

Generally, products prepared in this way have a limited shelf life under storage at chill conditions and the process does not destroy toxins or spores. More-over, these products are prone to contamination by *Clostridium botulinum* and good standards of hygiene control are necessary during the production process, subsequent storage and final preparation.

Chill control

Clostridium botulinum (Clostridium welchii)

Temperature control requirements

Spoilage of food

Food spoilage is associated with the gradual process of decomposition which takes place in all foods over a period of time, the rate of decomposition varying substantially according to the type of food and the conditions, particularly temperature, under which it is stored.

Decomposition takes place in meat following the slaughtering of animals, in vegetables and fruit after picking and in other food products following manu-facture or processing. All foods reach a stage where the degree of decomposition makes them unpalatable and eventually unfit for human consumption. Spoilage may also arise through contamination caused by chemicals, insects and rodents, oxidation of the product and through accidental physical damage.

Microbiological spoilage is, however, more important and is brought about by a complex degradation process in foods. Spoilage organisms will multiply partic-ularly in high risk food products, such as dairy products, fruit and vegetables, meat, fish and poultry.

Spoilage can result in the development of 'off' flavours and tastes in the food, together with changes in the appearance of the food, including consistency, nature and colour. Fermentation within food can result in the production of gases.

Whilst refrigeration will delay the onset of spoilage, it will not stop these changes taking place.

Bacteria

Freshness and fitness of food

Fungi

Milk and dairy products (food hazards)

Moulds in food

Poultry (food hazards)

Refrigerators

Stock control and rotation

Spore

A reproductive cell, the dormant survival form of some bacteria.

Bacteria

Endospore

Sporocyst

A parasitic fluke in the initial stage of infection.

Sporulation

The process whereby bacteria form spores.

Bacteria

Bacterial growth curve

Stabilisers

Additives, such as locust bean gum (E410) made from carob beans, which prevent ingredients from separating again after mixing.

Additives

E-numbers

Staphylococcus aureus

This micro-organism is found commonly on the human body, in the ear, nose and throat, and in septic skin lesions, such as boils, pimples, whitlows, burns and cuts. *Staphylococcus aureus* produces exotoxins and the foods most commonly associated in food poisoning outbreaks are poultry, ham, dairy products, raw milk and egg products.

Contamination is commonly associated with poor personal hygiene, infected food handlers contaminating food, inadequate temperature control, preparation of food too far in advance of serving, resulting in high risk foods standing at ambient temperatures, and inadequate temperature control of food during processing.

Bacteria

Bacterial food poisoning

Carriers of disease

Chill holding requirements

Exotoxins

Food handler

Food handling (practice)

Food-borne infection

Food poisoning (food-borne illnesses)

Food contamination

Personal hygiene

Temperature control (premises)

Temperature control requirements

Toxin

Stationary phase

A stage of bacterial growth where the population of bacteria has reached its maximum.

Bacteria

Bacterial growth curve

Statutory Codes under the Food Safety Act

Section 40 of the Food Safety Act incorporates a number of enabling powers for Ministers in relation to the enforcement by local food authorities. This has resulted in the production, as a joint exercise by the former Ministry of Agriculture, Fisheries and Food, Department of Health, Scottish Office and Welsh Office, of a series of codes of practice, incorporating guidance, predominantly aimed at ensuring uniformity of interpretation and enforcement of the Act by local food authorities. Reference should be made to the actual Codes and guidance for further information in specific situations.

The significance of these codes must be appreciated by both enforcement officers and persons representing operators of food businesses charged with offences under the Act and regulations made under the Act. Under section 40, food authorities 'shall have regard to any relevant provision of any such code' in their enforcement procedures.

Codes of Practice include:

1. *Responsibility for enforcement of the Food Safety Act 1990*

2. *Legal matters*

3. *Inspection procedures – general*

4. *Inspection, detention and seizure of suspect food*

5. *The use of Improvement Notices*

6. *Prohibition procedures* etc

In these Codes, those parts of a typeface in bold type are classed as the actual Code detail, whereas that in ordinary type is for guidance only.

Authorised officer

Codes of Recommended Practice – Food Hygiene (England) Regulations

Competent authority

Food Alerts

Food hygiene inspections

Food Safety Act 1990

Food Standards Inspection

Prohibition action

Prohibition of a person

Prohibition Orders

Prohibition procedures

Sterile

A state or condition where all living organisms have been destroyed.

Sterilisation

Sterilisation is, fundamentally, any heat or chemical process that destroys all micro-organisms in or on a food product.

Sterilisation has been used in the heat treatment of milk for many years, whereby raw milk is heated to a temperature of 110°C for approximately 30 minutes. Similar products, such as ice cream, are dealt with in this way.

It is important that the distinction between *sterilisation* and *disinfection* is recognised. Sterilisation implies the total destruction of all living micro-organisms and their spores. In many cases, this is difficult to achieve. Disinfection, on the other hand, implies the control of micro-organisms to a safe level, and is more significant in cleaning activities.

Stock control and rotation

All organisations should, for a variety of reasons, have a recognised system of stock control, whereby a record is maintained of all stock held at a point in time.

In the case of perishable foods in particular, stock rotation demands that a system of 'first in, first out' be operated, whereby older stock is used first, thereby minimising the risks of spoilage, 'blowing' in the case of canned goods, contamination by infestation and loss of food quality.

Canned goods

Food purchase and delivery

Food safety management systems

High risk foods

Spoilage of food

Stored product pest

These are insects, such as beetles, weevils and moths, which infest a range of mainly dry products stored for long periods, such as flour, grain, nuts and spices. Most damage to stored products is caused by the larval form of the insect.

The more common stored product pests are:

a) biscuit beetle (*Stegobium paniceum*)

b) mealworm beetle *(Tenebrio molitor)*

c) saw-toothed grain beetle *(Oryzaephilus surinamensis)*

d) confused flour beetle *(Tribolium confusum)*

e) grain weevil *(Sitophilus granarius)*

f) Mediterranean flour moth *(Ephestia kuehniella)*

Dry goods

Flour mite

Fumigation

Infestation prevention and control

Larva

Pest

Pesticides

Streptococci

The *Streptococcus* species are non-sporing Gram positive bacteria. They take the form of spherically-shaped bacterial cells which appear as long chains remaining attached after cell division.

Streptococcus faecalis can be transmitted to man through food. It is commonly present in the intestines of man and animals. This bacterium is highly resistant to heat and likely to survive heat treatment processes, such as pasteurisation. It can grow in alkaline conditions and has a temperature range for growth of 5°C to 50°C.

Bacteria

Bacterial food poisoning

Bacteriological standards

Food poisoning bacteria

Food poisoning (food-borne illnesses)

Food poisoning incidents

Strict (absolute) liability

Many duties on people under food safety legislation are of a strict or absolute nature, prefaced by the term 'shall' or 'must', and not qualified by terms such as 'so far as is practicable' or 'so far as is reasonably practicable', as with certain health and safety legislation. On this basis, failure to comply with such requirements may result in prosecution.

In the case of food safety legislation, however, it may be possible to submit a defence of 'all reasonable precautions and all due diligence', but much will depend upon the nature of the offence.

All reasonable precautions and all due diligence

Structural requirements for food premises

Annex II to Regulation (EC) No. 852/2004 on the hygiene of foodstuffs (General Hygiene Requirements for All Food Business Operators) – specifies:

a) General requirements for food premises (Chapter 1); and

b) Specific requirements in rooms where foodstuffs are prepared, treated or processed (Chapter 2)

In particular, Chapter 2 lays down particular requirements with respect to:

a) floor surfaces;

b) wall surfaces;

c) ceiling surfaces (or inner roof surfaces where no ceiling is installed);

d) windows and other openings;

e) doors; and

f) surfaces (including surfaces of equipment).

Generally, all surfaces must be maintained in a sound condition, be easy to clean and, where necessary to disinfect. This will require the use of impervious, non-absorbent, washable and non-toxic materials.

Ceilings in food premises

Cleaning, disinfection and housekeeping

Disinfection

Doors

Equipment requirements

Floor surfaces

Food rooms

Layout of food premises

Regulation (EC) No. 852/2004 on the hygiene of foodstuffs

Structural requirements for food premises

Wall surfaces

Supplier monitoring

The quality and safety of the finished product relies largely on the standard of raw materials used in its production. On this basis it is essential that suppliers are monitored to ensure that they are capable of providing a satisfactory product which complies with an agreed buying specification. Knowledge of specific sources of foodstuffs and the relative standards of hygiene maintained by such producers is important in establishing 'all due diligence'.

Factors to be considered in supplier monitoring include:

a) structural condition of the premises;

b) layout and location;

c) environmental factors, for example lighting and ventilation;

d) food storage arrangements;

e) food delivery arrangements;

f) processing and temperature control systems;

g) product protection procedures, such as foreign body control;

h) health surveillance arrangements for staff;

j) infestation control procedures;

k) hygiene control arrangements; and

l) food safety training procedures.

Much will depend on the nature of the product, the relative risks, the number of employees, past complaints and the attitude of local management as to the degree and extent of supplier monitoring required. However, there should be a formal procedure established agreeing inspections on a pre-determined basis.

Delivery of food

Environmental control

Foreign bodies

Hazard Analysis: Critical Control Point (HACCP)

Health surveillance

Hygiene audit

Infestation prevention and control

Lighting recommendations

Stock control and rotation

Structural requirements for food premises

Temperature control (premises)

Temperature control requirements

Training of food handlers

Surfactants

These are chemical substances which increase the wetting or penetrating action of a detergent. In effect, they reduce the surface tension of a liquid, thereby increasing penetration of the detergent.

Detergents

Swabbing

A bacterial monitoring and testing method involving the measurement of the take up of bacteria from a surface followed by incubation in a standard or selective medium.

Testing methods

Sweeteners

Lower in calories and safer for teeth, sweeteners are often used instead of sugar in carbonated drinks, chewing gum and yoghurt.

'Intense sweeteners', such as aspartame (E951), saccharin (E954) and acesulfame-K (E950) are many times sweeter than sugar and so only very small amounts are used in food.

Bulk sweeteners, such as sorbitol (E420), have about the same sweetness as sugar and should be used in similar amounts to sugar.

Additives
E-numbers

Symbiosis

The close association between two species, particularly where there is a benefit to both species.

Commensal

T

Taenia saginata

This tapeworm inhabits the small intestines of man and can grow up to 8m in length. The head incorporates four suckers (but no hooks) and is known as 'the unarmed tapeworm of man'. The tapeworm excretes 8 – 10 ripe segments daily. The cystic stage of the tapeworm, *Cysticercus bovis*, is found in cattle and is known as 'measles of beef' or 'measly beef'.

Cysticerci

Tapeworms (Cestodes)

Taenia solium

This tapeworm, encountered in pigs, can grow up to 5m in length. The head of the adult tapeworm has a ring of hooklets and is known as 'the armed tapeworm of man'. Its occurrence in the UK is rare. The cystic stage of *Taenia solium*, *Cysticercus cellulosae*, gives rise to 'measles of pork' or 'measly pork' and is found in the musculature of the pig, chiefly the muscles of the heart, diaphragm and tongue.

Cysticerci

Tapeworms (Cestodes)

Tapeworms (Cestodes)

These are parasitic worms with a small head and long body which increase in length due to the formation of additional segments below the head region. Adult worms may reach a length of 20 metres and can survive in a suitable host animal for as long as 25 years. The head incorporates suckers which enable the worm to attach itself to the intestinal lining. Tapeworms go through a series of stages of development from the egg stage to the adult worm.

Adult tapeworms are hermaphroditic and develop in the intestines of the host. They produce eggs which are excreted in the faeces of the host animal. These eggs are subsequently consumed by an intermediate host where development of the larval stages takes place. Larvae move then through the intestinal layers of this host passing into the lymphatic and circulatory systems and, subsequently, into the musculature and organs of the host. At this stage, a larval cyst is produced. This cyst incorporates buds in which immature tapeworms develop and are eventually released.

Taenia saginata and *Taenia solium* are typical tapeworms of cattle and pigs respectively.

Other species include:

    a)   *Diphyllobothrium latum* – fresh water fish;

    b)   *Echincoccus granulosus* – dogs, sheep and cattle;

    c)   *Taenia pisiformis* – rabbits and hares; and

    d)   *Taenia ovis* – sheep .

Definitive (primary) host

Echinococcus granulosus

Host

Parasites

Taenia saginata

Taenia solium

Target level

A specified value for a particular control measure that will either eliminate or control the risk from a hazard at a critical control point.

Critical Control Points (CCPs)

Hazard analysis

Hazard Analysis: Critical Control Point (HACCP)

Taxonomy

The naming, classification and description of organisms.

Technical defences

Where charged with an offence under food safety legislation, a defendant may be in a position to submit one or more of the following defences.

Duplicity

Duplicity, namely charging more than one offence in a summons, can have a deleterious effect. Each summons should relate to one specific offence only.

Identity of person summoned

It is vital that the correct person and/or company are identified in any summons. In certain cases it may be necessary to make use of the Local Government Act or Freedom of Information Act to obtain accurate information as to identity. The implications of charging the wrong person and/or company are well established in case law.

The role of the authorised officer

Here it is necessary to ensure that the authorised officer acted in accordance with, in particular, section 32 (powers of entry) and the appropriate statutory codes issued with the Act. It may also be necessary to establish the specific role of the authorised officer within the food authority and the decision-making process by that authority with regard to prosecutions and other sanctions imposed.

All reasonable precautions and all due diligence

Appeals to Crown Court

Authorised officer

Enforcement procedure

Food Safety Act 1990

Offences and penalties

Powers of entry

Prosecution

Statutory Codes under the Food Safety Act

Temperature control (premises)

A particular area of food safety practice in which control of temperature is used as a measure to eliminate or control a food hazard.

In terms of the workplace environment, temperature control further implies maintenance of a working temperature in production areas of approximately 16 – 20°C, irrespective of the season, in order to ensure reasonable comfort conditions for operators.

Excessive temperatures promote both bacterial growth and infestation by crawling and flying insects.

Environmental control

Infestation prevention and control

Regulation (EC) No. 852/2004 on the hygiene of foodstuffs

Temperature control requirements

Workplace (Health, Safety and Welfare) Regulations 1992

Temperature control requirements

Temperature control requirements for food are laid down in the Food Hygiene (England) Regulations 2006.

These regulations require certain foods to be kept at temperatures that will prevent the growth of harmful bacteria. It is an offence to allow food to be kept at temperatures that would cause a risk to health.

- Foods that need to be kept hot should be kept at 63°C or above.

- Foods that need to be kept cold should be kept at 8°C or below (preferably at 5°C or below).

- Foods that need to be kept frozen should be kept between – 18°C to – 24°C.

Chill control

Chilled storage

Chill holding requirements

Codes of Recommended Practice – Food Hygiene (England) Regulations

Cold holding/service

Cooling of food

Frozen food

Freezers

Hot cabinets

Hot holding requirements

Microwave ovens

Pasteurisation

Quick freezing

Refrigerators

Reheating of food

Sterilisation

Temperature control (premises)

Thawing of frozen food

Temperature measurement equipment

The measurement of the temperature of food products at various stages of manufacture and storage is an essential feature of a food safety management system. It is also frequently undertaken by authorised officers as part of a food hygiene inspection.

The following forms of thermometer are available:

Electronic probe thermometers

This form of thermometer comprises a temperature sensor located at its tip linked to an electronic unit incorporating a digital display. These probe thermometers can be used for monitoring both hot and cold temperatures in a variety of applications:

a)   air temperatures in refrigerators and freezers;

b)   food temperatures in refrigerators, hot cabinets and normal display;

c)   internal food temperatures of products, meat joints and poultry during cooking, reheating and cooling; and

d)   the temperature of food delivered by suppliers.

Authorised officers use instruments with a high specification, for example:

a)   accuracy of +/- 0.5°C or better (in the range 0°C to 20°C);

b)   accuracy must not be significantly affected by changing ambient temperatures, i.e. they must not change by more than 0.3°C across the ambient range of 0°C to 30°C;

c)   the display must be readable at 0.1°C intervals or less;

d)   the system should reach 90% of its final reading within 3 minutes;

e)   the system should be robust and shockproof; and

f)   the probe should be designed to promote good thermal contact.

Whilst probe thermometers used in manufacturing processes and catering may not need to be so specific in specification as above, in the selection of an instrument key qualities will be speed of response, relative accuracy and the ability to clean same easily.

The electronic display unit should be checked annually. Manufacturers may offer a service facility or calibration devices used.

The probe and system should be checked together monthly as follows:

Cold: Agitate the probe in a mixture of ice and a small amount of water until a steady reading is achieved. This should be – 1°C to + 1°C. If outside this range, the unit needs attention or repair.

Hot: Agitate the probe in boiling unsalted water until a steady reading is achieved. This should be between 99°C and 101°C. If outside this range, the unit needs attention or repair.

Liquid crystal thermometers

These relatively cheap plastic strip thermometers can be useful in storage units that do not have any other type of thermometer incorporated. They must be read *in situ* because their reading changes quickly if removed from the unit. Fixing such thermometers to the door or wall of the unit will 'damp' their response.

Glass mercury thermometers

These thermometers are not recommended as they pose a serious risk to food safety both from broken glass and the mercury. On no account should food be probed with a glass thermometer.

Chill control

Chill holding requirements

Chill holding tolerance periods

Cold chain

Cold holding/service

Cold store

Cook-chill

Cook-freeze

Cooling of food

Core (centre) temperature

Deep freeze

Delivery of food

Temporary premises

A premises which is to be used on a short-term basis or for a limited period of time prior to the establishment of permanent premises.

Moveable and temporary structures

Testing methods

The monitoring of potential bacterial contamination is an essential element of the food manufacturing industry. It entails the sampling of particular foods on a regular basis as part of a sampling programme, the growing of organisms from these samples under laboratory conditions and eventual assessment of the bacterial status of the samples. A number of physical, biological, immuno-logical and biochemical testing techniques are used.

Physical tests

Radiometry

This test measures the speed of consumption or ingestion of a particular substance, such as radioactive glucose, which is introduced into the culture medium. An indication of the number of micro-organisms present is given by the time, which is inversely related to the total micro-organisms in the sample, for total ingestion, i.e. the greater the number of micro-organisms present, the swifter the ingestion of the glucose.

Impedance

In this test, electrical resistance is used to determine the presence of bacteria. This is indicated on the basis of the greater the number of micro-organisms present, the more metabolic products produced and the greater the electrical resistance. Whilst this method gives a quick result, it is not specific about the actual nature of the micro-organisms present.

Microcalorimetry

Microcalorimetry operates on the basis of detecting temperature change caused by micro-organisms breaking down food.

Biological tests

Swabbing

Swabbing, or contact technique, is used for checking the bacteriological status of critical food contact surfaces in food manufacturing processes. The technique entails swabbing the surface and growing a colony of micro-organisms from the sample swab. Following staining, micro-organisms are identified by microscopic examination, or by simple counting methods.

Most probable number (MPN)

This technique is particularly appropriate for detecting and determining the density of faecal coliforms, such as *Escherichia coli*. The growth of bacteria in a series of dilutions of food samples is compared with MPN tables in order to estimate the total number of organisms present in the original sample.

Biochemical tests

MUG test

This test uses a particular nutrient, methyl umbelliferyl glucuronide (MUG) and operates on the basis that certain bacteria, in particular some strains of *Escherichia coli* and *Salmonellae,* incorporate a specific enzyme which splits this nutrient. This test detects and measures the reaction that takes place.

APT bioluminescence

Living organisms actually emit light, the process of bioluminescence. This test measures the light emitted when an enzyme, luciferase, is in the presence of adenosine triphosphate (ATP). ATP is the principal source of cellular energy in living organisms. Whilst this test has its limitations in terms of interpretation of levels of contamination, it has particular value in assessing the total levels of microorganisms in raw materials and the effectiveness of cleaning procedures.

Immunological tests

Phage typing

Many bacteriophages, i.e. viruses that attack bacteria, attack only one bacterial strain. The process entails identifying when a reaction has taken place using a particular bacteriophage, thereby identifying the actual strain of bacteria. The strains identified in this way are known as phage types.

Serotyping

This technique uses specific known antibodies to identify unidentified bacteria. When a reaction occurs, this can identify the nature of the bacteria present. In this test, antisera, groups of known antibodies are mixed with the food samples. Results can be visible as a result of physical changes in samples exposed on agar plates.

In the ELISA (enzyme-linked immunosorbant assay) test, presence of bacteria can be detected through changes in colour of the enzymes of particularly susceptible bacteria.

Genetic tests

There are several methods using strands of genetic material, such as ribonucleic acid (RNA) or DNA to assist in the identification of bacteria.

Polymerase chain reaction (PCR)

This test tends to have limited use due to the cost involved. The test examines the activity of a particular enzyme during genetic replication.

Bacteria

Bacterial growth curve

Bacteriophage (phage) typing

Coliforms

Colony count

Detection methods

Escherichia coli (E. coli)

Faecal organisms (bacteriological standards)

Micro-organisms (Microbes)

Organism

Viruses

Thawing of frozen food

It is essential that, particularly in the case of large meat joints and poultry, full thawing takes place before cooking, preferably in a thawing cabinet operating at between 10°C and 15°C. Where thawing is incomplete, much heat will be lost to completing the thawing process during the early cooking stages and the cooking temperature may be reduced, resulting in incomplete cooking. However, small items of frozen food may be cooked direct from the frozen state.

The thawing of frozen food in microwave ovens may be satisfactory but there is a risk of cold spots developing and the thawing process may not be consistent. Where frozen food is thawed in a refrigerator, extra thawing time should be allocated.

Cooking of food

Frozen food

Meat

Meat products (food hazards)

Microwave ovens

Refrigerators

Temperature control requirements

Thermophiles

Heat-loving micro-organisms that thrive at a temperature between 40°C and 80°C.

Micro-organisms (Microbes)

Thickeners

Additives which help give body to food.

Additives

E-numbers

Time limit for prosecutions

No prosecution for an offence under the Food Safety Act which is punishable under section 35(2) shall be begun after the expiry of:

    a)   three years from the commission of the offence; or

    b)   one year from its discovery by the prosecutor,

whichever is the earlier.

[Food Safety Act 1990]

No prosecution for an offence under the Hygiene Regulations which is punishable under paragraph (2) of Regulation 17 shall be begun after the expiry of:

    a)   three years from the commission of the offence; or

    b)   one year from its discovery by the prosecutor,

whichever is the earlier.

[Food Hygiene (England) Regulations 2006]

Offences and penalties

Prosecution

Toilets

Water closets and urinal accommodation.

Amenity areas

Sanitary conveniences

Welfare amenity provisions

Tolerance

A specified variation from the target level which is deemed to be acceptable for food safety.

Critical Control Points (CCPs)

Hazard Analysis: Critical Control Point (HACCP)

Target level

Total viable count

The total number of living cells detectable in a food sample.

Bacteriological standards

Sampling and analysis

Toxin

A poisonous substance produced by some bacteria and fungi. They can be classified by their effects on the body. Neurotoxins affect nerve functions and the central nervous system. Enterotoxins, on the other hand, have a direct effect on the intestinal system.

Endotoxins exist within the cell, whereas exotoxins are secreted by the cell as waste.

Endotoxin

Enterotoxin

Exotoxins

Mushroom toxin

Natural toxins

Neurotoxin

Toxoplasmosis

A number of protozoan parasites, *Toxoplasma gondii* and *Toxoplasma cati*, infest cats, causing neurological disorders in man where the cysts or tachyzoites (the early stage of the life cycle) are consumed. These cysts may be found in under-cooked meat and milk.

Toxoplasmosis is also associated with the fact that cats shed the cysts in their faeces and may infect man through contact. Symptoms in man vary from a mild infection to life-threatening disease. The disease is rare in the UK.

Meat

Meat products (food hazards)

Milk and dairy products (food hazards)

Parasites

Protozoa

Traceability requirements

An essential element of any food manufacturing process is that of tracing the final product once it has left the premises. This is particularly important where it may be necessary to recall products.

Food business operators shall be able to identify any person from whom they have been supplied with a food, a feed, a food producing animal, or any substance intended to be, or expected to be, incorporated into a food or feed. To this end, such operators shall have in place systems and procedures that allow for this information to be made available to the competent authorities on demand.

Food business operators shall have in place systems and procedures to iden-tify the other businesses to which their products have been supplied. This information shall be made available to the competent authorities on demand.

[Food Safety Act 1990 as amended]

Food business operator

Hazard Analysis: Critical Control Point (HACCP)

Product recall systems

Training of food handlers

Food handlers must receive appropriate supervision, and be instructed and/or trained in food hygiene to enable them to handle food safely. Those responsible for developing and maintaining the business's food safety procedures, based on HACCP principles, must have received adequate training. The requirements for training should be seen in the context of the nature and size of the business.

Regulation (EC) No 852/2004 on the hygiene of foodstuffs lays down the following requirements with respect to training of food handlers:

Food business operators are to ensure:

1. That food handlers are supervised and instructed and/or trained in food hygiene matters commensurate with their work activity.

2. That those responsible for the development and maintenance of the product referred to in Article 5(1) of this Regulation or for the operation of relevant guides have received adequate training in the application of the HACCP principles.

3. Compliance with any requirements of national law concerning training programmes for persons working in certain food sectors.

A number of accredited courses for food handlers are available under the auspices of the Chartered Institute of Environmental Health, Royal Society for the Promotion of Health and the Royal Institute of Public Health.

European food hygiene legislation

Food handling (practice)

Hazard Analysis: Critical Control Point (HACCP)

Information, instruction and training

Regulation (EC) No 852/2004 on the hygiene of foodstuffs

Training records

The European food hygiene legislation requires food handlers to receive appropriate instruction and training in food safety and hygiene measures. Furthermore, the maintenance of training records is an important aspect of a food safety management system, such as Hazard Analysis: Critical Control Point (HACCP).

Simple training records should incorporate:

a) the details of individuals who have received training, including the dates of same;

b) the format of the training, such as accredited courses through professional bodies such as the Chartered Institute of Environmental Health, Royal Institute of Public Health, etc;

c) the form of training, such as formal lectures, group discussion, case studies, etc;

d) the theoretical and practical aspects of training received, such as hygiene management procedures, food handling techniques, food hygiene inspections and preparation of reports; and

e) the results in terms of tests and examinations passed and qualifications achieved.

European food hygiene legislation

Hazard Analysis: Critical Control Point (HACCP)

Regulation (EC) No 852/2004 on the hygiene of foodstuffs

Training of food handlers

Transport of foodstuffs

Regulation (EC) No 852/2004 on the hygiene of foodstuffs lays down requirements in respect of the transport of foodstuffs thus:

1. Conveyances and/or containers used for transporting foodstuffs are to be kept clean and maintained in good repair and condition to protect foodstuffs from contamination and are, where necessary, to be designed and constructed to permit cleaning and/or disinfection.

2. Receptacles in vehicles and/or containers are not to be used for transporting anything other than foodstuffs where this may result in contamination.

3. Where conveyances and/or containers are used for transporting anything in addition to foodstuffs or for transporting different foodstuffs at the same time, there is to be effective separation of products

4. Bulk foodstuffs in liquid, granular or powder form are to be transported in receptacles and/or containers/tankers reserved for the transport of foodstuffs if otherwise there is a risk of contamination. Such containers must be marked in a clearly visible and indelible fashion, in one or more Community languages, to show that they are used for the transport of foodstuffs, or are to be marked FOR FOODSTUFFS ONLY.

5. Where conveyances and/or containers have been used for transporting anything other than foodstuffs or for transporting different foodstuffs, there is to be effective cleaning between loads to avoid the risk of contamination.

6. Foodstuffs in conveyances and/or containers are to be so placed and protected as to minimise the risk of contamination.

7. Where necessary, conveyances and/or containers used for transporting foodstuffs are to be capable of maintaining foodstuffs at appropriate temperatures and allow those temperatures to be monitored.

Cleaning, disinfection and housekeeping

Conveyances and containers

Contamination

Cross contamination

Food receptacles

Regulation (EC) No. 852/2004 on the hygiene of foodstuffs

Temperature control requirements

Trematodes

These are flatworm parasites of animals and man, the most common being the liver fluke, *Fasciola hepatica*.

Fasciola hepatica

Trichinella spiralis

This is a small round worm occurring in the intestines of man, pigs and rats and responsible for the disease, trichinosis. The larvae invade the muscles and when the flesh is consumed, these larvae are liberated into the stomach, passing into the intestine where they quickly mature, thereby completing the cycle.

Nematodes

Parasites

Trisodium phosphate

A sanitiser wash or rinse used to reduce the level of *E. coli* on the surface of carcass meat.

Sanitiser

Washing of food and food equipment

Turbidity test

This is a test undertaken following the processing of sterilised milk based on soluble proteins being denatured by heating above 100°C. A positive result will indicate inadequate heating of the milk or the presence of raw milk.

Raw milk (restrictions on sale)

Sterilisation

Two sink system

A commonly-used manual method of washing up in kitchens involving the use of a double sink or two sinks.

Initial washing and the removal of soil is carried out in the first sink which contains hot water with a detergent at a temperature of 55°C. Those items which are lightly soiled, such as glassware, are washed first. Heavily soiled items, such as plates, must be pre-cleaned or scraped to remove excessive soiling, prior to initial washing.

This process basically entails:

- pre-cleaning and rinsing to remove excessive food residues
- hand washing and cleaning in the first sink at a temperature of 55°C using a detergent to remove grease in particular
- subjecting dishes and utensils to a disinfecting rinse in the second sink at a temperature of 85°C; (where a chemical sanitiser is used, the temperature can be lower)
- air drying in racks.

Subsequent rinsing of items takes place in the second sink which contains water at a temperature of 82 – 88°C or, in some cases, cooler water incorporating a chemical disinfectant.

These items are then air-dried prior to storage.

Dish and utensil washing

Sanitiser

Washing of food and food equipment

U

Ultra Heat Treatment (UHT)

A high temperature heat treatment process, commonly applied to milk, which is directed at extending shelf life to around six months without refrigeration, achieving commercial sterility and reducing food spoilage organisms.

In this process, milk is heated to 132°C for one second followed by aseptic filling to sterile containers made from plastic laminated material.

Aseptic packaging

Milk and dairy products (food hazards)

Shelf life (definition)

Spoilage of food

Sterilisation

Unfitness for human consumption

This term applies to all food that is not safe to eat, rendered injurious to health and contaminated to such an extent that it would not be reasonable to expect it to be consumed.

Food which does not meet the food safety requirements under the Food Safety Act is also deemed as unfit.

All food must meet the food safety requirements of the Food Safety Act.

Food hazard

Food Safety Act 1990

Food safety requirements

Unprocessed products

Foodstuffs that have not undergone processing, and includes products that have been divided, parted, severed, sliced, boned, minced, skinned, ground, cut, cleaned, trimmed, husked, milled, chilled, frozen, deep-frozen or thawed.

[Regulation (EC) No 852/2004 on the hygiene of foodstuffs]

Raw materials

Upward variation of the 8°C temperature by manufacturers, etc

In any proceedings for an offence consisting of a contravention of sub-paragraph 1 of paragraph 2, it shall be a defence for the accused to prove that:

a) a food business responsible for manufacturing, preparing or processing the food, including, where relevant, the accused, has recommended that it is kept:

   i) at or below a specified temperature between 8°C and ambient temperatures; and

   ii) for a period not exceeding a specified shelf life;

b) that recommendation has, unless the accused is that food business, been communicated to the accused either by means of a label on the packaging of the food or by means of some other appropriate form of written communication;

c) was kept at a temperature above 8°C or, in appropriate circumstances, the recommended temperature for an unavoidable reason, such as:

   i) to accommodate the practicalities of handling during and after processing or preparation;

   ii) the defrosting of equipment; or

   iii) temporary breakdown of equipment,

and was kept at a temperature above 8°C or, in appropriate circumstances, the recommended temperature for a limited period only and that period was consistent with food safety.

[Food Hygiene (England) Regulations 2006]

Food business (definition)

Food Hygiene (England) Regulations 2006

Labelling requirements

Shelf life (definition)

'Use by' date

This date is applied to the packaging of high risk and perishable foods, such as meat products and those subject to cook-chill, which could cause food poisoning. The 'use by' date indicates the last day at which the food is safe for consumption.

'Best before' date

Date marking

High risk foods

Cook-chill

Shelf life (definition)

Utensils

Utensils include knives, spoons, whisks and other items used by hand in food manufacture and catering processes. As such, they can transfer infection to food if not cleaned properly.

In particular, utensils with wooden handles should not be used due to the absorbent nature of such handles.

Equipment requirements

V

Vacuum packing

A form of food packaging for, particularly, meat and fish where air is removed from the laminated plastic or nylon package or pouch to create a vacuum, thereby preventing the growth of aerobic micro-organisms.

On opening of the package, food prepared in this manner should be consumed immediately or refrigerated prior to consumption.

Packaging

Sous vide

Vector

Any organism which assists in the transmission of disease. Vectors may be living organisms, such as animals, birds, insects and man, or non-living organisms, such as food, water, contaminated surfaces and saliva.

Bacteria

Vehicle of contamination

A vehicle of contamination is any person, animal, bird, insect, substance or object that transmits contamination indirectly to food.

Vehicles of contamination in food premises include dish cloths, wipers, the hands and clothing of food handlers, rodents, crawling and flying insects, birds, food contact surfaces such as cutting boards, and surfaces coming into contact with hands such as utensils and tap handles.

Cleaning, disinfection and housekeeping

Equipment requirements

Extrinsic factor

Food contact surfaces

Food hazard

Indirect contamination

Proofing of buildings

Vending machines

The use of food and beverage vending machines has increased universally and the range of products dispensed from vending machines is extensive. Current food safety and hygiene legislation applies in the case of food sold and dispensed from vending machines.

Vending machines can, broadly, be classed as:

a) beverage vending machines:

  i) simple drink dispensers, where drink constituents are dispensed to a cup followed by hot water;

  ii) in-cup dispensers, where the ingredients are already contained in the cup to which hot water is added; and

  iii) post-mix machines, where ready-mixed cold or hot drinks are dispensed direct to a cup.

b) food vending machines:

  i) column and drawer machines for dispensing solid items, such as bars of chocolate; and

  ii) rotating drum machines, which contain simple items, such as pre-packed sandwiches, or whole meals stored under refrigeration and stored in separate compartments on shelves which rotate. The pre-cooked meals are commonly reheated in microwave ovens adjacent to the machine.

A number of principles apply in the safe and correct operation of vending machines, namely:

a) machines should be constructed of smooth, impervious, corrosion-resistant and non-toxic materials

b) they should be maintained in an efficient state, in efficient working order and in good repair to ensure the safety and wholesomeness of food being sold from same;

c) they should be sited away from direct sunlight and other sources of heat;

d) they should be subject to regular cleaning, both internally and externally, with a specific cleaning schedule, including the frequency of cleaning, displayed on the inside surface in a prominent position ;

e) they should be appropriately located to enable cleaning of surrounding floor and wall surfaces;

f) stock should be correctly rotated and all items should be provided with a 'Use by' date or date coded, with outdated stock being removed;

g) where dispensing high risk foods stored under refrigeration or at a temperature above 63°C, they should incorporate a temperature recording device; and

h) the name, address and telephone number of the operator should be permanently displayed in a prominent position on the machine.

Cleaning schedules

Equipment requirements

Exposing food for sale

Food Hygiene (England) Regulations 2006

High risk foods

Preventive maintenance

Stock control and rotation

Temperature control requirements

'Use by' date

Ventilation requirements

Ventilation of food premises may be by both natural and artificial means. Artificial ventilation is clearly far more efficient and reliable. Depending upon ambient temperatures, ventilation rates should be between 6 and 20 air changes per hour to maintain reasonable comfort conditions. Local exhaust ventilation should be provided over heat sources, such as the mouths of ovens. Ventilation requirements for workplaces generally are covered by the Workplace (Health, Safety and Welfare) Regulations 1992 and Approved Code of Practice.

[Workplace (Health, Safety and Welfare) Regulations 1992]

There are to be suitable and sufficient means of natural or mechanical ventilation. Mechanical airflow from a contaminated area to a clean area is to be avoided. Ventilation systems are to be so constructed as to enable filters and other parts requiring cleaning or replacement to be readily accessible.

[Regulation (EC) No. 852/2004 on the hygiene of foodstuffs]

Cross contamination

Environmental control

General requirements for food premises

Regulation (EC) No. 852/2004 on the hygiene of foodstuffs

Temperature control requirements

Workplace (Health, Safety and Welfare) Regulations 1992

Verification

The reviewing and checking of the entire HACCP procedure to ensure correct operation according to plan.

Hazard Analysis: Critical Control Point (HACCP)

Appendix A: The HACCP Decision Tree

Viruses

A virus is a very small infective and parasitic organism that can only multiply within living cells and not in food. However, they can remain viable in food and water for varying periods of time and are responsible for a range of illnesses linked to food. In most cases, viruses are destroyed during normal cooking procedures and bacterial control is achieved through temperature and time controls.

Contamination of food can take place at source, particularly in the case of food which is eaten raw and not subject to any processing, such as oysters and salad foods. In this case, the need for contamination by sewage tests, in particular, must be considered along with water purity tests of the water at oyster beds.

Contamination by viruses can further arise from poor or inadequate standards of personal hygiene on the part of food handlers.

The viruses that are particularly significant are those associated with Hepatitis A (HAV), Norwalk virus and similar viruses, and Rotavirus.

Hepatitis A

Norwalk virus

Rotaviruses

Voluntary closure

In certain situations, where there are breaches of food safety legislation, the owner of a food business may offer to close the premises on a voluntary basis.

Most food authorities are prepared to accept such an offer. In these cases, Statutory Code of Practice No. 6 *Prohibition Procedures* recommends that the officer should:

    a)   consider whether there is any risk of the premises being reopened without his knowledge and/or agreement;

b) recognise that there is no legal sanction against a proprietor who reopens for business after offering to close; and

c) explain to the proprietor that, by making the offer to close, he is relinquishing rights to compensation if a court subsequently declines to make a Prohibition Order.

The Code recommends that where an authorised officer accepts an offer to close voluntarily, he should obtain written confirmation of the proprietor's offer to close and an undertaking not to reopen without specific permission. Moreover, he should make frequent checks on the premises to ascertain that they have not reopened. It should be appreciated that the person giving any such undertaking should have authority to take such action.

Authorised officer

Powers of entry

Prohibition action

Statutory Codes under the Food Safety Act

Voluntary surrender

Voluntary surrender

The practice of voluntary surrender of food by an owner to the food authority has operated for many years and is covered in Statutory Code of Practice No. 6 *Prohibition Procedures*. This may be on the instigation of the owner or the authorised officer.

Where food is voluntarily surrendered for destruction, a receipt should be issued by the authorised officer and the description of the food should include the phrase voluntarily surrendered for destruction. The receipt should be signed by the person surrendering the food.

Prohibition action

Statutory Codes under the Food Safety Act

Voluntary closure

VTEC (Verocytotoxin)

The term 'verocytotoxin' refers to the type of cells this micro-organism affects in laboratory work. Verocytotoxin-producing *E.coli* (VTEC) is a particularly virulent serotype of the bacterium which is also referred to as the serotype 0157:H7 and as EHEC (enterohaemorrhagic *E.coli.*)

Verocytotoxin producing *E.Coli* (VTEC) produces potent toxins and can cause severe illness in man. VTEC are responsible for a range of illnesses which may be severe and sometimes fatal, particularly in infants, young children and the elderly. The most important VTEC strain associated with human disease is 0157 VTEC.

0157 VTEC can lead to a range of symptoms, including bloody diarrhoea and haemolytic uremic syndrome (HUS). HUS is characterised by acute renal failure and haemolytic anaemia. It is the major cause of acute renal failure in children in Britain as well as several other countries.

HUS develops in up to 10% of patients infected with 0157 VTEC. Some patients, usually adults, also show neurological complications.

The incubation period prior to diarrhoea is usually 3 days, but can be from 1 to 14 days. In fit adults, symptoms will disappear within 2 weeks. Renal or neurological complications can remain for life. Bacteria are excreted for up to a week, but can survive much longer, particularly in children.

Asymptomatic carriers of 0157 VTEC have been reported. The fatality rate of 0157 VTEC infection is 1-5%, but can be much higher.

Escherichia coli (E. coli)

Incubation period

Serotyping

Toxin

W

Wall surfaces

Wall surfaces in food rooms must be impervious and capable of being readily cleaned. Light colours should be used to enable the state of cleanliness to be assessed easily.

Ideal wall surfaces include ceramic tiles, plastic-coated panels, stainless steel and polypropylene sheeting. Painted surfaces need regular examination to ensure there is no flaking of the paint.

Where appropriate, wall surfaces should be protected by some form of barrier to prevent damage to same from trolleys, trucks, lift trucks, etc

Regulation (EC) No. 852/2004 on the hygiene of foodstuffs

Structural requirements for food premises

Washing facilities

Food premises

Regulation (EC) No 852/2004 on the hygiene of foodstuffs lays down specific requirements for washing facilities in food premises thus:

- An adequate number of washbasins is to be available, suitably located and designated for cleaning hands. Washbasins for cleaning hands are to be provided with hot and cold water, materials for cleaning hands and for hygienic drying. Where necessary, the facilities for washing food are to be separate from the hand-washing facility

Workplaces

In the case of workplaces, the Workplace (Health, Safety and Welfare) Regulations 1992 lay down requirements for washing facilities in workplaces thus:

1. Suitable and sufficient washing facilities, including showers if required by the nature of the work or for health reasons, shall be provided at readily accessible places.

2. Washing facilities shall not be suitable unless:

   a) they are provided in the immediate vicinity of every sanitary convenience, whether or not provided elsewhere as well;

   b) they are provided in the vicinity of any changing rooms required by these regulations, whether or not provided elsewhere as well;

   c) they provide a supply of clean hot and cold, or warm water (which shall be running water so far as is practicable);

d) they include soap or other suitable means of cleaning;

e) they include towels or other suitable means of drying;

f) the rooms containing them are sufficiently ventilated and lit;

g) they and the rooms containing them are kept in a clean and orderly condition and are properly maintained; and

h) separate facilities are provided for men and women, except where and so far as they are provided in a room the door of which is capable of being secured from inside and the facilities in each such room are intended to be used by only one person at a time.

3. The above shall not apply to facilities which are used for washing the hands, forearms and face only.

Amenity areas

Food Hygiene (England) Regulations 2006

Regulation (EC) No 852/2004 on the hygiene of foodstuffs

Welfare amenity provisions

Workplace (Health, Safety and Welfare) Regulations 1992

Washing of food and food equipment

Requirements for washing food and food equipment are outlined in Regulation (EC) No 852/2004 on the hygiene of foodstuffs, thus:

1. Adequate facilities are to be provided, where necessary, for the cleaning, disinfecting and storage of working utensils and equipment. These facilities are to be constructed of corrosion-resistant materials, be easy to clean and have an adequate supply of hot and cold water.

2. Adequate provision is to be made, where necessary, for washing food. Every sink or other such facility provided for the washing of food is to have an adequate supply of hot and/or cold potable water consistent with the requirements of Chapter VII (Water Supply) and be kept clean and, where necessary, disinfected.

Equipment requirements

Food Hygiene (England) Regulations 2006

Potable water

Regulation (EC) No 852/2004 on the hygiene of foodstuffs

Sinks

Waste food storage and disposal

Regulation (EC) No 852/2004 on the hygiene of foodstuffs lays down requirements for food waste thus:

1. Food waste, non-edible by-products and other refuse are to be removed from rooms where food is present as quickly as possible, so as to avoid their accumulation.

2. Food waste, non-edible by-products and other refuse are to be deposited in closable containers, unless food business operators can demonstrate to the competent authority that other types of containers or evacuation systems used are appropriate. These containers are to be of appropriate construction, kept in sound condition, be easy to clean and, where necessary, disinfect.

3. Adequate provision is to be made for the storage and disposal of food waste, non-edible by-products and other refuse. Refuse stores are to be designed and managed in such a way as to enable them to be kept clean and, where necessary, free of animals and pests.

4. All waste is to be eliminated in a hygienic and environmentally friendly way in accordance with Community legislation applicable to that effect, and is not to constitute a direct or indirect source of contamination.

Cleaning, disinfection and housekeeping

Cleaning schedules

Food business operator

Regulation (EC) No 852/2004 on the hygiene of foodstuffs

Structural requirements for food premises

Water-borne infections

Drinking water can become polluted in many ways – by sewage, a range of chemical substances, insects and animals remains. In the same way, polluted water can contaminate food if used, for example, in shellfish beds or for the washing of fruit and raw vegetables. Water-borne infections include typhoid fever, paratyphoid fever and dysentery.

Typhoid and paratyphoid fevers

The more severe water-borne infection, typhoid fever (or enteric fever), is caused by the micro-organism, *Salmonella typhyi,* and still occurs in many countries where water treatment and purification systems are sparsely-located or inadequate. *Salmonella typhi* has a long incubation period (3 to 56 days) and is responsible for many deaths. The micro-organism is excreted in the faeces of patients and carriers, with up to 5% of the persons infected becoming carriers for life and with the potential for relapses.

Symptoms include fever, severe diarrhoea, enlargement of the spleen and, in some cases, rose-coloured spots on the body.

Paratyphoid, caused by *Salmonella paratyphi,* is less severe, with symptoms comparable with typhoid fever.

Control strategies for preventing these infections include:

a)   ensuring high standards of personal and structural cleanliness in the handling and preparation of food;

b)   strict control over the bacteriological quality of the water supply;

c)   ensuring the prevention of cross contamination between water services and sewage systems;

d)   the installation and use of water closets connected to a main drainage system;

e)   careful control in cooking with particular reference to times and temperatures for different classes of food;

f)   exclusion of food handlers manifesting symptoms and/or who are, or may be, carriers; and

g)   well-managed infestation prevention and control procedures.

Shigella dysentery

Commonly known as *bacillary dysentery,* Shigella dysentery is caused by direct transmission from person to person and outbreaks are associated with human carriers of the disease. Water and food, however, frequently act as vehicles in the chain of infection, particularly in areas where insanitary conditions prevail.

Shigella dysentery can be caused by four specific pathogenic micro-organisms, *Shigella sonnei, Shigella dysenteriae, Shigella flexneri* and *Shigella boydii.* The most serious symptoms are associated with infection by *Shigella dysenteriae* and mortality rates can be high, particulary in the case of babies and young children.

The incubation period varies from one to seven days, and infection can arise from very low doses of the micro-organism. Illness is associated with the Shiga toxin, a bacterial enzyme that affects the synthesis of protein in the body. The illness (Shigellosis) is spread through consumption of contaminated food or via the faecal-oral route of an infected person.

Following infection, the bacterial cells invade the lining of the patient's colon, causing death of parts of the tissue and severe diarrhoea. This results in blood-stained faeces in many cases. Vomiting and fever are also typical symptoms of Shigellosis.

Preventive and control measures include emphasis on personal hygiene, strict attention to the risk of direct or indirect faecal contamination, for instance by flying insects, control over the purity of drinking water and the avoidance of insanitary conditions.

Bacteria

Carriers of disease

Coliforms

Cross contamination

Direct contamination

Dysentery

Enzymes

Exclusion of food handlers

Faecal coliform

Fish and shellfish (food hazards)

Flying insect control

Incubation period

Infestation prevention and control

Personal hygiene

Sanitary conveniences

Structural requirements for food premises

Temperature control requirements

Toilets

Toxin

Water supply

Regulation (EC) No 852/2004 on the hygiene of foodstuffs lays down particular requirements with respect to water supply to food premises thus:

1. There must be an adequate supply of potable water which is to ensure foodstuffs are not contaminated.

2. Where non-potable water is used, for example for fire control, steam production, refrigeration or other similar purposes, it is to circulate in a separate duly identified system. Non-potable water is not to connect with, or allow reflux into, potable water systems.

3. Recycled water used in processing or as an ingredient is not to present a risk of contamination. It is to be of the same standard as potable water, unless the competent authority is satisfied that the quality of the water cannot affect the wholesomeness of the foodstuff in its finished form.

4. Ice which comes into contact with food or which may contaminate food is to be made from potable water or, when used to chill whole fishery products, clean water. It is to be made, handled and stored under conditions that protect it from contamination.

5. Steam used directly in contact with food is not to contain any substance that presents a hazard to health or is likely to contaminate the food.

6. Where heat treatment is applied to foodstuffs in hermetically sealed containers it is to be ensured that water used to cool the containers after heat treatment is not a source of contamination for the foodstuff.

Canning processes

Competent authority

Heat treatment

Ice

Potable water

Regulation (EC) No 852/2004 on the hygiene of foodstuffs

Washing of food and food equipment

Welfare amenity provisions

Welfare amenity provisions include:

- sanitary conveniences
- hand washing and showering arrangements
- facilities for the changing of clothing and clothing storage arrangements
- the provision of drinking water
- facilities for rest and to take meals.

The legal requirements for welfare amenity provisions in workplaces generally are incorporated in the Workplace (Healthy, Safety and Welfare) Regulations 1992 and accompanying Approved Code of Practice.

Any arrangement of welfare amenities must take account of two basic aspects, namely:

a) ensuring compliance with the minimum legal requirements; and

b) preventing cross-contamination of food.

Welfare amenity areas should be designed on the following principles:

Design aspects

In sanitation, hand washing and shower areas the surfaces of floors, walls, ceilings, doors and fittings should be capable of being readily cleansed and maintained. There should be an intervening ventilated space between any sanitation area and a food room. Facilities for the disposal of sanitary dressings should be provided in female sanitation areas. Lighting and ventilation should be adequate. Walls, doors and fittings should be of vandal-proof design.

Wash-hand basins and showers should have adequate supplies of hot and cold water or of hot water at a suitably controlled temperature. Supplies of soap, clean towels and nail brushes should be provided. The provision of wall-mounted liquid soap dispensers and disposable paper towels, or the continuous non-returnable type of roller towel cabinet, are recommended as opposed to tablet soap and simple roller towels. In food manufacture and catering, the use of a bactericidal hand cleanser is recommended. Lidded containers should be provided for the storage of soiled paper towels.

In clothing storage and changing areas, suitable seats, preferably of the wall-mounted type, should be provided to permit easy changing of footwear. There must be effective means for drying clothing.

Layout

The layout of the amenity area should ensure that employees have separate access to clothing storage, sanitation, hand cleansing and shower facilities, and are not required to pass through food rooms or processing areas in outdoor clothing. Ideally, an amenity area should be designed for a maximum of 100 persons and where a labour force exceeds this number, further separate amenity areas should be provided. Care should be taken to avoid overcrowding at shift changeovers.

Clothing storage, sanitation and hand cleansing facilities should be arranged so that they lead from one to another in a sequential flow in that order before access to the working area is possible.

For the storage of outdoor clothing, coat hangers captive to single-tier metal stands are recommended in preference to lockers. These rails should be free-standing with ample room between rails. Protective clothing should be hung separately, for instance on parallel or adjoining rows, or separated from outdoor clothing by the sanitation and hand cleansing facilities in a food production area. Small lockers should be provided in the outdoor clothing storage area for the storage of valuable items, such as wrist watches, wallets, etc.

Where hand cleansing facilities occupy a common area with the sanitation facilities, the wash-hand basins should be placed as near as possible to the exit from the area, and in such a position that they make a striking impact on the user of the sanitation facilities. Where hand cleansing facilities occupy a separate area from the sanitation facilities, they should be so sited that access to the sanitation facilities is only possible through the hand cleansing area. Wash-hand basins should be positioned at the point of greatest vantage, as described above.

Showers should be provided to enable staff to cleanse themselves after physical work in a dirty and/or hot environment, to enhance the standards of personal hygiene in food manufacture or catering, and to enable staff to proceed from work to other activities. Whilst there are no legal requirements with regard to the number of showers to be provided in an amenity area, a standard of one shower unit per forty employees is recommended.

Drinking water facilities are not recommended for installation in amenity areas. They should be sited in or adjacent to working areas.

Amenity areas

Changing facilities

Hand washing facilities

High risk foods

Liaison with authorised officers

Lighting recommendations

Personal hygiene

Potable water

Regulation (EC) No. 852/2004 on the hygiene of foodstuffs

Sanitary conveniences

Structural requirements for food premises

Toilets

Washing facilities

Water supply

Workplace (Health, Safety and Welfare) Regulations 1992

Windows

Regulation (EC) No 852/2004 on the hygiene of foodstuffs lays down requirements for windows thus:

- Windows and other openings are to be constructed to prevent the accumulation of dirt.

- Those which can be opened to the outside environment are, where necessary, to be fitted with insect-proof screens which can be easily removed for cleaning. Where open windows would result in contamination, windows are to remain closed and fixed during production.

Infestation prevention and control

Proofing of buildings

Regulation (EC) No 852/2004 on the hygiene of foodstuffs

Structural requirements for food premises

Workplace (Health, Safety and Welfare) Regulations 1992

These regulations impose absolute duties on employers to maintain the workplace, ensure cleanliness, ensure adequate environmental control and safe structural elements, and to provide adequate welfare facilities, i.e. sanitary accommodation, washing facilities, drinking water, clothing storage and changing facilities for employees.

Wrapping

The placing of a foodstuff in a wrapper or container in direct contact with the foodstuff concerned, and the wrapper or container itself.

[Regulation (EC) No 852/2004 on the hygiene of foodstuffs]

Packaging

Wrapping and packaging of foodstuffs

Wrapping and packaging of foodstuffs

Regulation (EC) No 852/2004 on the hygiene of foodstuffs lays down the following provisions applicable to the wrapping and packaging of foodstuffs.

1. Materials used for wrapping and packaging are not to be a source of contamination.

2. Wrapping materials are to be stored in such a manner that they are not exposed to a risk of contamination.

3. Wrapping and packaging operations are to be carried out so as to avoid contamination of the product. Where appropriate and in particular in the case of cans and glass jars, the integrity of the container's construction and its cleanliness is to be assured.

Contamination

Cross contamination

Packaging

Xerophile

An organism that flourishes in dry conditions and survives low A_w values.

A_w *(water activity)*

Y

Yeast

Yeasts are a form of unicellular fungus which reproduce by budding and rapid growth on specific foods, particularly those containing sugar (glucose and fructose), resulting in spoilage of the foods involved.

Yeasts are relatively resistant to heat and multiply over a broad range of temperatures. Some yeasts produce ascospores, a type of spore, and many yeast spores can be spread through airborne routes.

Yeasts are used in fermentation processes converting sugars into alcohol.

Ascospores

Fungi

Spoilage of food

Yersinia enterocolitica

This bacterium found in meat, in particular pork, and raw milk causes the foodborne illness yersiniosis. The disease is characterised by symptoms of gastro-enteritis, such as diarrhoea and/or vomiting, together with fever and abdominal pain comparable with appendicitis.

Gastro-enteritis

Meat

Meat products (food hazards)

Z

Zoonoses

The zoonoses are that group of diseases which are transmissible from animal to man. This may be through direct contact with infected animals and rodents, contamination of water and food, or through consumption of infected animal products.

Contact with an animal infected with *Brucella abortus* may cause the disease, brucellosis. Veterinary surgeons and artificial inseminators are at risk of contracting this disease. Similarly, those coming into contact with the urine of a rat infected with the organism, *Leptospira incterohaemorrhagicae,* such as people working in sewers or pest control operators, may contract leptospirosis or Weil's disease.

Infestation prevention and control

Meat

Meat products (food hazards)

Appendices

Appendix A
The HACCP Decision Tree

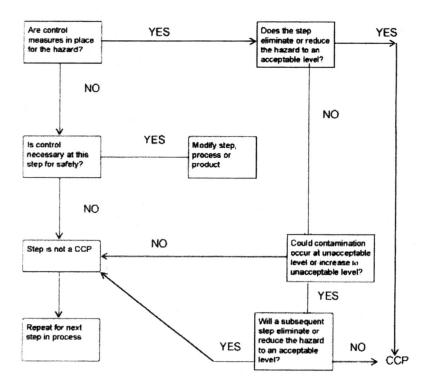

Appendix B
Food Safety Act Forms

Authority: . . . .

Food Safety Act 1990 – Section 9
DETENTION OF FOOD NOTICE

Reference Number:

1. To: . . . .
    Of: . . . .
    . . . .

2. Food to which this notice applies:
    Description   : . . . .
    Quantity   : . . . .
    Identification marks   : . . . .

3. *THIS FOOD IS NOT TO BE USED FOR HUMAN
    CONSUMPTION.*
    In my opinion, the food does not comply with food safety require-
    ments because: . . . .
    . . . .
    . . . .

4. The food must not be removed from:
    . . . .
    . . . .
    *unless it is moved to:
    . . . .
    . . . .
    (*Officer to delete if not applicable)

5. Within 21 days. either this notice will be withdrawn and the food
    released, or the food will be seized to be dealt with by a justice of
    peace. or in Scotland a sheriff or magistrate. who may condemn it.

    Signed: . . . . Authorised Officer
    Name in capitals: . . . .
    Date: . . . .
    Address: . . . .
    . . . .
    . . . .
    Tel: . . . . Fax: . . . .

> *Please read the notes overleaf care-*
> *fully. If you are not sure of your rights*
> *or the implications of this notice. you*
> *may want to seek legal advice.*

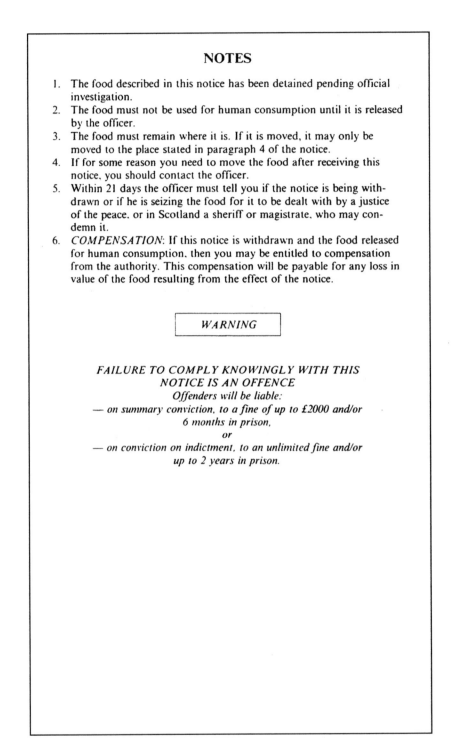

NOTES

1. The food described in this notice has been detained pending official investigation.
2. The food must not be used for human consumption until it is released by the officer.
3. The food must remain where it is. If it is moved, it may only be moved to the place stated in paragraph 4 of the notice.
4. If for some reason you need to move the food after receiving this notice, you should contact the officer.
5. Within 21 days the officer must tell you if the notice is being withdrawn or if he is seizing the food for it to be dealt with by a justice of the peace, or in Scotland a sheriff or magistrate, who may condemn it.
6. *COMPENSATION:* If this notice is withdrawn and the food released for human consumption, then you may be entitled to compensation from the authority. This compensation will be payable for any loss in value of the food resulting from the effect of the notice.

> *WARNING*

*FAILURE TO COMPLY KNOWINGLY WITH THIS
NOTICE IS AN OFFENCE*
Offenders will be liable:
— *on summary conviction, to a fine of up to £2000 and/or
6 months in prison,*
or
— *on conviction on indictment, to an unlimited fine and/or
up to 2 years in prison.*

Authority:

Food Safety Act 1990 – Section 9
WITHDRAWAL OF DETENTION OF FOOD NOTICE

1. To: . . . .
    Of: . . . .
    . . . .

2. Detention Notice Number . . . ., dated . . . . and served
    on you on . . . . (date) is now withdrawn. The food described
    in paragraph 3 below can now be used for human consumption.

3. Food released for human consumption:
    Description   : . . . .
    Quantity   : . . . .
    Identification marks   : . . . .

    Signed: . . . . Authorised Officer
    Name in capitals: . . . .
    Date: . . . .
    Address: . . . .
    . . . .
    . . . .
    Tel: . . . . Fax: . . . .

> *Please read the notes overleaf care-
> fully. If you are not sure of your rights
> or the implications of this notice, you
> may want to seek legal advice.*

NOTES

1. The food described in this notice has been released for human consumption.
2. If this notice does not relate to all of the food originally detained, then the rest has been seized under section 9(3)(b) of the Food Safety Act 1990.
3. *COMPENSATION*: If you can show that any of the food now released for human consumption has lost value, you may be entitled to compensation from the authority. Compensation will be payable for any loss in value resulting from the effect of the notice.

Authority:

Food Safety Act 1990 – Section 9
FOOD CONDEMNATION WARNING NOTICE

Reference Number:

1. To: . . . .
   Of: . . . .

2. This Notice applies to the following food which has been seized by an officer of this authority:
   Description   : . . . .
   Quantity   : . . . .
   Identification marks   : . . . .

3. *IT IS MY INTENTION TO APPLY TO A JUSTICE OF THE PEACE, OR IN SCOTLAND A SHERIFF OR MAGISTRATE,* AT
   . . . .
   ON . . . . (DATE) AT . . . . AM/PM FOR THE ABOVE FOOD TO BE CONDEMNED,
   because . . . .

4. As the person in charge of the food, you are entitled to attend and to bring witnesses.

5. A copy of this notice has also been given to:
   . . . .
   . . . .
   who may also attend and bring witnesses.

   Signed: . . . . Authorised Officer
   Name in capitals: . . . .
   Date: . . . .
   Address: . . . .
   . . . .
   . . . .
   Tel: . . . . Fax: . . . .

> *Please read the notes overleaf carefully. If you are not sure of your rights or the implications of this notice, you may want to seek legal advice.*

NOTES

1. You are being warned that the Authority will be applying to a justice of the peace, or in Scotland a sheriff or magistrate, for the food that has already been seized to be condemned.
2. The justice of the peace, or in Scotland the sheriff or magistrate, will listen to the authority's case that the food fails to comply with food safety requirements and should be condemned. You may say why it should not be condemned.
3. You may bring your own evidence and witnesses to challenge the view of the authority and you may be represented by a lawyer.
4. You are not being charged with an offence. The hearing is only to decide whether the food complies with food safety requirements. But the court may order the food to be condemned. However you may be prosecuted for offences under the Food Safety Act 1990.
5. *EXPENSES*: If the justice of the peace, or in Scotland the sheriff or magistrate, orders the food to be condemned, then the owner of the food will have to pay reasonable expenses for it to be destroyed or disposed of.
6. *COMPENSATION*: If this justice of the peace, or in Scotland the sheriff or magistrates, does not condemn the food, the owner of the food may be entitled to compensation from the authority for any loss in its value as a result of the action taken by the authority.

Authority:

Food Safety Act 1990 – Section 10
IMPROVEMENT NOTICE

Reference Number:

1. To: . . . . (Proprietor of the food business)
   At: . . . .
   . . . .
   . . . . (Address of proprietor)

2. In my opinion the:
   . . . .
   . . . .
   [Officer to insert matters which do not comply with the Regulations]
   in connection with your food business . . . .
   . . . . (Name of business)
   at . . . .
   . . . . (Address of business)
   do/does* not meet the requirements of . . . .
   of the . . . . Regulations
   because:
   . . . .
   . . . .
   [*Officer to delete as appropriate]

3. In my opinion, the following measures are needed for you to comply
   with these Regulations: . . . .
   . . . .
   . . . .

4. These measures or measures that will achieve the same effect must be
   taken by: . . . . (date)

5. *It is an offence not to comply with this improvement notice by the date
   stated.*
   Signed: . . . . Authorised Officer
   Name in capitals: . . . .
   Date: . . . .

   Address: . . . .
   . . . .
   Tel: . . . . Fax: . . . .

> *Please read the notes overleaf care-
> fully. If you are not sure of your rights
> or the implications of this notice, you
> may want to seek legal advice.*

NOTES

1. In the opinion of the officer you are not complying with the Regulations under Part II of the Food Safety Act 1990 described in paragraph 2 of the notice. The work needed in the officer's opinion to put matters right is described and it must be finished by the date set.
2. Your are responsible for ensuring that the work is carried out within the period specified, which must be at least 14 days.
3. *You have a right to carry out work that will achieve the same effect as that described in the notice.* If you think that there is another equally effective way of complying with the law, you should first discuss it with the officer.

YOUR RIGHT OF APPEAL

4. If you disagree with all or part of this notice, you can appeal to the magistrates' court, or in Scotland to the sheriff. You must appeal within one calendar month of the date of the notice or the period ending with the date stated in paragraph 4 of the notice, whichever ends earlier.
5. If you decide to appeal, the time set out in the notice is suspended and you do not have to carry out the work described until the appeal is heard. *However, if you are not complying with the Regulations mentioned in the notice, you may still be prosecuted for failure to comply with those Regulations.*
6. When the appeal is heard, the magistrates' court, or in Scotland the sheriff, may confirm, cancel or vary the notice.

WARNING

FAILURE TO COMPLY WITH THIS NOTICE IS AN OFFENCE
Offenders are liable to be fined and/or
imprisoned for up to 2 years.

Autnority:

Food Safety Act 1990 – Section 12
EMERGENCY PROHIBITION NOTICE

Reference Number:
1. To: . . . . (Proprietor of the food business)
   At: . . . .
   . . . .
   . . . . (Address of proprietor)

2* I am satisfied that: . . . .
   . . . .
   . . . .
   at . . . .
   . . . . (Address of business)

POSES AN IMMINENT RISK FO INJURY TO HEALTH because:
   . . . .
   . . . .
   . . . .
(*See Note 1 overleaf)

3. *YOU MUST NOT USE IT FOR THE PURPOSES OF THIS/ANY/*
   THIS OR ANY SIMILAR* FOOD BUSINESS.
   [*Officer to delete as appropriate]
   Signed: . . . . Authorised Officer
   Name in capitals: . . . .
   Date: . . . .
   Address: . . . .
   . . . .
   Tel: . . . . Fax: . . . .

> *Please read the notes overleaf care-*
> *fully. If you are not sure of your rights*
> *or the implications of this notice, you*
> *may want to seek legal advice.*

NOTES

1. *When you receive this notice you must IMMEDIATELY stop using the premises, process, treatment or equipment described by the officer in paragraph 2 of the notice and located at the address stated.*
2. Within 3 days of service of this notice, the authority must apply to a magistrates' court, or in Scotland to a sheriff, for an order confirming the prohibition. You will be told the date of the hearing which you are entitled to attend and at which you may call witnesses if you wish.
3. If you believe that you have acted to remove the imminent risk of injury to health, you should apply in writing to the authority for a certificate which would allow you to use the premises, process, treatment or equipment again. You can do this even if the court hearing has not taken place.
4. You are not allowed to use the premises, process, treatment or equipment for the purpose specified in paragraph 3 of the notice (see section 11(3) of the Food Safety Act 1990) until (a) a court decides you may do so; (b) the authority issues you with a certificate as in paragraph 3 above; (c) 3 days have passed since the service of the notice and the authority has not applied to the court as in paragraph 2 above; or (d) the authority abandons the application.
5. A copy of this notice must, by law, be fixed on the premises or equipment which is not to be used. It is an offence (under section 1 of the Criminal Damage Act 1971 or, in Scotland, section 78 of the Criminal Justice (Scotland) Act 1980) to deface it.
6. *COMPENSATION:* If the authority does not apply to the magistrates' court, or in Scotland to the sheriff, for an order confirming its action within 3 days of the date of service of this notice, you will be entitled to compensation for any losses you have suffered because you could not use the premises, process, treatment or equipment because you were complying with this notice. You will also be entitled to such compensation if the magistrates' court, or in Scotland the sheriff, decide at the hearing that the authority's action was wrong.

WARNING

ANY ONE WHO KNOWINGLY CONTRAVENES THIS
NOTICE IS GUILTY OF AN OFFENCE
Offenders are liable to be fined and/or
imprisoned for up to 2 years.

Authority:

Food Safety Act 1990 – Section 12
NOTICE OF INTENTION TO APPLY FOR AN
EMERGENCY PROHIBITION ORDER

Reference Number:
1. To: ....
   Address: ....
   ....
   ....

   You are the proprietor of the food business at:
   ....
   ....
   ....

2. *I give notice that I shall be applying to the* ....
   Magistrates' Court/Sheriff sitting at ....
   for an emergency prohibition order because ....
   ....
   ....

3. If an order is made by the court you will not be able to use the prem-
   ises, process, treatment or equipment described:
   ....
   ....
   ....
   for the purpose of this/any or any similar* food business.
   [*Officer to delete as appropriate]
   Signed: .... Authorised Officer
   Name in capitals: ....
   Date: ....
   Address: ....
   ....
   Tel: .... Fax: ....

> *Please read the notes overleaf care-*
> *fully. If you are not sure of your rights*
> *or the implications of this notice, you*
> *may want to seek legal advice.*

NOTES

1. This notice tells you that the authority intend to apply to the magistrates' court, or in Scotland the sheriff, for an emergency prohibition order which, if granted, would mean that you could not use the premises, process, treatment or equipment described for the purposes specified in paragraph 3 of the notice (see section 11(3) of the Food Safety Act 1990).
2. The court will consider the evidence from the authority as to why they believe there is an imminent risk of injury to health from the operation of your food business or part of it. You may bring you own evidence and witnesses to put before the court and you may choose to be represented by a lawyer.
3. *If the court is convinced by the authority's evidence, then an order will be made stating what you may not do. The order will be served on you by the authority. A copy of it must be fixed by the authority at your premises and it is an offence to deface it. (Section 1 of the Criminal Damage Act 1971 or, in Scotland, section 78 of the Criminal Justice (Scotland) Act 1980).*
4. In England and Wales, you have the right to appeal to the Crown Court against the decision of the magistrates' court if you think that it is wrong. In Scotland the position is governed by the Rules of Court.
5. The making of an order does not mean you are guilty of an offence but the authority may seek to prosecute you for offences under the Food Safety Act 1990 or associated regulations.
6. If you have been issued with an emergency prohibition notice from the authority, you will know what steps should be taken to remove the imminent risk to health.
7. *If the court is not satisfied by the authority's evidence and an order is not issued, then you will be entitled to continue your business. If the authority has already issued you with an emergency prohibition notice and you have suffered loss because you have complied with it, then you will also be entitled to compensation from the authority.*

Authority:

Food Safety Act 1990 – Section 11 & 12
CERTIFICATE THAT THERE IS NO LONGER A RISK TO HEALTH

1. To: . . . . (Name of proprietor)
   At: . . . . (Address of proprietor)
   Proprietor of: . . . .
   Address of food business: . . . .
   . . . .

2. *The enforcement authority certifies that it is satisfied that you have taken sufficient measures to secure the removal of the imminent* risk of injury to health described in the*:

   emergency prohibition notice*
   emergency prohibition order*
   prohibition order*
   [*Officer to delete as appropriate]
   served on you on . . . . (date).

   Signed: . . . . Authorised Officer
   Name in capitals: . . . .
   Date: . . . .
   Address: . . . .
   . . . .
   Tel: . . . . Fax: . . . .

THIS CERTIFICATE MEANS THAT YOU MAY NOW USE THE PREMISES, PROCESS, TREATMENT OF EQUIPMENT AGAIN.

> *Please read the notes overleaf carefully. If you are not sure of your rights or the implications of this notice, you may want to seek legal advice.*

NOTES

1. The authority is now satisfied that the imminent* risk of injury to health no longer exists in respect of the circumstances that caused the authority to issue you with an emergency prohibition notice or the court to impose a prohibition order or emergency prohibition order.
2. *The relevant notice or order is now lifted and you may use the premises, process, treatment or equipment again.*
   [*Officer to delete as appropriate]

Authority:

Food Safety Act 1990 – Sections 11 & 12
NOTICE OF CONTINUING RISK TO HEALTH

1. To: . . . . (Name of proprietor)
   At: . . . . (Address of proprietor)
   Proprietor of: . . . .
   Address of food business: . . . .
   . . . .

2. *The authority is NOT satisfied that you have taken sufficient measures to secure the removal of the imminent* risk of injury to health described in the:*

   emergency prohibition notice*
   emergency prohibition order*
   prohibition order*
   [*Officer to delete as appropriate]

   served on you on . . . . (date), a further copy of which is attached.
   The authority is not satisfied because: . . . .
   . . . .
   . . . .

3. *You must not use the premises, process, treatment of equipment in question until the authority notifies you that you may do no.*
   Signed: . . . . Authorised Officer
   Name in capitals: . . . .
   Date: . . . .
   Address: . . . .
   . . . .
   Tel: . . . . Fax: . . . .

> *Please read the notes overleaf carefully. If you are not sure of your rights or the implications of this notice, you may want to seek legal advice.*

NOTES

1. The authority is not yet satisfied that the imminent* risk of injury to health has been removed at your business. The reasons why the authority is not satisfied are given.
2. You still cannot use the premises, process, treatment or equipment in question for the purposes described in the emergency prohibition notice/emergency prohibition order/prohibition order* even if you are appealing against the terms of this notice.
3. You are entitled to appeal against this notice. If you want to do so, you should apply to the magistrates' court, or in Scotland to the sheriff, within one calendar month of the date on which this notice is served on you.
4. As soon as you think that there is no longer a/an imminent* risk of injury to health, because of actions you have taken, you may apply to the authority for the prohibition notice or order to be lifted.
    [*Officer to delete as appropriate]

> *WARNING*

*FAILURE TO COMPLY WITH THE ORIGINAL NOTICE
OR ORDER IS AN OFFENCE*
*Offenders are liable to be fined and/or imprisoned for
up to 2 years.*

Appendix C
Health Screening Documentation

PRE-EMPLOYMENT HEALTH SCREENING QUESTIONNAIRE

Surname
Mr
Mrs_____
Miss

Work location_____

Forenames_____ Date of birth_____

Marital status_____ Position applied for_____

National Insurance No_____

SECTION A

Please circle if you are at present suffering from, or have suffered from:

* Giddiness
* Fainting attacks
* Epilepsy
* Fits or blackouts
* Mental illness
* Anxiety or depression
* Recurring headaches
* Serious injury
* Serious operations

* Severe hay fever
* Asthma
* Recurring chest disease
* Recurring stomach trouble
* Recurring bowel trouble
* Recurring bladder trouble
* Stroke
* Heart trouble
* High blood pressure
* Varicose veins

* Diabetes
* Skin trouble
* Ear trouble or deafness
* Eye trouble
* Defective vision (not corrected by spectacles or contact lenses)
* Defective colour vision
* Back trouble
* Muscle or joint trouble
* Hernia/rupture

SECTION B

Please circle if you have any disabilities that affect:

* Standing
* Walking
* Stair climbing

* Lifting
* Use of your hands
* Driving a motor vehicle

* Working at height
* Climbing ladders
* Work on staging

SECTION C

How many working days have you lost during the last 3 years due to illness or injury?

_____days

Are you at present having any tablets, medicine or injections prescribed by a doctor?

YES/NO

Are you a registered disabled person? YES/NO

Additional questions to be answered by any prospective employee who will handle food or enter food production areas in the course of his/her employment.

SECTION D

Please circle if you **have ever** suffered from:

* Typhoid fever	* A perforated ear drum	* Recurring skin condition
* Paratyphoid fever	* A running ear	* Hepatitis (liver disorder)
* Dysentery	* Frequent sore throats	* Tuberculosis
* Salmonella		

SECTION E

Please circle if you are **at present** suffering from:

* Cough with phlegm	* A running ear	* Diarrhoea/Vomiting
* Abdominal pain	* Raised temperature	* Boil(s)
* Acne	* Septic finger(s)	* Styes

SECTION F

When did you last visit your dentist?_____

If treatment is necessary are you willing to visit your dentist for treatment?   YES/NO

The answers to these questions are accurate to the best of my knowledge.

I acknowledge that failure to disclose information may require reassessment of my fitness and could lead to termination of employment.

Signed_____Prospective employee   Date_____

FITNESS CERTIFICATE

Mr/Mrs/Miss_____

employed at_____

Occupation_____

has had a medical/health assessment and you are advised that he/she is :

FIT   FIT WITH RESTRICTIONS   UNFIT

Notes

To be reviewed on_____(Date)

Signed_____   Date_____

Occupational health physician/nurse

FOOD HANDLER'S QUESTIONNAIRE ON RETURN TO WORK

FOLLOWING ABSENCE DUE TO ILLNESS, INJURY OR TRAVEL

ABROAD

Surname_____Forenames_____

Work location_____Department_____

Date of absence from_____to_____

Reason for absence_____

Holiday destination (where appropriate)_____

PART 1

Please circle if you have you been suffering from, or have been in contact with anyone suffering from:

* Vomiting   * Diarrhoea   * Any bowel disorder

Please circle if you have you been suffering from any infection affecting:

* Skin   * Nose   * Throat   * Eyes   * Ears

Have you had any severe flu-like symptoms?   YES/NO

PART 2

Please circle if you have been suffering from, or have been in contact with anyone suffering from, any of the following communicable diseases:

* Typhoid   * Paratyphoid   * Cholera   * Dysentery

* Tuberculosis   * Hepatitis   * Salmonella

PART 3

Have you made a full recovery from your illness?   YES/NO

Are you now free of all symptoms?   YES/NO

Signed_____Employee_____Date

Signed _____Manager_____Date

Appendix D
Food Hygiene Audit

FOOD HYGIENE AUDIT

This Audit has been undertaken with a view to ensuring compliance with the Food Hygiene (England) Regulations 2006 and Regulation (EC) No.852/2004 on the hygiene of foodstuffs.

Location of Premises   Date

	YES/NO

GENERAL

1. All food is prepared, processed, manufactured, packaged, stored, transported, distributed, handled and offered for sale or supply in a hygienic way.

2. A formally-established food safety management system, such as Hazard Analysis: Critical Control Point (HACCP) or Assured Safe Catering (ASC) is currently operated within the organisation.

3. There is a formal procedure whereby persons suffering from food borne infections, any infected wound, skin infection, sores, diarrhoea or with any analogous medical condition report such conditions to the proprietor of the food business or his representative.

4. In situations listed above, persons are prohibited from from handling food.

PREMISES

5. Food premises are kept clean and maintained in good repair and condition.

6. The layout, design, construction and size of the food premises:

    (a) permits adequate cleaning and/or disinfection;   yes

    (b) is such as to protect against the accumulation of dirt, contact with toxic materials, the shedding of particles into food and the formation of condensation or undesirable moulds on surfaces;

    (c) permits good food hygiene practices, including protection against cross contamination between and during operations, by foodstuffs, equipment, materials, water, air supply or personnel and external contamination such as pests;   and

    (d) provides, where necessary, suitable temperature conditions for the hygienic processing and storage of products.

7.   An adequate number of washbasins are available, suitably located and designated for cleaning hands.

8.   An adequate number of flush lavatories are available and connected to an effective drainage system.

9.   Lavatories do not lead directly into rooms in which food is handled.

10. Washbasins for cleaning hands are provided with hot and cold (or appropriately mixed) running water, materials for cleaning hands and for hygienic drying.

11. The provision for washing food is separate from the hand-washing facility.

12. There are suitable and sufficient means of natural or mechanical ventilation.

13. Ventilation systems are so constructed as to enable filters and other parts requiring cleaning or replacement to be readily accessible.

14. All sanitary conveniences within the food premises are provided with adequate natural or mechanical ventilation.

15. The food premises has adequate natural and/or artificial lighting.

16. Drainage facilities are adequate for the purpose intended, and are constructed to avoid the risk of contamination of foodstuffs.

17. Adequate changing facilities are provided for personnel.

18. In rooms where food is prepared, treated or processed:

    (a)   floor surfaces are maintained in a sound condition, are easy to clean and, where necessary, disinfect;

    (b)   wall surfaces are maintained in a sound condition and are easy to clean and, where necessary, disinfect;

    (c)   ceilings and overhead fixtures are designed, constructed and finished to prevent the accumulation of dirt and reduce condensation, the growth of undesirable moulds and the shedding of particles;

    (d)   windows and other openings are constructed to accumulation of dirt;

(e)   openable windows and doors are fitted with insect screens which can be easily removed for cleaning;

(f) open windows remain closed and fixed during food production, where the opening of such windows would result in contamination of foodstuffs;

(g) doors are easy to clean and, where necessary, disinfect;

(h) surfaces (including surfaces of equipment) in contact with food are maintained in a sound condition, are easy to clean and, where necessary, disinfect;

19. Adequate facilities are provided for the cleaning and disinfecting of work tools and equipment.

20. Adequate provision is made for the washing of food, where necessary.

TRANSPORT ARRANGEMENTS

21. Conveyances and/or containers used for transporting foodstuffs are kept clean and maintained in good repair and condition, and are designed and constructed to permit adequate cleaning and/or disinfection.

22. Receptacles in vehicles and/or containers are not used for transporting anything other than foodstuffs where this may result in contamination of foodstuffs.

23. Bulk foodstuffs in liquid, granular or powder form are transported in receptacles and/or containers reserved for the transport of foodstuffs.

24. Containers for the transport of foodstuffs are marked in a clearly visible and indelible fashion to indicate they are used for transport purposes.

25. Conveyances and/or containers are effectively cleaned between loads where there may be a risk of contamination.

26. Foodstuffs in conveyances and/or containers are so placed and protected as to minimise the risk of contamination.

27. Where necessary, conveyances and/or containers used for transporting foodstuffs are capable of maintaining foodstuffs at appropriate temperatures and, where necessary, designed to allow those temperatures to be monitored.

EQUIPMENT

28. All articles, fittings and equipment with which food comes into contact are kept clean and –

(a) are so constructed, of such materials and kept in such good order, repair and condition, as to minimise any risk of contamination of the food;

(b)   with the exception of non-returnable containers and
      packaging, are so constructed, of such materials and
      kept in such good order, repair and condition, as to
      enable them to be thoroughly cleaned and, where
      necessary, disinfected, sufficient for the purpose
      intended;

(c)   installed in such a manner as to allow adequate
      cleaning of the surrounding area.

FOOD WASTE

29.   Food waste and other refuse is not allowed to accumulate in
      food rooms, except so far as is unavoidable for the proper
      functioning of the business.

30.   Food waste and other refuse are deposited in closable
      containers or other forms of appropriate containers.

31.   Waste containers are of an appropriate construction, kept
      sound condition, and where necessary, easy to clean and
      disinfect.

32.   Adequate provision is made for the removal and storage of
      food waste and other refuse.

33.   Refuse stores are designed and managed in such a way as to
      enable them to be kept clean, and to protect against access
      by pests, and against contamination of food, drinking water,
      equipment or premises.

PERSONAL HYGIENE

34.   Every person working in a food handling area maintains a
      degree of personal cleanliness and wears suitable, clean
      and, where appropriate, protective clothing,

35.   No person, known or suspected to be suffering from, or to
      be a carrier of, a disease likely to be transmitted through
      food or while afflicted, for example, with infected wounds,
      skin infections, sores or with diarrhoea, is permitted to
      work in any food handling area in any capacity in which
      there is any likelihood of directly or indirectly
      contaminating food with pathogenic micro-organisms.

PROVISIONS APPLICABLE TO FOODSTUFFS

36.   No raw materials or ingredients are accepted by the business
      if they are known to be, or might reasonably be expected to
      be, so contaminated with parasites, pathogenic micro-
      organisms, or toxic, decomposed or foreign substances, that
      after normal sorting and/or preparatory or processing
      procedures hygienically applied by the food business, they
      would still be unfit for human consumption.

37. Raw materials and ingredients stored in the establishment are kept in appropriate conditions designed to prevent harmful deterioration and to protect them from contamination

38. All food which is handled, stored, packaged, displayed and transported, is protected against any contamination likely to render the food unfit for human consumption, injurious to health or contaminated in such a way that it would be unreasonable to expect it to be consumed in that state.

39. Food is so placed and/or protected as to minimise any risk of contamination.

40. Adequate procedures are in place to ensure pests are controlled.

41. Hazardous and/or inedible substances, including animal feedstuffs, are adequately labelled and stored in separate and secure containers.

TRAINING

42. Food handlers engaged in the food business are supervised and instructed and/or trained in food hygiene matters commensurate with their work activities.

TEMPERATURE CONTROL

43. Food which is likely to support the growth of pathogenic micro-organisms or the formation of toxins is kept at a temperature below 8°C.

44. Food which –

    (a) has been cooked or reheated;

    (b) is for service or on display for sale;

    (c) needs to be kept hot in order to control the growth of pathogenic micro-organisms or the formation of toxins,

    is kept at a temperature above 63°C.

45. Raw materials, ingredients, intermediate products or finished products, and those likely to support the growth of micro-organisms are not kept at temperatures which would result in a risk to health.

ACTION PLAN

1.   **Immediate action**

2.   **Short-term action (14 days)**

3.   **Medium-term action (6 months)**

4.   **Long-term action (2 years)**

Auditor_____Date_____

Authorising Manager_____Date_____

Appendix E
Cleaning Schedule

Date_____

Equipment/Area Cleaned	Time	Cleaning Equipment/ Method	Carried out by (Signature)	Checked by (Signature)	Any problems/ Action Taken

Appendix F
Temperature Control Record – Cabinet/Cold Stores

Date_____

Time	Cabinet/Coldstore	Required Temperature	Actual Air Temperature	Checked by (Signature)	Action Taken if not Required Temperature

Appendix G
Temperature Control Record – Deliveries

Date_____

Time	Delivery From	Lorry/Product Temperature if applicable	Checked by (Signature)	Accept	Reject	Reason for Rejection

Other titles from Thorogood

THE A-Z OF HEALTH AND SAFETY

Jeremy Stranks

P/B • 658 pages   **£19.99**
ISBN(10): 1 85418 387 7 • (13): 978-185418387-3

R/B • 658 pages   **£55.00**
ISBN(10): 1 85418 382 6 • (13): 978-185418382-8

Health and safety law and practice has changed considerably in recent years and all organisations must be fully up to speed with best practice. In accessible A-Z format, this book is a major new reference work by an acknowledged expert in an area of crucial importance to every organisation, large and small, private and public.

THE A-Z OF THE ENVIRONMENT

Jeremy Stranks

P/B • 520 Pages   **£19.99**
ISBN(10): 1 85418 415 6 • (13): 978-185418415-3

R/B • 520 Pages   **£55.00**
ISBN(10): 1 85418 420 2 • (13): 978-185418420-7

A very timely addition to the A-Z series by an acknowledged expert on a subject of huge relevance to organisations across all sectors. Full coverage of all the latest changes to the law, theory and practice as at mid 2007.

THE A-Z OF EMPLOYMENT PRACTICE

David Martin

P/B • 712 pages • 2nd edition   **£19.99**
ISBN(10): 1 85418 327 3 • (13): 978-185418327-9

R/B • 712 pages • 2nd edition   **£55.00**
ISBN(10): 1 85418 322 2 • (13): 978-185418322-4

This book comes at a time when managers are faced with still more new legislation, obligations and potential penalties. It explains what the law is and then what to do, providing expert advice on every aspect of employment practice from recruitment, pay and incentives to maternity/paternity leave, personnel records, contracts and holidays.

"This book covers everything you need to know about good employment practice... This is a really useful book. Every manager should have one."   PROFESSIONAL MANAGER

"This book will be of value to all businesses, particularly perhaps smaller businesses where the director/owner needs to be his or her own personnel or HR manager... a valuable guide for every manager and would-be leader."

JOHN SUNDERLAND. CHAIRMAN, CADBURY SCHWEPPES PLC

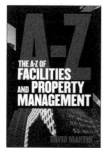

THE A-Z OF FACILITIES AND PROPERTY MANAGEMENT

David Martin

P/B • 416 pages   **£19.99**
ISBN(10): 1 85418 313 3 • (13): 978-185418313-2

R/B • 416 pages   **£55.00**
ISBN(10): 1 85418 3184 • (13): 978-185418318-7

A major new reference work, in an easy-to-use A-Z format, covering all aspects of facilities and property management, strategy, administration and control, backed up by a wealth of practical suggestions. Covers all the latest legislation on waste, energy consumption and environmental issues and offers valuable insights into the management of property assets.

THE A-Z OF MANAGEMENT CONCEPTS AND MODELS

Bengt Karlof and Fredrik Lövingsson

P/B • 440 pages   **£18.99**
ISBN(10): 1 85418 390 7 • 13): 978-185418390-3

H/B • 440 pages   **£35.00**
ISBN(10): 1 85418 385 0 • (13): 978-185418385-9

An A-Z of all the essential concepts and models applied in business and management. A superb and comprehensive source of reference for professionals and students, with 124 detailed entries from Balanced scorecard to Zero-based planning.

MANAGE TO WIN

Norton Paley

P/B • 448 pages   **£15.99**
ISBN(10): 1 85418 395 8 • (13): 978-185418395-8

H/B • 448 pages   **£29.99**
ISBN(10): 185418 301 X • (13): 978-185418301-9

Learn how to reshape and reposition your company to meet tougher challenges and competitors, when to confront and when to retreat, how to assess risk and opportunity and how to move to seize opportunities and knock out the competition.

"This book is a 'must have' for any manager intent on success."
EDWARD J. FRED, CEO & PRESIDENT, CPI AEROSTRUCTURES, INC.

MANAGING PEOPLE FOR THE FIRST TIME

Julie Lewthwaite

P/B • 352 pages   **£12.99**
ISBN(10): 1 85418 332 X • (13): 978-185418332-3

"The value of this book is that it makes a worthwhile attempt to help the first-time manager. Combining training material with a storyline involving real people makes it a lot more digestible than a textbook."
PEOPLE MANAGEMENT

"There are books on managing people by the truckload, but little specifically for the first time manager. The whole range of management knowledge, theory and practice is contained in this easily absorbed text."   BUSINESS EXECUTIVE

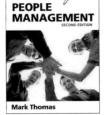

MASTERING PEOPLE MANAGEMENT

Mark Thomas

P/B • 232 pages • 2nd edition   **£14.99**
ISBN(10): 1 85418 328 1 • (13):978-185418328-6

How to build and develop a successful team by motivating, empowering and leading people. Based on in-depth experience of developing people and initiating change within many organisations, Mark Thomas provides a shrewd, practical guide to mastering the essential techniques of people management.

MASTERING LEADERSHIP

Michael Williams

P/B • 288 pages • 2nd edition   **£14.99**
ISBN(10):1 85418 308 7 • (13):978-185418308-8

Without a grasp of what true leadership implies you cannot hope to develop a really effective team. With telling insight, Michael Williams shows what distinguishes truly high-achieving teams from the rest of the pack.

"A must-read for anyone who wants to become a better leader. Easy to read and packed full of practical advice about how to make things happen. A complete course on business leadership and personal development."
DR PATRICK DIXON, CHAIRMAN, GLOBAL CHALLENGE LTD AND FELLOW, LONDON BUSINESS SCHOOL

BUSINESS SEMINARS

Focused on developing your potential

Falconbury, the sister company to Thorogood publishing, brings together the leading experts from all areas of management and strategic development to provide you with a comprehensive portfolio of action-centred training and learning.

We understand everything managers and leaders need to be, know and do to succeed in today's commercial environment. Each product addresses a different technical or personal development need that will encourage growth and increase your potential for success.

- Practical public training programmes
- Tailored in-company training
- Coaching
- Mentoring
- Topical business seminars
- Trainer bureau/bank
- Adair Leadership Foundation

The most valuable resource in any organization is its people; it is essential that you invest in the development of your management and leadership skills to ensure your team fulfil their potential. Investment into both personal and professional development has been proven to provide an outstanding ROI through increased productivity in both you and your team. Ultimately leading to a dramatic impact on the bottom line.

With this in mind Falconbury have developed a comprehensive portfolio of training programmes to enable managers of all levels to develop their skills in leadership, communications, finance, people management, change management and all areas vital to achieving success in today's commercial environment.

What Falconbury can offer you?

- Practical applied methodology with a proven results
- Extensive bank of experienced trainers
- Limited attendees to ensure one-to-one guidance
- Up to the minute thinking on management and leadership techniques
- Interactive training
- Balanced mix of theoretical and practical learning
- Learner-centred training
- Excellent cost/quality ratio

Falconbury In-Company Training

Falconbury are aware that a public programme may not be the solution to leadership and management issues arising in your firm. Involving only attendees from your organization and tailoring the programme to focus on the current challenges you face individually and as a business may be more appropriate. With this in mind we have brought together our most motivated and forward thinking trainers to deliver tailored in-company programmes developed specifically around the needs within your organization.

All our trainers have a practical commercial background and highly refined people skills. During the course of the programme they act as facilitator, trainer and mentor, adapting their style to ensure that each individual benefits equally from their knowledge to develop new skills.

Falconbury works with each organization to develop a programme of training that fits your needs.

Mentoring and coaching

Developing and achieving your personal objectives in the workplace is becoming increasingly difficult in today's constantly changing environment. Additionally, as a manager or leader, you are responsible for guiding colleagues towards the realization of their goals. Sometimes it is easy to lose focus on your short and long-term aims.

Falconbury's one-to-one coaching draws out individual potential by raising self-awareness and understanding, facilitating the learning and performance development that creates excellent managers and leaders. It builds renewed self-confidence and a strong sense of 'can-do' competence, contributing significant benefit to the organization. Enabling you to focus your energy on developing your potential and that of your colleagues.

Mentoring involves formulating winning strategies, setting goals, monitoring achievements and motivating the whole team whilst achieving a much improved work life balance.

Falconbury – Business Legal Seminars

Falconbury Business Legal Seminars specialises in the provision of high quality training for legal professionals from both in-house and private practice internationally.

The focus of these events is to provide comprehensive and practical training on current international legal thinking and practice in a clear and informative format.

Event subjects include, drafting commercial agreements, employment law, competition law, intellectual property, managing an in-house legal department and international acquisitions.

For more information on all our services please contact: Falconbury on:
Telephone +44 (0)20 7729 6677 or visit the website at: www.falconbury.co.uk.